Preface

This is the third in a series of math books designed to help students excel on the SAT and ACT.

When I first started tutoring 11 years ago, I never imagined I would one day write a book, let alone three books, that would reach many more students than I could possibly tutor in person or even virtually.

It is my fervent hope that students all over the country, and even the world, will find these books useful and provide them with that extra edge that will push their SAT or ACT exam scores high enough to gain them admission to the college or university of their dreams.

That has been, is, and will continue to be my goal. And, it is to that end that I put my years of experience tutoring down into a permanent record that will help students of all math levels reach their highest goals.

Contents

Introduction 3

Systems of Equations 4

Inequalities 39

Percentages 73

Probability 98

Linear Relationships 131

Measures of Central Tendency 157

Quadratic Relationships 184

Proportions 206

Geometry 224

Trigonometry 258

Statistics 291

Miscellaneous 311

Conclusion 341

Introduction

Nothing strikes fear into the the hearts of high school students preparing to take the SAT and ACT like math word problems.

When the College Board revamped their SAT exams back in 2016, they decided to include more of those dreaded word demons than ever before.

I suspect they did so to address the constant complaints that math teachers hear from students all the time: "Why do I need math if it doesn't relate to the 'real' world?"

As the saying goes, "Be careful what you wish for." The unintended consequence of such a complaint has been a substantial increase in the number of word problems dealing with hypothetical but realistic scenarios involving math. It is then the student's job to translate these scenarios into mathematical solutions. What fun, right?

Well, like it or not, you're stuck with this new reality and it would be in your best interest to strengthen your skills at solving word problems if you want a high score on the test, whether it's the SAT or ACT.

That's why I wrote this book, to help you deal with word problems as painlessly as possible.

The examples I present are not exhaustive. No book ever could be. But, this book presents the majority of likely types of words problems you'll encounter based on actual ones that appeared on past tests.

So, buckle in and enjoy the ride as you embark on a journey to becoming an SAT and ACT word problem pro.

Systems of Equations

Since so many word problems boil down to a simple system of linear equations, this topic deserves its own chapter. And this is it. It's the very first chapter because it happens with more word problems than any other type. So, let's dive right in and see how these kinds of word problem show up over and over again, and how to solve them.

1. Last week Rob worked 13 more hours than Amy. If they worked a combined total of 61 hours, how many hours did Amy work last week?

    A) 24

    B) 35

    C) 40

    D) 48

This kind of word problem is probably one of the most typical you'll see on either the SAT or ACT exam because it tests your ability to set up a system of equations based on a real life scenario. As stated in the introduction, creators of the SAT and ACT are very aware that students throughout the country feel that math is boring because it doesn't deal with the real world and things that matter. So, they try to come up with problems that shatter the myth that math is not useful.

Getting back to this problem, we can create a mathematical relationship **immediately** from the information given in the very first sentence:

$$R = A + 13$$

You should be able to guess that R represents Rob's working hours and A represents Amy's. Here we should stop to consider that, although you have seen countless problems where **x** and **y** are the given variables, you do NOT have to use those variables when setting up your own equations. It makes more sense to use *descriptive variables* which let you know right away what you're dealing with, instead of having to remember which variable represents what. So, clearly, it makes sense to call Rob's hours **R**, and Amy's hours **A**.

Then, according to the first sentence, Rob worked 13 hours **more** than Amy. So, mathematically, that means R = A + 13.

Here, we notice there are **2** variables but only one equation. Now, we need to understand a basic rule: *If you are solving for 1 variable, you only need one equation. For 2 variables, you need 2 equations. For 3 variables, 3 equations, etc*. So, in this case, we need another equation.

Can you see what the other equation would be? Reading on we see that they worked a **combined** total of 61 hours. That's our second equation:

$$R + A = 61$$

Now we have our system of equations! The next question is how to solve them.

You should have learned that the two primary ways of solving any system of linear equations is by *Elimination* or *Substitution*. Choosing which one is usually a matter of preference, but one way is usually faster than the other, depending the particular system we are dealing with.

In this case, we already know that R = A + 13, so it would be logical to **substitute** A + 13 for R in the second equation to get:

$$A + 13 + A = 61$$

Combining like terms and subtracting the 13 we get : 2A = 48, and so A = 24. Choice **A**.

That was quite a lengthy explanation of how to solve a relatively simple word problem using a system of linear equations. If you fully understood it, then you are well on your way to solving just about any other similar type of word problem they might ask. But, it will require practice before you'll be able to do it quickly and accurately because there are countless ways they can create problems which will test your ability to set up the system of equations correctly.

Let's look at some more...

2.

A school cafeteria sells cheeseburgers for $4.50 and hot dogs for $2.50. If the revenue from selling cheeseburgers and hot dogs was $549.00 and the total number of cheeseburgers and hot dogs sold was 182, how many cheeseburgers did they sell that day?

A) 37

B) 47

C) 57

D) 67

Although this one seems a bit more complicated, it follows the same approach as the previous problem. Once again, it would be a good idea to use descriptive variables. Let's call the number of cheeseburgers C and the number hot dogs H. Easy enough. So then, we have **2** variables, which means we need **2** equations. Now, it's just a matter of determining how to translate the problem into 2 equations.

From the information given in the problem, we know that each cheeseburger costs $4.50 and each hot dog costs $2.50. We also know that the **revenue**, which is the total money collected from selling the cheeseburgers and hot dogs, is $549.00. Therefore, our first equation should be:

$$4.5C + 2.5H = 549$$

If you're not sure why, think about how much money you would make selling one cheeseburger. It would be $4.50, right? And it would be that much for every cheeseburger you sell. So, the total amount you would make for any number of cheeseburgers would $4.50 **times** the number of cheeseburgers you sell, which is shown mathematically as 4.50C or just 4.5C. The same goes for the hot dogs, which is shown mathematically as 2.50H or just 2.5H.

So, the first equation is in the bag. But, we need another. Can you see the other?

Since the total number of cheeseburgers and hot dogs is 182, the second equation is just:

$$C + H = 182$$

Now, we have all we need to solve for C and H. But, they are only asking about C, so we should be looking to **eliminate** the H.

We can do that by multiplying the entire second equation by 2.5 to get 2.5C + 2.5H = 455.

Then, setting up the system of equations we have:

$$4.5C + 2.5H = 549$$

$$2.5C + 2.5H = 455$$

Subtracting the second from the first leaves us with 2C = 94. So then C = 47. Choice **B**.

You may be wondering you could have also solved the system of equations using *substitution*. The answer is yes.

Using substitution, we look at the original second equation, C + H = 182, and put H in terms of C by simply subtracting C to the other side. That gives us H = 182 − C.

Then, we can substitute the H in the original first equation with 182 − C to get:

$$4.5C + 2.5(182 - C) = 549$$

Then, 4.5C + 455 − 2.5C = 549

2.5C = 94, and so C = 47. Same answer. So, as you can see, you had a choice. In this case, either way would have taken about the same amount of time to solve.

3.
An ice cream truck sells soft ice cream cones for $4.50 each and cups of Italian ices for $3.00 each. The ice cream truck's revenue from selling a total of 154 cones and cups in one day was $582.00. How many cups of Italian ice were sold that day?

A) 56

B) 74

C) 88

D) 99

Here's another one, very similar to the previous problem. The more you see problems like these, the faster you'll become at solving them. As you are well aware by now, time is a very important factor on the SAT and ACT exams.

We should be able to set this one up very quickly. Let's call the number of soft ice cream cones S and the number of Italian ices I. Then we can set up the 2 equations right away:

$$4.5S + 3I = 582$$

$$S + I = 154$$

Once again, for this one, you can use either substitution or elimination to solve for I.

Using substitution: $S = 154 - I$. Therefore, $4.5(154 - I) + 3I = 582$. Continuing to solve...

$693 - 4.5I + 3I = 582$

$111 = 1.5I$

$I = 74$. **B**.

4.
Mrs. Haley has a pitcher containing x ounces of lemonade to distribute to the kids at her daughter's birthday party. If she gives each child 6 ounces of lemonade she will have 6 ounces left over. In order to give each child 8 ounces of lemonade, she will need an additional 8 ounces. How many children are at the party?

A) 11

B) 9

C) 8

D) 7

This problem might seem confusing, but if you take it step by step you can set up the system of equations with relative ease.

Here, they tell us the variable to use for the amount of lemonade in pitcher is x. But we can use our own variable for the number of kids at the party. Let's call it k.

Then we can set up two equations. The first is based on the information that when 6 ounces of lemonade was given to each child, there was an excess of 6 ounces left in the pitcher. That means the amount of lemonade **used** was x – 6 ounces. So, the equation is:

$$6k = x - 6$$

For the second equation we read that if 8 ounces is given to each child, then there will not be enough lemonade in the pitcher to do it. In fact, Mrs. Haley will need an additional 8 ounces to fill all their glasses. So, the second equation is:

$$8k = x + 8$$

If these two equations are confusing to you, think of it in terms of how much lemonade is needed to fulfill the 6 ounce per cup requirement and the 8 ounce per cup requirement.

So, now that we have our system of equations we can solve. Let's put the first equation under the second and subtract to eliminate the x's:

$$\begin{aligned} 8k &= x + 8 \\ -\ 6k &= x - 6 \\ \hline 2k &= 14 \end{aligned}$$

Make sure you're careful to remember that when you subtract a negative number it is the same as adding a positive. That's why 8 – (-6) = 14. Then, solving for k we get k = 7. Choice **D**.

5.

Between 1609 and 1611, Henry Hudson embarked on two voyages along a body of water now known as the Hudson River. According to his logs, the first voyage lasted

13 days longer that the second voyage, and the two voyages combined lasted a total of 253 days. How many days did the second voyage last?

A) 110

B) 120

C) 130

D) 140

By now you should be thinking of systems of equations, which will require 2 linear equations. Again, let's use descriptive variables. Let's say F = the number of days of the first voyage, and
S = the number of days of the second voyage. Then, based on the given information we can set up the 2 equations right away:

$$F = S + 13$$

$$\text{And, } F + S = 253$$

If you questions about these 2 equations, read the problem carefully and you'll see they are correct.

Since we are only interested in the **second voyage**, we can *substitute* F in terms S, which is already shown in the first equation. Then, plugging that into the second equation we get:

$$S + 13 + S = 253$$

Continuing to solve for S: 2S = 240, and so S = 120. **B**. Are you starting to get the hang of this?

6.

An online video game store sells new and used games. Each new game sells for $10, and each used game sells $4. If Sal purchased a total of 12 new and used games that have a combined selling price of $72, how many new games did he purchase?

- A) 2
- B) 3
- C) 4
- D) 5

So, here again, we can set up the necessary equations with little trouble. First, let's choose our descriptive variables. How about N for the number of new games and U for the number of used games? Then the system of equations becomes:

$$10N + 4U = 72$$

$$N + U = 12$$

Since we are interested in the number of **new games**, we want to solve for N. Again, substitution looks like the best way to go here. Then we put U in terms of N in the second equation to get U = 12 − N. Substituting that into the first equation we get:

$$10N + 4(12 - N) = 72$$

Then, 10N + 48 − 4N = 72

6N = 24

N = 4. Choice **C**.

7. A candy manufacturing company is selling two different boxes of chocolates for Valentine's Day, a standard box and a deluxe box. The standard box has a volume of 30 cubic inches, and the deluxe box is 50 cubic inches. The company receives an order for 80 boxes of both types, and the total volume of the order to be shipped is 2,150 cubic inches. Which of the following systems of

equations can be used to determine the number standard boxes, *s*, and deluxe boxes, *d*, that were ordered?

A) $80 - s = d$
       $30s + 50d = 2,150$

B) $80 - s = d$
       $50s + 30d = 2,150$

C) $s - d = 80$
       $40(s + c) = 2,150$

D) $s - c = 80$
       $50s + 30d = 2,150$

In this SAT word problem you are not asked to solve anything! You only need to **set up** the proper system of equations. We will do that as we have been doing all the others so far, except, in this case they are giving us the descriptive variables s and d.

They tell us that the standard box has a volume of 30 cubic inches and the deluxe box is 50 cubic inches. The total volume to be shipped is 2,150 cubic inches. So, we have enough information to write our first equation:

$$30s + 50d = 2,150$$

Let's stop right there and look at the choices. The **only** choice that shows that relationship is choice **A**. So we're done!

But, let's assume that there were two choices that showed this relationship, which is very common on the SAT. Then you will need find another equation to find the answer.

In this case, they tell that the company receives an order of 80 boxes of both types. Then, the other equation would be:

$$s + d = 80$$

But you'll notice that that equation is not among the choices. However, if we simply rearrange that equation, we get 80 − s = d, which **is** among the choices.

Of course, they could not give two choices with the same equations, because there can only be **one** right answer. But they would be varied the first equation, in that case, and then you would have been able to pick the only choice that had both correct equations.

8.

A group of 36 people went on a ski trip. To reach the top of the mountain they needed to use a ski lift which had two different size chairs. One carried 2 people at a time, the other carried 4. The group needed a total of 12 chairs to make it up the mountain. Assuming all the chairs were filled to capacity and every person in the group used the ski lift, exactly how many of the chairs used were the two-person size.

A) 6

B) 8

C) 10

D) 12

This one may be worded a little differently than the others but it is solved the same way. We need a system of equations with 2 variables. One variable is the number of **two-person chairs**, and the other is the number of **four-person chairs**. Using the first letter of each variable, let's call them **T** and **F**. Again, you can call them x and y as long as you remember which is which.

Since we know there were a total of 36 on the ski trip, and all the chairs were filled to capacity, then our first equation will be:

$$2T + 4F = 36$$

And, since there are a total of 12 chairs of both types, our second equation will be:

$$T + F = 12$$

Once again, you have a choice of using substitution or elimination to solve this system for T. And, as is typically the case, either one will work fine. Let's go with elimination on this one just for practice. Since we are solving for T, we want to get rid of the F variable by first multiplying the second equation by 4:

$$4T + 4F = 48$$

Now we can set up a simple system of equations to solve:

$$4T + 4F = 48$$
$$- \ 2T + 4F = 36$$
$$2T = 12$$

Then, T = 6. Choice **A**.

As you can see, problems like these are just a matter of translating English into math. And, as with any new language, practice is the key to mastery.

Try doing the same problem using substitution so that you can become equally proficient at using both methods.

9. Rapid Taxi Service charges a $4 fee plus $1 per mile to take a passenger anywhere within a 5-mile radius. Jiffy Cab Service charges a $2 fee plus $2 per mile. How many miles must a passenger travel to be charged the same amount by either company?

A) 1
B) 2
C) 3
D) 4
E) 5

This problem is modeled after a problem that appeared on an actual ACT exam. That's why you see 5 choices. As with the SAT, the ACT tests you on similar topics with problems that can be solved the same way.

Let's call the total amount charged T and the number of miles traveled by a passenger using each taxi service M. Then our two equations will be:

$$M + 4 = T \text{ for the Rapid Taxi Service ride, and}$$

$$2M + 2 = T \text{ for the Jiffy Cab Service ride}$$

Notice that T is the same for both equations because the problem specifically asks us to find the miles traveled such that the total charge is the **same** for either company.

Then, subtracting the first equation from the second we get:

$$2M + 2 = T$$
$$- \underline{M + 4 = T}$$
$$M - 2 = 0$$

Then, solving, M = 2. Choice **B**.

Setting up a system of equations is not necessarily the only way to solve this problem, but it illustrates how effective the system of equations method is in solving a host of linear relationship problems.

10.

Sam runs a concession stand at a basketball game. He is selling hot dogs and sodas. Each hot dog costs $2.50 and each soda costs $0.75. At the end of the night he made a total of $88.00. He sold twice as many sodas as he did hot dogs. How many sodas did he sell?

A) 22

B) 36

C) 44

D) 52

The second equation here is a little different, but the set up is the same as the others. We have two unknowns, so we need two equations. Let's call the number of hot dogs H and the number of sodas S. Then the first equation should be:

$$2.5H + 0.75S = 88$$

Again, we get rid of the extraneous zeros that aren't necessary to solve the equation. Now, we need the second equation. This time, the information provided leads us to a different equation than in prior examples. Here, they tell us that Sam sold twice as many sodas as he did hot dogs. Mathematically, that can be written as:

$$S = 2H$$

Translating back to English, that equation says that the number of sodas (S) is (=) two (2) times the number of hot dogs (H). So, we know it must be correct.

Now we have a choice. Since the question asks for the sodas sold, we can put H in terms of S and solve for S. But, that would mean H = S/2, based on the second equation. We really do not want to have to deal with fractions if we don't have to. So, let's just substitute S with 2H and solve for H. Then just double the answer to solve for S. Then, the first equation becomes:

2.5H + 0.75(2H) = 88

Continuing to solve...

2.5H + 1.5H = 88

4H = 88

H = 22

So, now we know the number of hot dogs sold was 22. Then the number of sodas sold must have been 2(22) = 44. Choice **C**.

11.
Shari and a friend go to Tacos Galore for lunch. She orders three soft tacos and three burritos and her total bill is $11.25. Her friend's bill is $10.00 for four soft tacos and two burritos. How much does a soft taco cost?

A) $1.25

B) $1.50

C) $1.75

D) $2.00

We should be able to set this one up quickly by now. Calling the soft tacos T and the burritos B we have our 2 equations:

$$3T + 3B = 11.25$$

$$4T + 2B = 10$$

Here's where a lot of students go astray creating unnecessary work in solving. Typically they will go directly to the *elimination* method and multiply the first equation by 2 and the second equation by 3 so that both equations will have a 6B that will cancel when the two equations are subtracted from each other.

While, that's fine, it's not necessary. How about doing this instead:

Divide the first equation by 3 to get T + B = 3.75 and the second equation by 2 to get 2T + B = 5.

Now, subtracting the first equation from the second we get T = 1.25. Choice **A**. Done.

Notice, you should not be too robotic when solving systems of equations. Sometimes there are shortcuts that should not be overlooked.

Let's check out another one.

12.

Margot can buy 2 notebooks and 3 packs of markers for $12.00.
Peter can buy 3 notebooks and 2 packs of markers for $13.00.
How much is one notebook and one pack of markers?

A) $3

B) $4

C) $5

D) $6

Set up the system of equations the usual way. Using N for the number of notebooks and M for the number of packs of markers you should get:

$$2N + 3M = 12$$

$$3N + 2M = 13$$

Here again, the temptation is to use elimination to solve for N and M and then add them together to get the answer. But, if you're clever and observant, you should notice what happens when you **add** the two equation:

$$\begin{aligned} 2N + 3M &= 12 \\ + \quad 3N + 2M &= 13 \\ \hline 5N + 5M &= 25 \end{aligned}$$

Do you see what just happened? We now have a new equation that's divisible by 5! And when we divide it by 5 we get N + M = 5, choice **C**.

Think of all the time you save doing it this way. So, pay attention, and try not to overlook these kind of shortcuts that happen quite frequent on the SAT and ACT.

13.
The admission fee at a small fair is $1.50 for children and $4.00 for adults. On a certain day, 2100 people enter the fair. If twice as many children than adults entered, how much money was collected?

A) $3,800

B) $4,200

C) $4,900

D) $5,050

This one may cause a little confusion because we can't use the $1.50 and $4.00 amounts right away to set up our first equation since we don't know how much money was collected. We will need another equation instead. Knowing that a total of 2100 people entered the fair, which includes adults and children, we can say:

$$A + C = 2100$$

Using descriptive variables, A, of course, would be the number of adults and C the number of children.

What else do we know? They tell us that there were twice as many children as adults. So that means our second equation is simply:

$$C = 2A$$

Now, substitution C for 2A in the first equation we get A + 2A = 2100. So, 3A = 2100, and then A = 700.

So then, having solved for A, we now know that C = 2(700) = 1400. And now we can answer the question. Since the cost of admission for each child is $1.50 and for adults is $4.00, the total amount collected is 1.5(1400) + 4(700) = $4,900. Choice **C**.

This problem illustrated that we can't always use the given numbers immediately to set up the system of equations. That's why practicing word problems is so necessary in order to get used to the many different ways problems can be worded and information presented.

14.

A landscaping company placed two orders with a nursery. The first order was for 13 bushes and 4 trees, and totaled $487. The second order was for 10 bushes and 1 trees, and totaled $199. The bills do not list the per-item price. What were the costs of one bush and of one tree?

A) $85

B) $96

C) $102

D) $115

This one looks pretty straightforward using a system of equations from the given information:

$$13B + 4T = 487$$

$$10B + T = 199$$

Here the temptation is to use substitution, since, from the second equation, T = 199 – 10B. But there's an even easier way to solve this.

You'll remember on a previous problem we added the system of equations and then divided by 5 to get the solution without having to solve for each variable and then adding them together.

Well, here, instead of adding, let's try **subtracting** the two equations:

$$\begin{array}{r} 13B + 4T = 487 \\ -\underline{\;10B + \;T = 199\;} \\ 3B + 3T = 288 \end{array}$$

Now, look what happens when you divide 3B + 4T = 288 by **3**. You get B + T = 96. Choice **B**.

Again, with a little attentive observation, we were able to solve this problem much faster than the conventional way of finding the value of each variable and then adding them together at the end. Remember, **time** is a big factor on both the SAT and the ACT. So, we want to use every available shortcut whenever possible.

Obviously, a problem like this would be found on Section 4 of the SAT, or anywhere on the ACT since you can use a calculator. However, a similar problem with easier numbers that don't require a calculator could also appear on Section 3 of the SAT where the use of a calculator is not permitted.

15.
A passenger jet took three hours to fly 1800 miles in the direction of the jetstream. The return trip against the jetstream took four hours. What was the jet's speed in still air?
A) 395
B) 425
C) 475
D) 525

What? We haven't seen one like this before? But don't panic. It will still just be a system of linear equations once we properly interpret the English and convert it into math.

In this problem we have a plane that travels at a certain when it flies **with the wind**, and another speed when it flies **against the wind**. The wind itself, which is called the jetstream in the problem, blows at a certain speed. So, let's first define our variables. We'll call the plane's speed <u>without the wind</u> **P** and the wind's speed **W**.

Let's now recall from Algebra 1 that **speed x time = distance**. If you forgot that, here's your opportunity to remember it for your test. And, also, let's consider that if the plane is traveling in the direction of (with) the jetstream (wind) then it will travel **faster**, right? They also tell us the time and the distance while traveling in this direction. So, now we have enough information to set up our first equation:

$$(P + W)(3) = 1800$$

If that confuses you, remember again that Speed x Time = Distance. The speed of the plane going **with** the wind is P + W, the amount of time traveling in that direction is 3 hours, and the distance traveled is 1800 miles.

Using the same reasoning, the second equation for the plane going **against** the wind should be:

$$(P - W)(4) = 1800$$

It would be a good idea at this point to distribute both equation to put them in standard linear form:

$$3P + 3W = 1800$$

$$4p - 4W = 1800$$

It looks like elimination would be the best way to go here to get rid of the W's and solve for P, but **first** let's reduce each equation to make our lives easier.

Dividing the first equation by 3 gives us **P + W = 600**, and dividing the second by 4 gives us **P − W = 450**. Then,

$$\begin{aligned} P + W &= 600 \\ +\ P - W &= 450 \\ \hline 2P &= 1050 \end{aligned}$$

Then we can finish it off by dividing by 2 to get P = 525mph. Choice **D**.

You may need to review this problem several times until it really clicks, but it would be well worth your while to do it so that you'll be ready if they throw something like this at you on the test.

Let's look at another one to help you solidify your understanding of such a problem.

16.
A boat can travel 16 miles up a river in 2 hours.
The same boat can travel 36 miles downstream in 3 hours.
What is the speed of the boat in still water?

A) 10

B) 12

C) 15

D) 17

This one is very similar to the previous problem, except that instead of a plane we have a boat, and instead of wind we have current.

It should be obvious that the boat is traveling more slowly up river, since it takes 2 hours to travel 16 miles, which means the speed is 16/2 = 8 mph. And traveling downstream its speed is 36/3 = 12 mph. So, traveling upstream it must going **against the current**, and traveling downstream it must be going **with the current.**

Let's call the speed of the boat in still water B, and the speed of the current C.

Then we can set up two equations based on the given information:

$$(B - C)(2) = 16$$

$$(B + C)(3) = 36$$

This time, without distributing, let's divide the first equation by 2 and the second by 3 to get:

$$B - C = 8$$

$$B + C = 12$$

Then, it would make sense to **add** the two equations so that the C variable cancels out:

$$B - C = 8$$
$$+\ \underline{B + C = 12}$$
$$2B = 20$$

Then, solving for B, B = 10. Choice **A**.

Note, that if they question asked for the speed of the <u>current</u> then we would have **subtracted** the two equations to get -2C = -4, and then C = 2.

17.

A psychological research study at a local university pays participants $15 if they are students and $10 if they are not students. If the study pays 10 participants a total of $120, how many of the participants were students?

A) 2

B) 4

C) 6

D) 8

Since descriptive variables here are not so evident, let's just go with x and y. So then, let x = the number of students, and y = the number of non-students. Then, it should be fairly clear that we can set up a system of equations based on the given information as:

$$15x + 10y = 120$$

$$x + y = 10$$

Since the question asks for the number of student participants we should put y in terms of x in the second equation to get y = 10-x. Then, substitute:

$$15x + 10(10 - x) = 120$$

Continuing to solve for x:

$15x + 100 - 10x = 120$

$5x = 20$

$x = 4$. Choice **B**.

18.

Connor and Joachim collaborated to write a computer program that consisted of 3,500 lines of code. If Joachim wrote 600 more lines of code than Connor did, how many lines of code did Connor write?

    A) 1200

    B) 1300

    C) 1450

    D) 2050

This one is pretty straightforward. We'll use C for the number of lines of code Connor wrote, and J for the number of lines of code Joachim wrote. Then, the system of equations should be:

$$J + C = 3,500$$

$$J = C + 600$$

Directly substituting the second equation into the first we get:

$$C + 600 + C = 3,500$$

Continuing to solve for C:

$2C = 2,900$

$C = 1450$. Choice **C**.

19.
Mrs. Brown has a bag of candy bars to hand out to the students of her class before they take their AP calculus exam. If she gives each student 3 candy bars, she will have 6 left over. In order to give each student 5 candy bars, she will need 50 more candy bars. How many students are in Mrs. Brown's class?

A) 18

B) 22

C) 28

D) 44

First, let's identify our unknowns, which will be our variables. There are the total number of candy bars in the bag. Let's call those C. And, there are the number of students in Mrs. Brown's class. We'll call them S.

Translating the statement, "If she gives each student 3 candy bars, she will have 6 left over.", into a mathematical equation, we can write:

$$3S + 6 = C$$

Translating, "In order to give each student 5 candy bars, she will need 50 more candy bars", into a mathematical equation, we have:

$$5S = C + 50$$

Let's put the S's and C's in the same columns so that we have a system of equations that are easy to solve:

$$3S - C = -6$$
$$5S - C = 50$$

Subtracting the first equation from the second we get:

$$5S - C = 50$$
$$-\ \underline{3S - C = -6}$$
$$2S = 56$$

Then, S = 28. Choice **C**. Be careful when you subtract the -6 !

20.

At a restaurant, each large order of fries has 350 more calories than one large soda. If 2 large orders of fries and 3 large sodas have a total of 1,500 calories, how many calories does one large order of fries have?

A) 510

B) 650

C) 750

D) 900

You should be able to set this one up right away using F for the number of calories for each large order of fries, and S for the calories in each soda:

$$F = S + 350$$

$$2F + 3S = 1500$$

Putting S in terms of F, the first equation becomes:

$$S = F - 350$$

Substituting that into the second equation we get:

$$2F + 3(F - 350) = 1500$$

Continuing to solve for F:

2F + 3F − 1050 = 1500

5F = 2550

F = 510. Choice **A**.

You could have also used <u>elimination</u> to solve this. Try it.

21.

John's weight is 3/5 of Peter's weight. If John were to gain 8 pounds, he would weigh 2/3 of Peter's weight. What is Peter's weight in pounds?

A) 100

B) 110

C) 115

D) 120

Using descriptive variables J and P for John's and Peter's weights, respectively, we can write down the equations as we translate the English into math:

John's weight is 3/5 of Peter's weight: **J = (3/5)P**

If John were to gain 8 pounds, he would weigh 2/3 of Peter's weight: **J + 8 = (2/3)P**

Now, we can just <u>substitute</u> the first equation into the second to get:

$$(3/5)P + 8 = (2/3)P$$

Then, it's just a matter of basic algebra to solve for P:

(2/3)P − (3/5)P = 8

If this were a Section 3 SAT problem, you would not be able to use your calculator. Then you would need to solve manually using common denominators:

(10/15)P − (9/15)P = 8

(1/15)P = 8

P = 8(15) = 120. Choice **D**.

22.

A smartphone costs $15 more than five times the cost of a basic cell phone. If the smartphone and the basic phone together cost $615, how much more does the smartphone cost than the basic phone?

A) $395

B) $415

C) $455

D) $500

Using S for the cost of the smartphone, and B for the cost of the basic cell phone, we can set up the system of equations right away:

$$S = 5B + 15$$

$$S + B = 615$$

To find out how much more the smartphone cost than the basic phone we'll have to solve for each and then take the difference.

It looks like direct substitution of the first equation into the second will work fine, although you *could* also use elimination. But, let's go ahead with substitution:

5B + 15 + B = 615

6B = 600

Then, B = 100

Solving for S using the second equation:

S + 100 = 615

S = 515

Then, the difference, S – B = 515 – 100 = 415. Choice **B**.

23.

Ken, Justin, and Tiff have read a total of 100 books from the library. Justin read 3 times as many books as Ken, and Tiff read 2 times as many as Justin. How many books did Ken read?

A) 12

B) 10

C) 9

D) 8

Here's one with **3** variables, so we will need 3 equations. Let's see what they are. First, they tell us that Ken, Justin, and Tiff read a total of 100 books. Using K, J, and T as our variables we have our first equation:

$$K + J + T = 100$$

Simple enough. So are our next 2 equations:

$$J = 3K$$

$$T = 2J$$

Since the question asks for how many books Justin read, we want to put everything in terms of K. J is already in terms of K, but T is not. Substituting J = 3K into T = 2J we get:

$$T = 2(3K) = 6K$$

Now, we can substitute all the variables in terms of K into the first equation to get:

$$K + 3K + 6K = 100$$

Solving for K:

10K = 100

K = 10. Choice **B**.

As you can see, problems with 3 unknowns is not necessarily harder than the typical 2 variable problem.

24.

There are 20 high school seniors who are taking the total of 85 AP classes this year. Some of them take 4 APs and the others take 5. How many seniors are taking 5 APs?

   A) 4

   B) 5

   C) 6

   D) 8

Again, we have a case where descriptive variables aren't very apparent or helpful. So, let's just call the number of seniors who take 4 AP classes, x, and the number who take 5 AP classes, y. Then, our system of equations are:

$$x + y = 20$$

$$4x + 5y = 85$$

We'll use <u>elimination</u> to solve this, although substitution would work just as well:

First, let's multiply the first equation by 4 to set up an elimination of the x variable.

So, $4x + 4y = 80$. Then, subtract that from the second equation:

$$\begin{aligned} 4x + 5y &= 85 \\ -\ \underline{4x + 4y} &= \underline{80} \\ y &= 5 \end{aligned}$$

Choice **B**. Done.

25.

There is $160 cash in John's pocket. John only has 10 and 20 dollar bills. If John has a total of 12 bills, how many 20 dollar bills are in his pocket?

A) 2

B) 4

C) 6

D) 8

Again, it seems like descriptive variables aren't too obvious here. So, let's go with x and y again. Then, let x = the number of 10 dollar bills, and y = the number of 20 dollar bills.

Then, based on the given information, our 2 equations should be:

$$10x + 20y = 160$$

$$x + y = 12$$

Again, elimination or substitution would work equally well here. I'll go with elimination, and then you can try it again with substitution.

Since we want to solve for the number of 20 dollar bills, we want to eliminate the x variable which represents the number of 10 dollar bills. So, let's multiply the second equation by **10**:

$$10x + 10y = 120$$

Now, it's just a matter of subtracting that equation from the first equation:

$$\begin{aligned} 10x + 20y &= 160 \\ -\ 10x + 10y &= 120 \\ \hline 10y &= 40 \end{aligned}$$

And, solving for y, we get y = 4. Choice **B**.

By now, your speed in solving these types of problems should be increasing significantly.

26.

Five erasers cost as much as 3 pencils. If Matt bought one eraser and one pencil for $1.60, how much does one pencil cost in dollars?

A) 0.50

B) 0.60

C) 1.00

D) 1.10

Translating into math as you read, if 5 erasers cost as much as 3 pencils, then:

$$5E = 3P$$

where E is the number of erasers and P is the number of pencils.

Then, we also know, if Matt bought one eraser and one pencil for $1.60:

$$E + P = 1.60$$

Now, we have a choice. We can either put E in terms of P in the <u>first</u> equation and substitute that into the second, **or** we can put E in terms of P in the <u>second</u> equation and substitute that into the first.

If we go with the first option we would have E = (3/5)P. That's not very desirable since E would be *fraction* of P and then we'd be dealing with fraction which are prone to more careless mistakes. So, let's go with the second option.

E = 1.60 – P

Then, substituting that into the first equation we get:

$$5(1.6 - P) = 3P$$

Continuing to solve for P:

8 – 5P = 3P

8P = 8

P = 1. Choice **C**.

Of course, you could have chosen the first option, and if you don't make a careless mistake you'll get the same answer.

27.

A company sells boxes of marbles in red and green. Helen purchased a box of marbles in which there were half as many green marbles in the box as red ones and 15 marbles were green. How many marbles were in Helen's box?

A) 30

B) 40

C) 45

D) 50

Here, descriptive variables should work nicely. We'll call R the number of red marbles, G the number of green marbles. Of course, your choices of variable letters is entirely up to you, so long as you remember what they belong to.

Once again, we'll set up the math equations as we are given the worded information.

"...there were half as many green marbles in the box as red ones and 15 marbles were green." There two equations we can write right away from this information:

$$G = (1/2)R$$

$$G = 15$$

Then, substituting G = 15 into the first equation, we solve for R: 15 = (1/2)R, then R = 15/(1/2) = 30.

Then, the total number of marbles in Helen's box were 15 + 30 = 45. Choice **C**.

You may be wondering why we even needed to set up a system of equations for such a simple problem. The answer is, you should get in the habit of translating English into math, setting up the worded information into logical math equations, and solving in a step by step process. This way, you'll become very proficient at the process, which will allow you to solve the harder ones.

28.

A car rental company calculates the price of renting a car by adding the fixed rental fee with an additional charge for every 10 miles traveled. If the charge to rent a car and drive 50 miles is $120 and the charge to rent a car and drive 200 miles is $165, what would be the price, in dollars, to rent a car and travel 300 miles?

  A) 178
  B) 186
  C) 195
  D) 225

Here's one that's a bit more challenging. Let's start, as usual, by defining our variables.

We'll call F the fixed price, and C the additional charge <u>for every 10 miles traveled</u>.

What do we do with that underlined information, you may wonder? Well, let's think about it. We will need to **divide the miles traveled by 10** to determine how many times the additional charge C is applied. But, it must be a *whole number* because C is applied only in 10 mile intervals.

That means a 50 mile drive has an additional charge of (50/10)C = 5C, and a 200 mile drive has an additional charge of (200/10)C = 20C.

Now we have all the information we need to set up the system of equations:

$$5C + F = 120$$

$$20C + F = 165$$

To answer the question in the problem, we will have to solve for both C and F, and use those values to solve for the price to rent the car and travel 300 miles.

The easiest thing to do is solve for C first by subtracting the first equation from the second:

$$20C + F = 165$$
$$- 5C + F = 120$$
$$15C = 45$$

Solving for C by dividing by 15 we get **C = 3**.

Now we can solve for F using the first equation: 5(3) + F = 120

F = 120 – 15 = **105**.

So, to rent a car and travel 300 miles, (300/10)(3) + 105 = 90 + 105 = 195. Choice **C**.

29.
Mrs. Peters provides some markers to her Art class. If each student takes 3 markers, there will be 1 marker left. If 5 students take 4 markers each and the rest of the students take 2 markers each, there will be no markers left. How many students are in Mrs. Peter's Art class?

A) 6

B) 7

C) 8

D) 9

With problems like these, you can't take it all in in one gulp. You must take it in smaller bites. So, first let's define our variables, as always. I'll call the number of markers M and the number of students S. But be careful here. M is the total number of markers, and you'll see why as we set up the equations.

35

Our first equation is derived from the statement, "If each student takes 3 markers, there will be 1 marker left." That means if we subtract the number of markers taken by the students from the total number of markers, then 1 marker will be left. Mathematically we can write it as follows:

$$M - 3S = 1$$

Hopefully, that was understandable enough. But the next statement is a bit more complicated, yet still quite doable as far as translating it into a math equation.

"If 5 students take 4 markers each and the rest of the students take 2 markers each, there will be no markers left."

Let's break down that statement. "If 5 students take 4 markers each..." Well, how many markers is that? It's simply (5)(4) = 20 markers, right?

Continuing on, "...and the rest of the students take 2 markers each..." How many are the rest of the students? Isn't it just S – 5, which are the original number of students minus the 5 who took 4 markers each? They tell us that remaining number of students took 2 markers each. So, the number of markers those students took can be represented by 2(S – 5). And finally, "...there will be no markers left" means that after all those markers are subtracted from the total original number of markers M, the result is 0. Then, putting all of that information into an equation we have:

$$M - 20 - 2(S - 5) = 0$$

Simplifying that equation we get

$$M - 2S = 10$$

We now have our system of equations, and we can solve:

$$M - 2S = 10$$
$$- \underline{M - 3S = 1}$$
$$S = 9$$

Choice **D**.

While that was more challenging than most of the others, you can see that it still doable if taken step by step, writing down the relationships you know, then putting it all together. However, it would be wise to skip a problem like this on the test and come back to it later if you have the time.

30.
> Twelve Smooth-Glide pens and eight Easy-Write pencils cost exactly $16.00 at Office World. Six Smooth-Glide pens and ten Easy-Write pencils cost $11.00 at the same location. How much will nine Smooth-Glide pens and nine Easy-Write pencils cost at Office World? (Disregard the dollar sign when gridding your answer.)

This is an example of a problem you might see on the SAT on the part where you must grid-in your answer. The only disadvantage is that you can't confirm your answer among a list of choices. So, you have to be very careful not to make a careless mistake.

It's solved the same way you would any other word problem using a system of equations. So, we'll approach it the same way, starting off by defining our variables.

Descriptive variables would work well here. Let's call the price of each Smooth-Glide pen, S, and the price of each Easy-Write pencil, E.

Then, from the first sentence, we can set up our first equation:

$$12S + 8E = 16$$

The next sentence gives us the information we need for the second equation:

$$6S + 10E = 11$$

The question asks for the cost of nine Smooth-Glide pens and nine Easy-Write pencils.

We *could* use elimination to find the cost of each variable and then multiply them by 9 and add them together. But, there's a much easier way to solve this.

Look what happens when we add the two equations:

$$\begin{array}{r} 12S + 8E = 16 \\ +\ \underline{6S + 10E = 11} \\ 18S + 18E = 27 \end{array}$$

Now, if we just divide the whole thing by 2 we get 9S + 9E = **13.50**. Done!

Try not to overlook these shortcuts on the test. They come up more often than you might think, and will save you a lot of time.

This chapter showed you 30 examples of word problems that could be solved using systems of linear equations. As you can imagine, there are limitless ways they can create a word problems of these types, but the approach to solving them is the same.

With practice, you will become proficient and answer these questions without wasting too much time. So, review the problems presented in this chapter until you feel comfortable doing all of them.

Now, let's move on to systems of **inequalities**...

Inequalities

Among the many types of word problems that could appear on the SAT and ACT, one that turns up quite frequently involves inequalities. As you have probably learned in your high school math courses, inequalities are solved very much like equalities, except for a few special rules that make them different. We'll go over them as we solve the problems in this chapter. But, with word problems, the differences are even greater because we must include the added factor of *translation*.

For example, here is a simple inequality that most of you can solve without any problem:

$$5x - 13 \geq 2x + 2$$

Here, like with equalities, we want to get the x variable on one side and the numbers on the side of the inequality sign. Then, continuing to solve:

$3x \geq 15$, and so $x \geq 5$. Done.

With word problems, it's not so straight forward. We can have the **same** inequality as the prior example, but written as a word problem like this:

"Thirteen less than five times a number is *at least* as great as two more than twice that number."

Do you see how that may appear more complicated, yet it is mathematically the same as the prior example?

Well, in this chapter we'll examine a variety of word problems commonly found on the SAT and ACT that will require you to properly interpret inequalities hidden in paragraphs written in plain English.

Let's get started...

1.
The posted weight limit for a freight elevator in a particular building is 3000 pounds. A delivery man that is carrying x identical boxes each weighing 15 pounds on a hand truck will use the freight elevator. If the combined weight of the delivery man and the empty hand truck is 250 pounds, what is the maximum possible value for x that will keep the combined weight of the delivery man, hand truck, and boxes below the posted weight limit of the freight elevator?

A) 175

B) 183

C) 192

D) 202

The variable representing the number of boxes carried by the delivery man is given as x, so we don't need to come up with our own descriptive variable.

Then, clearly, if each box weighs 15 pounds, x boxes weights 15x. Then, adding in the weight of the delivery man and the empty hand truck, there is a total weight of 15x + 250.

So far, so good. But how do we set up a mathematical relationship that will answer the question posed in this problem?

When dealing with inequality word problems there are always key words or phrases that reveal which operation sign to use. In this case, the key word is **below**, which appears in the last sentence. That tells us that the total weight must be *less than* the 3000 pound weight limit of the elevator.

The inequality sign for *less than*, as you probably already know, is <.

Then, the inequality as a math expression becomes:

$$15x + 250 < 3000$$

Continuing to solve:

15x < 2750

x < 183.33

Remember, x represents the <u>number of boxes</u>. And, since you can't have a fraction of a box, the answer is 183. Choice **B**.

2.

A worker uses a forklift to move boxes that weigh either 50 pounds or 75 pounds each. Let x be the number of 50-pound boxes and y be the number of 75-pound boxes. The forklift can carry up to either 35 boxes or a weight of 3,200 pounds. Which of the following systems of inequalities represents this relationship?

A) $\begin{cases} 50x + 75y \leq 3{,}200 \\ x + y \leq 35 \end{cases}$

B) $\begin{cases} \dfrac{x}{50} + \dfrac{y}{75} \leq 3{,}200 \\ x + y \leq 35 \end{cases}$

C) $\begin{cases} 50x + 75y \leq 35 \\ x + y \leq 3{,}200 \end{cases}$

D) $\begin{cases} x + y \leq 3{,}200 \\ 50x + 75y \leq 3{,}200 \end{cases}$

Here, again, the variables are defined for us, so we must use them. But, you'll notice that there is nothing to solve here. The problem only asks for the correct system of inequalities.

Setting up the inequalities is derived from the *third* sentence, "The forklift can carry <u>up to</u> either 35 boxes or a weight of 3,200 pounds."

Pay attention to the underlined words, "up to". That's the key to the proper set up.

Think about what "up to" means. It means any value <u>less</u> the given amount, *including* the amount itself. Then, up to 35 boxes written as an inequality is:

$$x + y \leq 35$$

The other inequality deals with the **weight**, which is calculated by the number of boxes times the weight of each type of box. The weight of each type box is given as 50 and 75 pounds, respectively. Then, the second inequality must be:

$$50x + 75y \leq 3{,}200$$

So, the choice with those two inequalities is **A**.

3.
On March 1, 2010, there were 150,000 tons of plastic at a recycling plant that had a processing capacity of 250,000 tons. Each year since then, the amount of plastic at the plant increased by 5,000 tons. If y represents the time, in years, after March 1, 2010, which of the following inequalities describes the set of years where the plant is at or above capacity?

A) $250{,}000 - 5{,}000 \leq y$

B) $250{,}000 \leq 5{,}000y$

C) $155{,}000 \leq 5{,}000y$

D) $150{,}000 + 5{,}000y \geq 250{,}000$

Here, the last sentence provides the key information needed to answer this problem. Notice the words "**at or above**". That translates to the inequality operation $\geq$, since "at" is *equal to* the value itself and "above" means over or *greater than*.

But what value are they talking about? It's the **capacity**, which is given as 250,000 tons.

So, looking at the choices we can stop right there, because the only choice that shows $\geq 250{,}000$ is choice **D**.

4.

Jack has two part-time jobs. In one job he works as a landscaper, which pays $10 per hour, and in the other he works as a delivery man, which pays $11 per hour. He can work no more than 30 hours per week, but he wants to earn at least $330 per week. Which of the following systems of inequalities represents this situation in terms of x and y, where x is the number of hours he does landscaping, and y is the number of hours he works as a delivery man?

A) $10x + 11y \leq 330$
   $x + y \geq 30$

B) $10x + 11y \leq 330$
   $x + y \leq 30$

C) $10x + 11y \geq 330$
   $x + y \leq 30$

D) $10x + 11y \geq 330$
   $x + y \geq 30$

Here's another system of inequalities problem. Our task is to determine which two inequalities fit the narrative of the paragraph.

The first key phrase is found in line 3: "no more than". Think about that. It means it *can be less than or equal to* but not greater than. Which inequality symbol describes that? It's the ≤ symbol, isn't it?

So then, based on the given information, one of the inequalities **must** contain ≤ 30. With that fact alone, we can *eliminate* choices A and D immediately since they show the opposite.

Then, it's a choice between B and C. That's where the second key phrase comes in:

"at least", which means it *can be greater than or equal to* but not less than. And, of course, that inequality symbol is ≥.

So, that leaves us with choice **C** as the only possible answer.

5.

Karen is working this summer as part of a group of census takers in a her community. She earned $10 per hour for the first 20 hours she worked this week. Because of her performance, her group leader raised her salary to $15 per hour for the rest of the week. Karen saves 90% of her earnings from each week. What is the minimum number of hours she must work the rest of the week to save at least $315 for the week?

A) 25

B) 20

C) 10

D) 5

Clearly, the inequality key term is found in the last sentence, "at least". But how to do we get to the solution?

Let's start with the information given at the beginning. Karen earned $10 per hour for the first 20 hours she worked this week. So, that means, so far, she earned (10)(20) = $200.

Then we're told she got a raise to $15 per hour for the rest of the week. We don't know how many hours that is, so let's use the descriptive variable **h** for those hours.

So, now we know she earned 15h + 200 dollars that week. However, she <u>saves</u> 90% of that each week. That means she saves (0.9)(15h + 200).

The question is what is the <u>minimum</u> number of hours she must work the rest of the week to save <u>at least</u> $315 for the week?

We already know how which inequality operation symbol to use for the term "at least", so we can now set up the inequality:

$$(0.9)(15h + 200) \geq 315$$

We can solve for h by first dividing by the 0.9 to get:

15h + 200 ≥ 350

15 h ≥ 150

h ≥ 10.

Then, the <u>minimum</u> number of hours she needs to work for the rest of the week is 10. Choice **C**.

Although this problem was a bit more involved than some others, if you take it step by step you can see that it is certainly not beyond your reach.

6.

Marty needs to hire at least 5 more workers to deal with increased demand in orders since he issued $5 off coupons on any large pizza. The new workers will be made up of pizza makers who will be paid $540 per week, and pizza delivery drivers who be paid $330 per week, not including tips. His budget for paying the new workers is no more than $3,500 a week. He must hire at least 3 pizza makers and at least 2 delivery drivers. Which of the following systems of inequalities represents the conditions described if x is the number of pizza makers and y is the number delivery drivers?

A) $540x + 330y \geq 3,500$
$x + y \leq 5$
$x \geq 3$
$y \geq 2$

B) $540x + 330y \leq 3,500$
$x + y \geq 5$
$x \geq 3$
$y \geq 2$

C) $540x + 330y \leq 3,500$
$x + y \geq 5$
$x \leq 3$
$y \leq 2$

D) $540x + 330y \leq 3,500$
$x + y \leq 5$
$x \geq 3$
$y \geq 2$

This system of inequalities actual has 4 relationships we have to account for. But, no matter. If we take it step by step it won't be a problem.

The first key term is in the very first sentence: "Marty needs to hire <u>at least</u> 5 more workers…"

They tell us x is the number of pizza makers and y is the number of delivery drivers, so that inequality must be:

$$x + y \geq 5$$

How fortunate, since that eliminates choice A and D immediately. Very often, with systems of inequalities, you have the opportunity to eliminate choices with the very first inequality.

If we're observant, we notice that choices B and C have the same inequality listed as the first among the four. So, that won't help us narrow down the choices. Then, it would be a good to skip the information in the paragraph dealing with that.

Then, the next key term appears in the sentence: "He must hire <u>at least</u> 3 pizza makers and <u>at least</u> 2 delivery drivers."

That means only **B** can be the correct choice.

As you can see, with *systems* of inequalities, the process of elimination is usually the best approach.

7.

At the fish food processing plant, Cynthia can clean at least 30 fish and at most 40 fish per hour. Based on this information, what is a possible amount of time, in hours, that it could take Cynthia to clean 105 fish?

We've seen the term "at least" several times now, so we should have a pretty solid understanding of what that means mathematically.

Now, we see the term "at most", which means the value *can be less than or equal to* but not greater than the given value.

Then, if we call the number of fish Cynthia can clean in an hour, F, we have a simple inequality:

$$30 \leq F \leq 40$$

Notice how we combined the two inequalities into a single inequality. That helps to clarify the situation. It means that Cynthia can clean between 30 and 40 fish per hour.

So, it would be a good idea to just pick a number between 30 and 40. How about 35?

Then, one possible amount of time that it could take Cynthia to clean 105 fish would just be 105/35 = **3** hours.

There were no choices because this was an SAT grid-in problem.

8.

A courier service delivers only 30-pound and 50-pound packages. On each delivery trip, the courier van can carry up to 20 packages, and the total weight of the packages cannot exceed 660 pounds. What is the maximum number of 50-pound packages that the van can carry per trip if the courier service is paid by the pound and wants to maximize profit?

A) 1

B) 2

C) 3

D) 4

Here is a system of inequalities that requires solving. So, let's start off by defining the variables.

We'll call x the number of 30-pound packages, and y the number of 50-pound packages.

We already know the term "up to" means less than or equal to. So, we can set up the first inequality as:

$$x + y \leq 20$$

For the next inequality we see the term "cannot exceed". That simply means the value *can be less than or equal to* but not greater than the given value. Then, based on the fact that the total weight of the packages cannot exceed 660 pounds, we can set up the second inequality as:

$$30x + 50y \leq 660$$

To maximize profit, the van needs to carry as many packages as possible, we want x + y = 20. Then, x = 20 – y, which we can substitute into the second inequality:

30(20 – y) + 50y ≤ 660

600 – 30y + 50y ≤ 660

20y ≤ 60

So, y ≤ **3**. Since we want the maximum number of 50-pound packages, the answer is 3. Choice **C**.

As you can see, solving a system of inequalities is very similar to solving a system of equations, although setting up the system can be a little trickier.

9.
Rapido Shipping Services puts a limit on the size of the boxes they are willing to ship. This limit states that for rectangular shaped boxes, the sum of the perimeter of the base of the box and its height cannot exceed 160 inches. The perimeter of the base is determined using the width and length of the box. If a box has a height

of 50 inches and its length is twice the width, which inequality shows the allowable width x, in inches, of the box?

A) $0 < x \le 15$

B) $0 < x \le 18\frac{1}{3}$

C) $0 < x \le 19\frac{1}{2}$

D) $0 < x \le 20$

This one will require some thinking, so we'll take it slow, step by step.

The second sentence tells us that sum of the perimeter of the base of the box and its height <u>cannot exceed</u> 160 inches.

If we call the perimeter P and the height H, then:

$$P + H \le 160$$

That doesn't get us very far, but at least it gets the ball rolling. The next question is how do find the perimeter? You should remember from algebra 1 and geometry that the perimeter of any rectangular shape is the sum of all the sides, which is twice the length plus twice the width. Mathematically, it's written as 2L + 2W.

Here, they tell us that the width is represented by x. Then, the perimeter of the base of the box is 2L + 2x. We also know that the height is 50 inches. So, let's put all that into our original inequality:

$$2L + 2x + 50 \le 160$$

That's a little better, but we still have two variables. We want to solve for the allowable width x, so we need to get rid of the length L or change it somehow. Do you see how?

They tell us that *the length is twice the width*, so that means L = 2x. Let's substitute that into the inequality to get:

2(2x) + 2x + 50 ≤ 160

Now we only have one variable x, and we can solve:

4x + 2x ≤ 110

6x ≤ 110

x ≤ 18.33

The width must have some measure greater than zero, so the correct expression is

0 < x ≤ 18.33. Choice **B**.

As you can see, if you take a harder problem step by step, using the information that is given, you can usually figure it out. Of course, time is luxury you don't have on the SAT or ACT, so you'd probably want to skip this one and come back to it later if time permits. Or, you can check out a shortcut solution to this problem in my other book, "SAT Math: Book of Shortcuts".

10.

Jeff tests how the total volume occupied by a fluid contained in a graduated cylinder changes when round marbles of various sizes are added. He found that the total volume occupied by the fluid, V, in cubic centimeters, can be found using the equation below, where x equals the number of identical marbles Jeff added, one at a time, to the cylinder, and r is the radius of one of the marbles.

$$V = 24\pi + x\left(\frac{4}{3}\pi r^3\right)$$

If the volume of the graduated cylinder is 96π cubic centimeters, then, what is the maximum number of marbles with a radius of 3 centimeters that Jeff can add without the volume of the fluid exceeding that of the graduated cylinder?

A) 1
B) 2
C) 3
D) 4

As intimidating as this problem may seem, it's really not that bad, as we shall see.

Fortunately, they are *giving us* the equation to use, so that automatically makes this problem less problematic. Now, all we have to do is define the variables and interpret the question correctly.

We see two variables, **x** and **r**. They tell us r is the radius of the graduated cylinder and x is the number of identical marbles Jeff adds to the graduated cylinder.

The question is presented in the last paragraph: "If the volume of the graduated cylinder is 96π cubic centimeters, then, what is the maximum number of marbles with a radius of 3 centimeters that Jeff can add without the volume of the fluid exceeding that of the graduated cylinder?"

From that last sentence we now know that the volume of the graduated cylinder is 96π cubic centimeters and r = 3. So, now we're down to one variable x, which is the one we're looking for to answer the question.

The phrase "without the volume of the fluid exceeding..." means that the volume *can be less than or equal to* but not great than. So we need to use the symbol ≤. Now, we can set up the inequality:

$$24\pi + x\left(\frac{4}{3}\pi(3^3)\right) \le 96\pi$$

Continuing to solve for x:

$24\pi + x\left(\frac{4}{3}\pi(27)\right) \le 96\pi$

24π + 36πx ≤ 96π

36πx ≤ 72π

x ≤ 72π/36π, therefore x ≤ 2. So, the *maximum* number of marbles that can be added are 2. Choice **B**.

11.

Sai is ordering new shelving units for his store. Each unit is 7 feet in length and extends from floor to ceiling. Sai's store has 119 feet of wall space that includes 21 feet of windows along the walls. If the shelving units cannot be placed in front of the windows, which of the following inequalities includes all possible values of r, the number of shelving units that Sai could use?

A) $r \leq \dfrac{119-21}{7}$

B) $r \geq \dfrac{119+21}{7}$

C) $r \leq 119 - 21 + 7r$

D) $r \geq 119 + 21 - 7r$

Here again, we're not asked to solve, but only to set up the proper inequality.

The variable r is given as the number of shelving units that Sai could use.

That number depends on the available wall space, which includes 21 feet of windows which must be *subtracted* since shelving units cannot be placed in front of windows.

Then, the available wall space is 119 − 21 feet. Since each shelving unit is 7 feet long, the maximum number of shelving units is $\dfrac{119-21}{7}$.

Since we cannot exceed the maximum, the possible number of shelving units can be any amount *less than or equal to* the maximum. Hence, choice **A**.

12.

Dogs need 8.5 to 17 ounces of water each day for every 10 pounds of their weight. Everett has two dogs—Ringo is a 35-pound black lab mix, and Elvis is a 55-pound beagle. Which of the following ranges represents the approximate total number of ounces of water, w, that Elvis and Ringo need in a week?

A) $77 \le w \le 153$

B) $109 \le w \le 218$

C) $536 \le w \le 1,071$

D) $765 \le w \le 1,530$

Inequalities are often used to represent a *range* of values, as illustrated in this problem.

Once again, this type of problem will require a series of step before we arrive at the correct choice.

The problem tells us that the *minimum* amount of water a dog needs is 8.5 ounces each day for every 10 pounds of weight. That can be represented mathematically by the ratio 8.5/10.

They also tells us that the *maximum* amount of water is 17 ounce for every 10 pounds, which is represented by 17/10.

The total weight of *both* dogs is 35 + 55 = 90 pounds. So, the minimum amount of water they need is (8.5/10)(90) = (8.5)(9) = **76.5 ounces** per day, and the maximum is (17/10)(90) = (17)(9) = **153 ounces** per day. So far, so good.

The question is asking for range of water required for both dogs in *a week*.

Well, we all know that there are 7 days in a week. So the range is a minimum of (7)(76.5) = **535.5** ounce of water, and a maximum of (7)(153) = **1,071** ounce.

That range is represented *approximately* by choice **C**.

Once again, we see, that a step by step approach renders a seemingly difficult problem quite doable.

13.

Lennon has 6 hours to spend in Ha Ha Tonka State Park. He plans to drive around the park at an average speed of 20 miles per hour, looking for a good trail to hike. Once he finds a trail he likes, he will spend the remainder of his time hiking it. He hopes to travel more than 60 miles total while in the park. If he hikes at an average speed of 1.5 miles per hour, which of the following systems of inequalities can be solved for the number of hours Lennon spends driving, d, and the number of hours he spends hiking, h, while he is at the park?

A) $1.5h + 20d > 60$
   $h + d \leq 6$

B) $1.5h + 20d > 60$
   $h + d \geq 6$

C) $1.5h + 20d < 60$
   $h + d \geq 360$

D) $20h + 1.5d > 6$
   $h + d \leq 60$

Here's another system of inequalities that does not require any solving, only the set up.

Although this word problem is rather lengthy, it can be solved relatively quickly by process of elimination.

The first, notice in the very first sentence, that Lennon has 6 hours to spend at the park, <u>and not more!</u> Although the no more part was not explicitly stated, it is certainly *implied.* That means the time he spends driving, d, and the time he spends hiking, h, together must be *less than or equal to* 6. The **only** choice that shows that fact is choice **A**. Done!

As an added confirmation that A is the correct choice, you could notice in the third sentence the term *more than* 60 miles. That means one of the inequalities must show **> 60**. Only choices A and B show this. But choice B has an incorrect inequality showing

54

that the hiking and driving time can be greater than 6 hours, which, as previously explained, is false.

You can see, that in problems like these, logic plays a bigger role than mathematical calculations.

14.
Samantha offers two different packages of yoga classes at her yoga studio. She offers two hot yoga sessions and three zero gravity yoga sessions at a total cost of $400. She also offers four hot yoga sessions and two zero gravity sessions at a price of $440. Samantha wants to offer a larger package for long-time clients in which the cost must exceed $800. If Samantha does not wish to include more than 13 sessions for the long-time client package, will she be able to create this package for her clients?

A) No, because the closest package that she can offer consists of three hot yoga and three zero gravity yoga sessions.

B) No, because the closest package that she can offer consists of four hot yoga and four zero gravity yoga sessions.

C) Yes, because she can offer five hot yoga and five zero gravity yoga sessions.

D) Yes, because she can offer six hot yoga and six zero gravity yoga sessions.

This is an interesting problem in that it involves systems of *equations* **and** *inequalities*.

How do we handle that? Well, we're going to need to know the cost of each hot yoga session and each zero gravity yoga session to determine which package fulfills all of Samantha's criteria for the larger package offer. In order to do that we'll need to set up a system of equations based on the given information of the current two packages of yoga sessions.

Let's start by choosing descriptive variables. How about **H** for the cost of each hot yoga session and **Z** for the cost of each zero gravity yoga session?

Then, according to the given information:

$$2H + 3Z = 400$$

$$4H + 2Z = 440$$

If you studied the previous chapter, this set up should be a piece of cake.

Let's use the elimination method to solve. We can eliminate the H variable first by multiplying the first equation by 2 and then subtracting the second equation from it.

$$4H + 6Z = 800$$
$$- \underline{4H + 2Z = 440}$$
$$4Z = 360$$

Then, **Z = 90**.

To solve for H, just plug the value for Z into either of the original equations. Let's use the first one again:

2H + 3(90) = 400

2H + 270 = 400

2H = 130

H = 65.

Now, we can use that information to see which of the choices cost *exceeds* 800, which is a requirement according to the problem, and also has no more than 13 sessions, which is another requirement.

The question asks if she will be able to create such a package based on those requirements. Let's look at the choices:

A) Three hot yoga and three zero gravity yoga sessions is far below the 13 session limit, which fulfills that requirement, but it does not exceed $800 in cost. Although it does not fulfill all of Samantha's requires, that does not mean there is not another package she can create that will.

B) This is also incorrect for same reasons that choice A is.

C) While five hot yoga and five zero gravity session is not more than 13 session, it also does not exceed the $800, since 5(65) + 5(90) = $775. So, that won't work.

D) Six hot yoga and six zero gravity yoga sessions is less than 13 **and** costs more than $800, since 6(65) + 6(90) = $930.

So, **D** is the answer.

Although this was a rather lengthy problem and explanation, it can be done relatively quickly once you understand the steps involved. But, as stated previously, a problem like is this best skipped and returned to later in the test, if time permits, unless you are confident you can solve it straight away. Remember, on the SAT and ACT all problems are worth the same points, regardless of their difficulty.

15.

The number of eggs that Farmer Jones has in his chicken coop will grow exponentially as Farmer Jones buys more chickens to increase production. The number of eggs Farmer Jones has in the coop can be modeled by the equation $y = 3^x$ beginning on Day 1, where x is given by $x = 1$, and y is the number of eggs currently in the coop. If the coop can support only 4,000 eggs, and Farmer Jones empties the coop every day, on which day will the chickens produce too many eggs for the coop to support?

A) Day 6
B) Day 7
C) Day 8
D) Day 9

You should not be intimidated by exponential equations. Remember, one of the given choices must be the answer, so we can plug them in to see which one answers the question correctly.

First we must correctly interpret the word problem. They tell us that y is the number of eggs currently in the coop. And they also tell us that 4000 the *maximum* number of eggs the coop can support.

They also tell us, implicitly, that x is the number of days that the chickens are laying eggs. I say *implicitly* because they don't directly state that in the problem, but you can see from the given equation that the number of eggs produced depends on the number of days.

The question asks on which day will the chickens produce *too many eggs* for the coop to support. That can be written mathematically by the inequality:

$$3^x > 4000$$

Although this can solved with logarithms, it's unnecessary since we can just check the choices to see which value of x makes 3^x greater than 4000.

This would most certainly be on section 4 of the SAT where calculators are permitted. Then, plugging in the choices we find $3^8 = 6561$, which is greater than 4000. So, choice **C** is the answer.

16. Shaun is developing a weight loss regimen, which includes both a workout plan and a calorie-restriction plan. Shaun wants to work out for no less than 30 minutes and no more than 60 minutes a day and consume no less than 2,000 and no more than 2,500 calories. If each minute, m, of his workout time burns 50 calories, which of the following inequalities represents the number of minutes, m, that Shaun can work out each day to burn off as many calories as he consumes?

    A) $30 \leq m \leq 60$
    B) $30 \leq m \leq 50$
    C) $40 \leq m < 50$
    D) $40 \leq m \leq 50$

Here's another system of inequalities. They are described by the second sentence: "Shaun wants to work out for *no less than* 30 minutes and *no more than* 60 minutes a day and consume *no less than* 2,000 and *no more than* 2,500 calories."

No less than means that the value can be greater than or equal to the given value, denoted by the symbol ≥ , and *no greater than* means the value can be less than or equal to the given value, denoted by the symbol ≤ .

Since they tell us the variable *m* represents the number of minutes of Shaun's workout, and each minute burns 50 calories, then our 2 inequalities are:

$$30 \leq m \leq 60$$

$$2{,}000 \leq 50m \leq 2{,}500$$

A system of inequalities is not as straightforward as a system of equations, where you can use elimination or substitution to solve.

If we substitute 30 for *m* from the first inequality, you can see that it doesn't work in the second inequality since 50(30) = 1500, which is **not** greater than or equal to 2000.

But, if we solve for *m* in the second inequality by dividing by 50 we get:

$$40 \leq m \leq 50$$

That range of values falls *within* the range of values of the first inequality, so it satisfies **both** inequalities. So, choice **D** is the answer.

17.

In a certain ancient farming community, anthropologists determine that new dwellings were constructed monthly as modeled by the function $f(x) = 2x + 100$, where x is the current month of the year and $f(x)$ is the number of dwellings constructed by the end of that month. Additionally, they determine that the population grew exponentially each month, thanks to the discovery of more fertile land for farming. This growth is modeled by the equation $g(x) = 3^x$, where $g(x)$ represents the current population at the end of a given month. What is the smallest integer value of x, with 1 representing the end of January and 12 representing the end of December, at which the population surpasses the number of dwellings built?

A) 2

B) 5

C) 8

D) 10

Again, we see a problem that might seem too intimidating to tackle at first. But, in the end, you'll see that it is a relatively simple inequality problem.

As always, interpreting the words is our primary challenge. Several variables are defined and certain equations are given. We are told that in an ancient farming community, new dwelling were constructed monthly according to a given function where **x** is the current month of the year and **f(x)** is the number of dwellings constructed by the end of the month. We are also given a function that represents the population growth of the ancient community, where g(x) is the current population at the end of a given month.

The question asks us to find the smallest value of x at which the population surpasses the number of dwellings built.

So, basically we're looking for the smallest value of x at which the g(x) function is greater than the f(x) function.

When you understand that is all that is really being asked here, the math becomes quite simple:

$$3^x > 2x + 100$$

Now, it's just a matter of plugging in the choices to see which one is the smallest, yet true:

A) $3^2 = 9$ which is **not** greater than $2(3) + 100 = 106$

B) $3^5 = 243$ which **is** greater than $2(5) + 100 = 110$.

Therefore, **B** is the answer.

As you do more word problems like these, you'll become more confident and less intimidated by them. They will always boil down to one or more equations and/or inequalities that will not be too difficult to solve.

18.

David is planning a dinner for his birthday. At one restaurant, the cost per person for dinner is $15, with an additional one-time set-up charge of $35. David has a maximum budget of $150. If p represents the number of people (including David) who will attend the dinner, which of the following inequalities represents the number of people who can attend within budget?

A) $15p \leq 150 + 35$

B) $35 \leq 150 - 15p$

C) $15p \geq 150 - 35$

D) $35 \geq 150 - 15p$

This one is much easier than the past few, and more typical of what you might expect on your test.

Still, it's not trivial and should not be taken lightly. Here, we'll need to first determine the right linear relationship between the cost of the party and the number of people.

We're told from the beginning that the cost per person is $15, with an additional set-up charge of $35. We're also given the variable that represents the number of people who will attend the dinner party as *p*.

So, the total cost can be represented mathematically as **15p + 35**.

If David has a maximum budget of $150, then the maximum cost is $150 and we can now set up an equality to determine how many people can attend without exceeding David's budget:

$$15p + 35 \leq 150$$

You'll notice that none of the choices show this inequality. But wait, one really does. It's just written in a different form.

If you subtract 15p from both sides, you get 35 ≤ 150 − 15p. Choice **B**.

19.
Marco is ordering salt, which is only sold in 30-pound bags. He currently has 75 pounds of salt, and he needs to have a minimum of 200 pounds. Which of the following inequalities shows all possible values for the number of bags, b, that Marco needs to order to meet his minimum requirement?

A) $b \geq 4$

B) $b \geq 5$

C) $b \geq 6$

D) $b \geq 7$

If Marco already has 75 pounds of salt, he will need 200 – 75 = 125 more pounds to meet his minimum requirement of 200 pounds.

Since each bag weighs 30 pounds, and b represents the number of bags Marco needs to order to meet his minimum requirement, the inequality should be:

$$30b \geq 125$$

Solving for b:

b ≥ 125/30, so b ≥ 4.167.

But the bags are only sold as whole bags. So, he must order at least 5. Choice **B**.

20.
Clark's Rule is a formula used to determine the correct dosage of adult over-the-counter medicine a child can receive. The child's weight, in pounds, is divided by 150, and the result is multiplied by the adult dose of the medicine. A mother needs to give her daughter acetaminophen, which has an adult dose of 1,000 milligrams. She does not know her daughter's exact weight, but she knows the weight is

between 75 and 90 pounds. Which of the following gives the range of correct dosage, d, in milligrams of acetaminophen the daughter could receive?

A) $50 < d < 60$

B) $500 < d < 600$

C) $1{,}000 < d < 1{,}200$

D) $1{,}600 < d < 2{,}000$

Once again, we only need to find the *range of values*, not any specific value, by using inequalities.

While the mother does not know her child's exact weight, she know it is between 75 and 90 pounds, which means it's *greater than* 75 but *less than* 90.

But the question is asking about dosage which is calculated, according to the problem, by taking the child's weight, dividing it by 150, and multiplying by 1000.

Then, the dosage on the low end would be (75/150)(1000) = 500 milligrams. And, on the high end, it would be (90/150)(1000) = 600 milligrams.

Therefore, choice **B**.

21.

Amanda is trying to decide whether to buy a season pass to her favorite baseball team's 30 home games this season. The cost of an individual ticket is $12, and the cost of a season pass is $180. The season pass will admit Amanda to any home baseball game at no additional cost. What is the minimum number of home baseball games Amanda must attend this season in order for the cost of a season pass to be less than the total cost of buying an individual ticket for each game she attends?

A.   10
B.   12
C.   14

D. 15
E. 16

This is a problem you may see on the ACT exam, and for that reason it has 5 choices, as do all ACT math problems.

You'll notice that it's not really much different than a word problem that could appear on the SAT. That's because both exams test you on almost the same topics.

The inequality is defined in the last sentence which contains the question:

"What is the <u>minimum</u> number of home baseball games Amanda must attend this season in order for the cost of a season pass to be <u>less than</u> the total cost of an individual ticket for each game she attends?"

The key inequality terms are underlined. But what are they referring to? Well, the number of home games that Amanda must attend is the question and the unknown. Let's call it **x** since it's the only variable we need. We know each individual ticket cost $12, so 12x will tell us the total cost of those tickets. And we need to find x such that the cost of a season pass is *less than* the total cost of the individual tickets. Then, we can set up a simple inequality based on this question:

$$180 < 12x$$

But, let's turn it around so we don't make any careless mistakes:

$$12x > 180$$

That may seem trivial, but you'd be surprise at how many students make careless mistakes with inequality symbols.

Then, the solution is simply x > 15. And here is where the majority of careless mistakes occur, because **half** of students who get this far answering the problem, blow it by choosing D as the answer. They carelessly forget that the answer must be <u>greater than</u> 15! So, the correct answer is **E**.

Be on the lookout for these type of problems that have a common careless mistake among the choices.

22.

At her hot dog stand, Janie sells hot dogs for $3 each. Purchasing hot dogs and other supplies costs $300 per month. The solution of which of the following inequalities models the numbers of hot dogs, h, Janie can sell per month and make a profit?

A. $h - 300 > 0$
B. $h - 300 < 0$
C. $h + 300 > 0$
D. $3h - 300 < 0$
E. $3h - 300 > 0$

Here's another problem you might see on the ACT. Once again, you're not asked to solve anything. Just choose the correct inequality.

To "make a profit", Janie must earn <u>more</u> money from the sale of her hot dogs than from the total cost of her hot dog stand operation.

The amount of money she earns is simply 3h, since each hot dog sells for $3 and h is the number of hot dogs she can sell per month. Her total costs are $300. Then, we can set up an inequality according to the question:

$$3h > 300$$

Once again, that inequality doesn't appear to be among the choices given. However, a simple rearrangement by subtracting 300 from both sides will give the correct answer:

$$3h - 300 > 0$$

Don't forget your basic algebra! Choice **E**.

23.

A new club wants to attract customers who are at least 18 but not more than 30 years of age. One of the number lines below illustrates the range of ages, in years, of the customers the club wants to attract. Which number line is it?

F.
```
———+——————•———————•———
   0        18       30
```

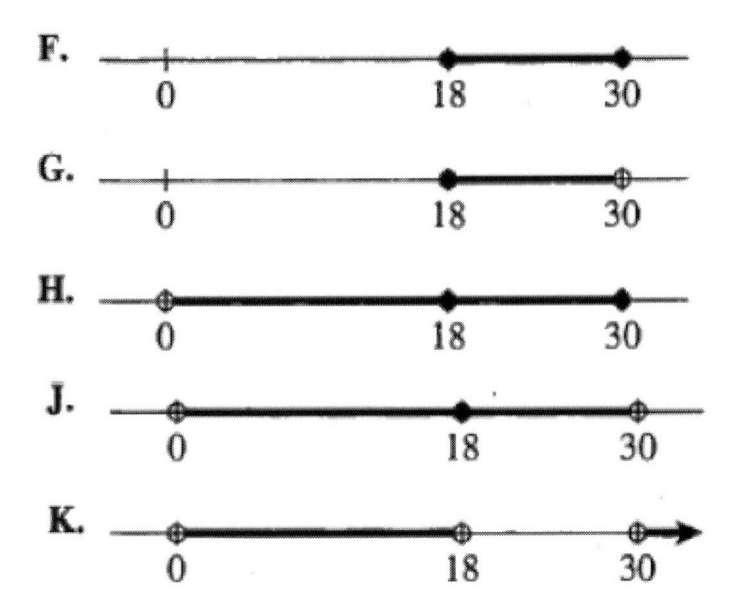

G.
```
———+——————•———————⊕———
   0        18       30
```

H.
```
———⊕——————•———————•———
   0        18       30
```

J.
```
———⊕——————•———————⊕———
   0        18       30
```

K.
```
———⊕——————⊕———————⊕——→
   0        18       30
```

Here's another ACT problem that has come up from time to time on prior tests.

If you remember what the key terms mean, then it should be a cinch.

If we let A be the age of the customers, then "…at least 18 but not more than 30 years of age", can be represented by the inequality:

$$18 \leq A \leq 30$$

If you're careful to remember that the key terms **include** the beginning and ending values, then you'll see that choice **F** is the answer.

Use the following information to answer the next 2 questions:

The Panthers athletic department at Frelley High School needs to raise $2,500.00 to fill a gap in its annual budget. The athletic department can choose 1 of the 2 options below to raise the needed funds.

Sell "Panthers baseball caps" option: After paying a one-time fee of $23.00 to rent the necessary equipment, the athletic department can sell baseball caps featuring the school's logo. The athletic department will buy plain caps and print the school logo on each, at a cost of $3.50 per cap. The athletic department will sell each cap for $5.00.

Sell "Panthers T-shirts" option: After paying a one-time fee of $19.00 to rent the necessary equipment, the athletic department can sell T-shirts featuring the school's logo. The athletic department will buy plain T-shirts and print the school logo on each, at a cost of $2.25 per T-shirt. The athletic department will sell each T-shirt for $4.00.

24.

For the "Panthers baseball caps" option, at least how many baseball caps must be sold in order to cover the one-time fee of renting the necessary equipment?

F. 14
G. 15
H. 16
J. 17
K. 23

These multi-part problems occur quite frequently on the ACT and SAT. The best way to handle them is to read the question first. Then, refer back to the passage.

To answer the first question, we refer back to the passage where we are told that the "one-time fee" is $23.00. We are also told that each cap will sell for $5 and costs $3.50. That means each cap has a profit of 5 – 3.50 = **$1.50**.

If we let x = the number of baseball caps sold, then, to find out how many baseball caps must be sold to at least cover the one-time fee, we can set up the following inequality:

$$1.50x \geq 23$$

Continuing to solve:

x ≥ 23/1.5. Therefore, x ≥ 15.33. And, since you can't sell a fraction of a cap, the answer must be 16. **H.**

Moving on to the next question from the same passage...

25.

The Panthers athletic department chose the "Panthers T-shirt" option and successfully filled the budget gap. What is the minimum number of T-shirts the athletic department must have sold?

F. 1,440
G. 1,664
H. 1,709
J. 1,726
K. 1,812

Again, referring back to the passage, if the cost of a T-shirt is $2.25 and the selling price is $4.00, then the profit is 4 – 2.25 = **$1.75**.

Also, the very beginning of the passage tells us that the budget gap is $2,500.

Taking into account a one-time fee of $19.00, and letting x = the number of T-shirts sold, we can set up an inequality to find the minimum number of T-shirts that must have been sold to fill in the budget gap:

$$1.75x - 19 \geq 2,500$$

Continuing to solve:

1.75x ≥ 2519

x ≥ 2519/1.75. Therefore x ≥ 1,439.43.

Again, since they can't sell a fraction of a T-shirt, the answer is **F**.

26.

If 3 times a number x is added to 12, the result is negative. Which of the following gives the possible value(s) for x?

F. All $x > 4$
G. All $x < -4$
H. 36 only
J. 4 only
K. 0 only

This one may not seem like an inequality problem but it actually is.

You just need to realize that all negative numbers are <u>less than</u> zero.

Then, the set up for this problem is just:

$$3x + 12 < 0$$

Continuing to solve:

$3x < -12$

$x < -4$. Choice **G**.

27.
Nick needs to order 500 pens from his supplier. The catalog shows that these pens come in cases of 24 boxes with 10 pens in each box. Nick knows that he may NOT order partial cases. What is the fewest number of cases he should order?

A. 2
B. 3
C. 18
D. 21
E. 50

This question may seem trivial but you'll notice that it does not contain any of the key terms that would indicate we're dealing with an inequality. Here, the inequality is *implied*.

If Nick <u>needs</u> to order 500 pens, then he must order <u>at least</u> 500 pens.

The problem tells us that each case has 24 boxes with 10 pens in each box. So, each case contains (24)(10) = 240 pens.

Then, if we let C be the number of cases, our inequality becomes:

$$240C \geq 500$$

Solving for C we get:

69

C ≥ 500/240. Therefore C ≥ 2.08. Even though that number is very close to 2, it's not enough since Nick cannot order partial cases. Therefore, he must order 3 cases. **B**.

28.

> Shannon is planning to tile a rectangular kitchen countertop that is 24 inches wide and 64 inches long. She determined that 1 tile will be needed for each 4-inch-by-4-inch region. What is the minimum number of tiles that will be needed to completely cover the countertop to its edges?
>
> A. 44
> B. 88
> C. 96
> D. 176
> E. 384

Since the question is asking for the *minimum* number of tiles, the amount can be *greater than or equal to* a certain value.

To determine that value we need to identify the how the tiles are involved in the problem. They will be used to cover a rectangular kitchen countertop that is 24 inches by 64 inches in *area*. That calculates to be 1536 *square inches.*

Shannon determined that 1 tile will be needed for each 4 x 4 inch region. That's another way of saying that each tile is 16 square inches in area. So, you can see how important it is to properly translate the paragraph.

Then, if we let T be the number of tiles needed, we can write an inequality to answer the problem:

$$16T \geq 1536$$

Continuing to solve for T:

T ≥ 96. Then the minimum number of tiles would be 96. Choice **C**.

This problem had a whole number solution, but if the solution instead would have been 96.35 tiles, for instance, then the answer would have been 97.

29.

The braking distance, y feet, for Damon's car to come to a complete stop is modeled by $y = \frac{3(x^2 + 10x)}{40}$, where x is the speed of the car in miles per hour. According to this model, which of the following is the maximum speed, in miles per hour, Damon can be driving so that the braking distance is less than or equal to 150 feet?

F. 10
G. 30
H. 40
J. 50
K. 60

This is not really too difficult to set up. They give you the braking distance formula and define the variable x as the speed of the car in miles per hour.

They are asking for the <u>maximum</u> speed at which the breaking distance will be <u>less than or equal</u> to 150 feet.

So, the set up is very straight forward:

$$\frac{3(x^2+10x)}{40} \leq 150$$

You *could* solve this by creating a quadratic inequality, but why bother? The answer is among the choices! Let's just plug them in:

F) $\frac{3(10^2+10(10))}{40} = \frac{3(200)}{40} = 15$. While that is less than 150, we're looking for the *maximum* speed which will produce a result closer to 150.

G) $\frac{3(30^2+10(30))}{40} = \frac{3(1200)}{40} = 90$. Getting closer, but still not there.

H) $\frac{3(40^2+10(40))}{40} = \frac{3(2000)}{40} = 150$. That's it. Can't go faster without exceeding 150 ft breaking distance. So, the answer is **H**.

Don't be intimidated by complicated formulas. Often, you can just plug in the choices to find the answer.

30.

Tickets for a community theater production cost $6 each when bought in advance and $8 each when bought at the door. The theater group's goal is at least $2,000 in ticket sales for opening night. The theater group sold 142 opening-night tickets in advance. What is the minimum number of tickets they need to sell at the door on opening night to make their goal?

A. 143
B. 144
C. 192
D. 250
E. 357

You should have the hang of this by now. There is nothing tricky about this problems.

As with systems of equations, we'll use descriptive variables for the two differently priced tickets. Let's call the tickets bought in advance, A, and the ones bought at the door, D.

The theater group's goal is at least $2000 in ticket sales. So, we can set up the inequality right away:

$$6A + 8D \geq 2{,}000$$

They tell us that 142 advance tickets were sold, so we can plug that into A immediately and solve for D:

$6(142) + 8D \geq 2{,}000$

$852 + 8D \geq 2{,}000$

$8D \geq 1148$

$D \geq 143.5$. Again, there are no fractions of tickets, so the answer is 144. **B**.

That concludes this chapter on Inequality word problems. Hopefully, 30 examples were enough to give you a good idea of the problems of these types to expect on the SAT or ACT. Remember to focus on the key inequality terms and underline them as you read the problems. If it's still confusing after doing that, skip it and come back to the problem later if time permits.

Percentages

Word problems involving percentages occur so frequently on the SAT and ACT that they deserve their own chapter. The creators of the tests like to present percentage problems because there are so many ways create them and so many kinds of problems that use percentages in one form or another that there are endless problems to put on present and future exams, while being certain that students will never see the same problem twice.

In this chapter I will show you the various types of word problem that require you to have a certain degree of mastery and understanding of percentages and how to use them in real-life scenarios, as they have appeared on numerous SAT and ACT exams in the recent past.

So, let's dive right in and see what you might expect to encounter on your upcoming exam.

1. Sarah bought a flat screen TV at a department store that gave a 15 percent discount off its original price. The total amount she paid to the cashier was d dollars, including a 6 percent sales tax on the discounted price. Which of the following represents the original price of the TV in terms of d?

   A) $0.91d$

   B) $\dfrac{d}{0.91}$

   C) $(0.85)(1.06)d$

   D) $\dfrac{d}{(0.85)(1.06)}$

Many students are completely befuddled by a problem like this. They never really grasped what it means, mathematically, when an item goes up or down in price by a certain percentage. Well, let's take the mystery out of it right now.

Any time something of any value **increases** by a certain percentage, the new amount can be mathematically calculated using what's called a **growth factor**. I discussed this at length in my first book, "SAT Math Book of Shortcuts". I'll reiterate it all here.

The growth factor is determined by adding the percentage increase written in decimal form to the number one.

So, for example, if a shirt costs $25 and the price increases by 12%, the growth factor would be 1 + 0.12 = **1.12**. Applying that to the old price, the new price is simply (1.12)(25) = **$28**. Done! What could be easier than that?

What if the same shirt is on sale at a discount of 12%? Well, in that case, we would apply a **decay** or **depreciation** factor, which is determined by subtracting the percentage decrease written in decimal form from the number one.

So, going back to the shirt example, at a discount of 12%, the decay factor would be 1 − 0.12 = **0.88**. Applying that to the pre-sale price, the sale price is simply (0.88)(25) = **$22**. Done!

If you remember these simple rules, suddenly percentage problems become a whole lot easier.

Now, let's see how this helps us solve the given SAT word problem.

In the problem we are told that Sarah bought a flat screen TV that 15% discounted off it's original price. So, right away, we know the decay factor is 1 − 0.15 = **0.85**.

So, if we call the original price P, then the discounted price would be 0.85P.

We are also told that a 6% sales tax was applied to the discounted price. Now, think. Does the sales tax increase or decrease the discounted price. It **increases** it, of course. So, we can treat the sales tax as a growth factor of 6%, which is 1 + 0.06 = **1.06**.

Since the amount she paid to the cashier is d, we can now set up an equation based on the given information:

$$(1.06)(0.85P) = d$$

Then, the original price P is $\dfrac{d}{(0.85)(1.06)}$. Choice **D**.

I hope that took the confusion out of that problem that **so** many students get wrong.

2.
>Karen is a stock broker who advises clients on which stocks to purchase for their portfolios. She noticed that stock A produced a 20 percent greater annual return than stock B. Based on Karen's observation, if

stock A produced $1440 in profit, how much did stock B
B produce?

A) 1150

B) 1200

C) 1240

D) 1730

This problem states that stock A produced a 20 percent greater annual return than stock B.

A 20 percent <u>greater</u> annual return means a <u>growth factor</u> of 1 + 0.2 = 1.2.

Are you beginning to see a pattern here? If we call A the amount of profit of stock A, and B the amount of profit of stock B, we can set up a simple equation:

$$A = 1.2B$$

They tell us that stock produced $1440 in profit, so all we have to do is plug that into the equation and solve for B:

1440 = 1.2B

B = 1440/1.2 = 1200. Choice **B**. Done.

Suddenly, these kind of percentage problems are not so intimidating anymore, are they?

3.

Jamie opened a bank account that earns 1 percent interest compounded annually. Her initial deposit was $1000, and she uses the expression $1000(x)^t$ to find the value of the account after t years. What is the value of x in the expression?

A) 10

B) 100

C) 1.01

D) 0.10

Here, the problem states Jamie's bank account, which is initially $1000, earn 1 percent interest <u>compounded annually</u>, which just means it increases by 1 percent <u>every year</u>.

But now we know that a 1 percent increase is a growth factor of 1 + 0.01 = **1.01**.

So, after one year the new amount is (1000)(1.01). Then, the next year it is [(1000)(1.01)](1.01) = 1000(1.01)^2 , etc. So, in t years it would be 1000(1.01)^t.

Then, x must be 1.01. Choice **C**.

4.

A radioactive substance decays at an annual rate of 15 percent. If the initial amount of the substance is 450 grams, which of the following functions f models the remaining amount of the substance, in grams, t years later?

A) $f(t) = 450(0.85)^t$

B) $f(t) = 450(0.15)^t$

C) $f(t) = 0.85(450)^t$

D) $f(t) = 0.15(450)^t$

The decay factor is practically revealed in the very first sentence.

If the substance decays by 15 percent every year, then the decay factor is just 1 − 0.15 = 0.85, which is applied to the remaining amount every year.

The only choice that shows this decay factor is **A**. Done.

5.

The atomic weight of an unknown element, in atomic mass units (amu), is approximately 15% less than that of boron. The atomic weight of boron is 10.8 amu. Which of the following best approximates the atomic weight, in amu, of the unknown element?

A) 5

B) 7

C) 9

D) 11

Here's the **decay factor** again. 15% less represents a decay factor of 1 − 0.15 = 0.85. So, (10.8)(0.85) = 9.18. Choice **C**.

6.

In planning the electric power distribution in a city, an electrical engineer estimates that, starting from the present, the population of the city will increase by 10 percent every 10 years. If the present population of the city is 100,000, which of the following expressions represents the engineer's estimate of the population x years from now?

A) $100,000(0.1)^{10x}$

B) $100,000(0.1)^{\frac{x}{10}}$

C) $100,000(1.1)^{10x}$

D) $100,000(1.1)^{\frac{x}{10}}$

This one may seem a little more confusing, but you can narrow it down to two choices right away using the growth factor.

When you read in the passage that the population of the city will increase by 10% every 10 years, you at least know that the growth factor must be 1 + 0.10 = **1.1**.

Just that fact alone allows to narrow down the choices to C or D. So, even if you had to guess, your chances of guess right just went up from 20% to 50%.

But, there is no need to guess. The growth factor is applied *every 10 years.* That means in 10 years the population goes up 10%. In 20 years it goes up another 10%, and so on. So, looking at the 20 example, 20/10 = 2 correctly describes the population going up 10% **twice.** So, **D** must be the answer.

If it were C, then in 20 years, according to that choice, the population would go up by 10 percent (10)(20) = 200 times, which would be absurd.

7.

Top Wheels Investment		
Car Model	Purchase Price (dollars)	Monthly lease price (dollars)
Turbo XL	34,000	350
Safari 4WD	42,000	433
Road Hog Sedan	29,500	304
Sprite Convertible	23,000	237
Sportster RX	32,500	335

Top Wheels dealership purchased the Turbo XL model and received a 40% discount off the original manufacturer's suggested retail price along with an additional 20% off the discounted price for purchasing the car in cash. Which of the following best approximates the original manufacturer's suggested retail price, in dollars, for the Turbo XL?

A) $85,000

B) $71,000

C) $63,000

D) $55,000

In this problem we're clearly dealing with decay factors because amounts are being **discounted** by a certain percentage.

The choices given are the **original** manufacturer's suggested retail prices. According to the table, the purchase price of the Turbo XL was $34,000. So, we just need to apply the decay factors of 1 – 0.4 = 0.6 and 1 – 0.2 = 0.8 to the given choices to see which one results in approximately $34,000.

A) (0.6)(0.8)(85,000) ≠ 34,000

B) (0.6)(0.8)(71,000) = 34,080 Done.

8.

A customer paid $48.50 for a jacket after a 5 percent sales tax was added. What was the price of the jacket before the sales tax was added?

A) $45.65
B) $46.19
C) $47.50
D) $48.00

Now, these type of problems should be starting to be easy for you.

We have already seen what an added sales tax represents. It's just a percentage increase in the original amount, and therefore can be calculated using a growth factor.

With a 5 percent sales tax, the growth factor is just 1 + 0.05 = **1.05**.

If we call P the price of the price of the jacket *before* the sales tax was added, then the equation to solve is:

$$1.05P = 48.50$$

Then, solving for P:

P = 48.5/1.05 = 46.19. Choice **B**.

9.

The United States' population has grown at an an average rate of 3.14 percent per year since 1948. There were approximately 238 million people in the US in 1985. Which of the following functions represents the United States' population P, in millions of people, t years since 1985 ?

A) $P(t) = 238(1.0314)^t$

B) $P(t) = 238(1.314)^t$

C) $P(t) = 3.14t + 238$

D) $P(t) = 1.0314t + 238$

Here again, some amount has increased or *grown* by a certain percentage.

Right away, we're dealing with a growth factor of 1 + 0.0314 = **1.0314**.

Many careless mistakes are made on this problem because students fail to write the percentage **in decimal form**. So, they think the growth factor is 1.314, which is wrong.

Then, since the growth factor is applied to the original amount of 238 million people, the only possible choice is **A**.

10.

Juanita purchased a figurine that had a value of $100. Every year, the figurine is estimated to increase 20% over its value from the previous year. The estimated value of the figurine, in dollars, 2 years after purchase can be represented by the expression 100a, where a is a constant. What is the value of a ?

A) 1.2

B) 2.4

C) 2.0

D) 1.44

From the given information, the figurine has a growth factor of 1 + 0.2 = **1.2.** This growth factor is applied **twice** because the 20% increase occurs **each year.** In two years, the increase is a factor of (1.2)(1.2) = **1.44**, which is then applied to the original $100 value. Therefore, $a = 1.44$. Choice **D**. Done.

11.

A video game was on sale for 30% off its original price. If the sale price of the video game was $28.00, what was the original price of the video game? (Assume there is no sales tax.)

A) $12.80

B) $24.50

C) $40.00

D) $42.50

Right away, we see that we're dealing with decay or depreciation factor. In this case it's 1 – 0.3 = **0.7**.

Then, after the decay factor is applied to the original price, it will give us the sale price.

So, again, if we call the original price P, we can now set up an easy equation to solve:

$$0.7P = 28$$

And, solving for P we get:

P = 28/0.7 = 40. Choice **C**.

By now, you should be really getting the hang of this. Soon you'll be able to answer questions like these in just a few seconds.

12.
In 2018 the populations of City X and City Y were equal. From 2013 to 2018, the population of City X increased by 30% and the population of City Y decreased by 20%. If the population of City X was 100,000 in 2013, what was the population of City Y in 2013?

A) 150,000

B) 162,500

C) 185,200

D) 202,500

This one is a bit more complicated, but using growth and decay factors will make it very doable.

First, let's establish the growth factor for the population of City X, which is 1 + 0.30 = 1.3.

Then, there is a decay factor for the population of City Y, which is 1 – 0.20 = 0.80.

Next, using the growth factor, let's calculate the population of City X in 2018.

If it was 100,000 in 2013, it is (1.3)(100,000) = 130,000 in 2018.

That means City Y is also 130,000 in 2018 since they tell us that both cities had equal populations in 2018 in the very first sentence.

To determine what the population of City Y was in 2013, we need to use the decay factor we already calculated, and apply it to the population in 2013, which we'll call Y.

Then, the equation to solve should be:

$$0.8Y = 130,000$$

Solving for Y, we get:

Y = 130,000/0.8 = 162,500. Choice **B**.

If this solution still confuses you, go over it a few times until it clicks. If it still doesn't click, just move on, and come back to it later and try again.

13.

Karen modeled the growth over several hundred years of an oak tree population by estimating the number of acorns per acre that were deposited each year within a forest's detritus, or floor. She estimated there were 800 acorns per acre the first year the acorns were deposited, with a 1% annual increase in the number of acorns per acre thereafter. Which of the following functions models $A(t)$, the number acorns per acre t years after the first year the acorns were deposited?

A) $A(t) = 800^t$

B) $A(t) = 800^{1.01t}$

C) $A(t) = 800(0.99)^t$

D) $A(t) = 800(1.01)^t$

Now you're reaching the point where you can knock off a problem like this in a few seconds, because you've seen several similar ones already.

A 1% annual increase in the number of acorns means there is a growth factor of 1 + 0.01 = 1.01.

Thanks to your newfound understanding of growth and decay factors you can stop right there, because the only choice showing this growth factor where it belongs is choice **D**. Done!

14.

A beverage store charges a base price of x dollars for one keg of root beer. A sales tax of a certain percentage is applied to the base price, and an untaxed deposit for the keg is added. If the total amount, in dollars, paid at the time of purchase for one keg is given by the expression $1.07x + 17$, then what is the sales tax, expressed as a percentage of the base price?

A) 0.07%

B) 1.07%

C) 7%

D) 17%

This one uses the growth factor in reverse, because they are giving you an expression that contains it. Do you see it?

If the base price of one keg of root beer is given as x, then number it is multiplied with must be the growth factor since it is greater than one and the sales tax increases the price by a certain percentage.

Let's look at that expression: 1.07x + 17.

Then, 1.07 = 1 + 0.07. So, the **0.07** must be the percentage increase written in decimal form.

Converting 0.07 back to a percentage, we get 7%. Choice **C**.

If you're wondering what the 17 represents in the given expression, it must be the *untaxed deposit for the keg* as stated in the second sentence.

15.

Hannah placed an online order for shirts that cost $24.50 per shirt. A tax of 7% is added to the cost of the shirts, before a flat, untaxed shipping rate of $6 is charged. Which of the following represents Hannah's total cost for s shirts, in dollars?

A) $0.07(24.50s + 6)$

B) $1.07(24.50 + 6)s$

C) $1.07(24.50s) + 6$

D) $1.07(24.50 + s) + 6$

Again, if we're adding a percentage increase to the cost of the shirt, it's the same as applying a growth factor.

In this case, it's a tax of 7%. So, the growth factor is 1 + 0.07 = 1.07. But be careful here. That tax is applied on to the shirts, not to the untaxed shipping rate of $6.

To determine the total cost of the shirts *before* the tax is added, we have to multiply the cost of each shirt, $24.50, and the number of shirts *s*, to get 24.50*s*.

Then applying the tax, using the growth factor, we get 1.07(24.50*s*). Adding the shipping rate separately, we get 1.07(24.50*s*) + 6. Choice **C**.

16.

Bryan, who works in a high-end jewelry store, earns a base pay of $10.00 per hour plus a certain percent commission on the sales that he helps to broker in the store. Bryan worked an average of 35 hours per week over the past two weeks and helped to broker sales of $5,000.00 worth of jewelry during that same two-week period. If Bryan's earnings for the two-week period were $850.00, what percent commission on sales does Bryan earn?

A) 1%
B) 2%
C) 3%
D) 4%

This problem doesn't deal with growth or decay factors at all, but it is still a percentage problem.

In this case, we are told Bryan's commission is a certain percentage of the sales that he helps to broker. And we're told those brokered sales over the past two weeks were $5,000.

If we let C = the percentage of Bryan's commission in decimal form, then the amount he earned in commission is just 5,000C.

But he also earns a base pay of $10.00 per hour. And, since he worked an average of 35 hours per week, he earned (10)(70) = $700 over the past two weeks.

Since they tell us his earnings for the two-week period were $850, we can now set up an equation to solve for C:

$$700 + 5000C = 850$$

Continuing to solve for C:

5000C = 150

C = 150/5000 = 0.03, which is 3%. Choice **C**.

As you can see, not every percentage problem involves growth or decay factors, although many do.

17.
> Mike consumes an average of 1,680 calories per day. Each day he has finals, Mike consumes 12% more calories per day than he usually does. During the last day of finals, he celebrates by consuming an additional 900 calories. Which of the following represents the total number of calories Mike consumes during *d* days of finals?
>
> A) 1.12(1,680*d* + 900)
> B) 1.12(1,680*d*) + 900
> C) 1.12(1,680 + 900)*d*
> D) (1,680 + 0.12*d*) + 900

Back to growth factors. If Mike consumes 12% more calories per day than he usually does, that means the growth factor will be 1 + 0.12 = 1.12.

If Mike usually consumes 1,680 calories per day, then during finals he consumes 1.12(1,680) per day. So, for *d* days he consumes 1.12(1,680*d*).

Adding 900 calories for the additional amount he consumes on the last day of finals in celebration, the total number of calories will be 1.12(1,680*d*) + 900. Choice **B**.

18.

The coal consumption of a factory at April was 460 tons. And the coal consumption of the factory at May decreased to 345 tons. What was the percentage decrease in the coal consumption of the factory?

A) 20%

B) 25%

C) 30%

D) 35%

Here we have a problem that's different from the others. In previous problems we were asked to find the new amount of something after a change in percentage. In this problem we are asked to find the change in percentage after a change in the amount.

For problems like these, we use the following formula:

Percentage change = $\dfrac{New\ Amount - Old\ Amount}{Old\ Amount}$ x 100

Then, applying this formula to this problem, the percentage decrease is:

$\dfrac{345-460}{460}$ x 100 = $\dfrac{-115}{460}$ x 100 = -25%.

The negative sign in the answer just means that there was a <u>decrease</u> in the percentage.

So, the answer is **B**.

19.

A truck driver transported 561 boxes of goods at the first time. And the number of boxes of goods at the second time increased to 748. What was the percentage increase in the number of boxes of goods?

A) $33\frac{1}{3}$%

B) 35%

C) $37\frac{1}{2}$%

D) 41%

Once again, just apply the formula for percentage change:

$\frac{748-561}{561}$ x 100 = $33.\overline{33}$. Choice **A**.

20.

Credit Load for Economics Majors

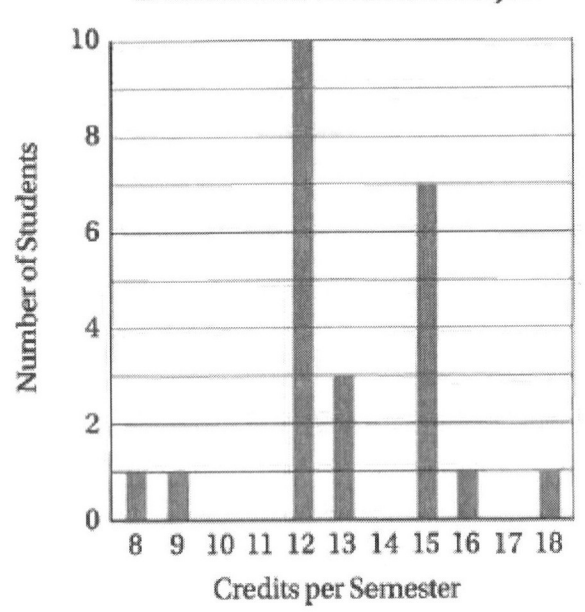

A university surveyed 24 economics majors and asked them how many credits they received the previous semester. The results are represented in the graph above. What percentage of these students received 15 or more credits that semester?

A) 29%

B) $33\frac{1}{3}$%

C) $37\frac{1}{2}$%

D) 54%

Here's another percentage problem that's different than the others we've seen. However, fortunately it's quite easy to solve if you know how to read a histogram.

The *number of credits* are given along the horizontal axis of the graph. Since the question asks for those students who received 15 or more credits, we're only interested the 3 bars at 15, 16 and 18.

The *height* of those bars are 7, 1, and 1 respectively. Those heights represent the *number of students* who received those credits.

Then, we're looking for the fraction of all the students who received 15 or more credits.

Since there are 24 students in total, the fraction is (7 + 1 + 1)/24 = 9/24.

Using your calculator, 9/24 = .375, which is equivalent to 37 ½ %. Choice **C**.

I think you know by now that to convert a decimal to its percentage equivalent you just need to move the decimal point two places to the right.

21.

Martha, a planner at the Springboro City Zoo, is developing a proposal for the new Animals of Africa trapezoidal shaped exhibit. The figure below shows her scale drawing of the proposed exhibit with 3 side lengths and the radius of a circular crocodile pit given in inches. In Martha's scale drawing, 1 inch represents 1.5 feet.

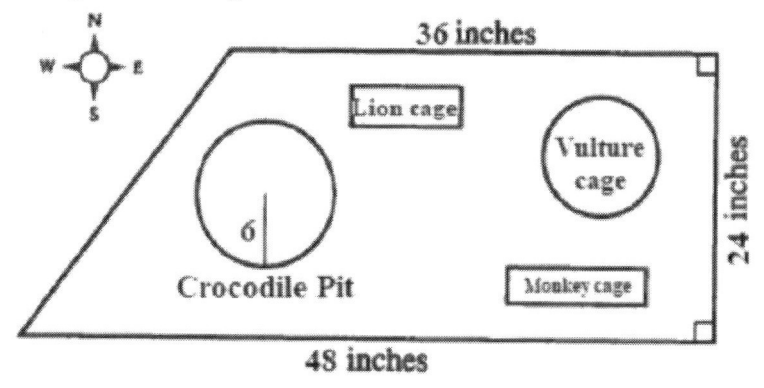

The length of the south side of the exhibit is what percentage of the length of the north side?

F. 111%
G. 123%
H. $133\frac{1}{3}$%
J. 135%
K. 140%

We see 5 choices, so we must be dealing with an ACT type problem, and we are. But, once again we notice that SAT and ACT problems are not much different from one another because they test basically the same math topics.

For this problem we're asked to compare the length of the south side of the exhibit to the north side and determine how they compare in terms of *percentage*.

Obviously, the south side is longer than the north side, so the percentage must be greater than 100. And all the choices reflect that fact. If any choice was less than 100% you could immediately eliminate it.

Then, to determine the actual percentage greater that the south side is to the north side, we simply take the ratio of the two sides and convert to a decimal:

48/36 = $1.\overline{333}$, which is equivalent to 133.33%. Choice **H**.

21.

The plans for a diving pool call for a rectangular prism that has a length of 20 meters, a width of 10 meters, and a depth of 5 meters. If the plans are changed to increase both the length and the width of the pool by 15%, what will be the increase, to the nearest 1%, in the volume of the pool?

A. 10%
B. 17%
C. 20%
D. 21%
E. 32%

90

Here we need to focus on only one thing: **the growth factor**.

Both the length and width of the pool will increase by 15%. That's a growth factor of (1 + 0.15) = **1.15** for each.

Now, the volume is just the product of the length, width, and depth. But, the depth is not changing, so we only need to factor in the changes in the length and width, which both increase by a factor of 1.15 as previously stated.

Then, the total increase in volume is just (1.15)(1.15) = 1.3225. But, we're only interested in the percent **increase**, which is the amount above 1. That's 0.3225 or 32.25%, which is 32% to the nearest 1%. Choice **E**.

22.

Students and adults from Eastern High School visited an amusement park on a field trip. The amusement park charged $20 for each adult ticket and $10 for each student ticket. Before the trip, the students were given this information about the Furious Falcon roller coaster: the average speed of the roller coaster is 50 miles per hour, and 1 ride on the roller coaster track is completed in 2.00 minutes. A graph showing the height above level ground, in feet, with respect to the time into the ride, in seconds, is given below.

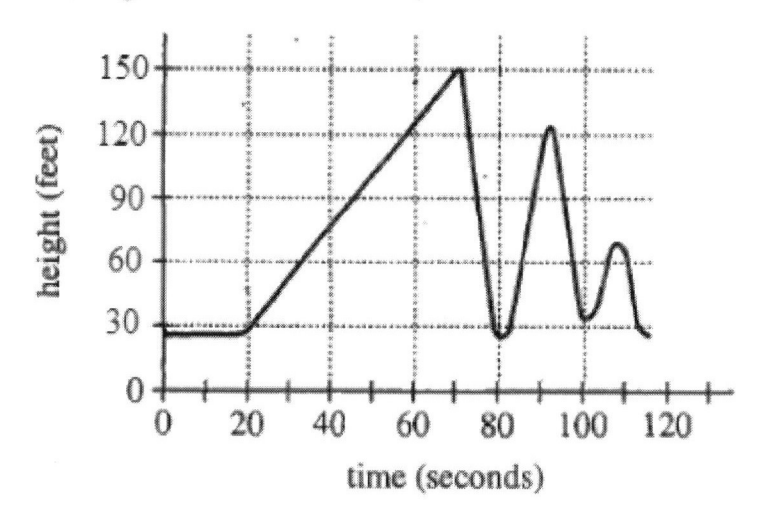

The roller coaster is at a height of at least 135 feet for a total of 5 seconds during each complete ride. Which of the following is closest to the percent of the time during a complete ride that the roller coaster is at a height of at least 135 feet?

F. 1%
G. 4%
H. 19%
J. 33%
K. 45%

This question was part of a multi-part problem modeled after an actual ACT problem.

Since this chapter is about percentage word problems, I'm only showing the question that deals with that.

Looking at the graph, we see that the roller coaster ride ends after about 120 seconds.

They also tell us that the roller coaster is at a height of at least 135 for a total of 5 seconds.

So, we have all the information we need to answer the question, which is very straightforward.

The percentage of the time the ride is at a height of at least 135 feet would then simply be 5/120 = 0.04167. Moving the decimal point two places to the right gives us about 4%. Choice **G**.

23.

There are 76 calories in 10 grams of grated Mozzarella cheese, and 67% of those calories are from fat. When measuring Mozzarella cheese, 5 grams is equal to 1 tablespoon. Which of the following is closest to the number of calories from fat per tablespoon of grated Mozzarella cheese?

F. 3
G. 8
H. 9
J. 13
K. 26

Here again, this percentage problem does not involve growth or decay factors, but rather a straightforward application of the percentage of a number.

If 67% of the calories in grated Mozzarella cheese are from fat, then 76 calories of grated Mozzarella cheese has (0.67)(76) = about **51** calories from fat.

Those 51 calories are in 10 grams of the cheese. One tablespoon is equivalent to 5 grams, which is **half** of 10 grams.

So, each tablespoon of cheese contains half of 51 calories, or about 26 calories. **K.**

24.

A 240-liter solution that is 8% salt is mixed with an 60-liter solution that is 13% salt. The combined solution is what percent salt?

A. 8%
B. 9%
C. 10%
D. 11%
E. 12%

Questions like these are fast and easy if you just remember this formula:

(amount of 1st solution)(% of 1st solution) +

(amount of 2nd solution)(% of 2nd solution) =

(amount of combined solution)(% of combined solution).

Then, the problem becomes, (240)(0.08) + (60)(0.13) = (240+60)x = 300x , where x is

the percent salt of the combined solution. Continuing to solve, 19.2 + 7.8 = 300x ,

27 = 300x, x = 27/300 = 0.09 = 9%. **B.**

25.

The changes in a city's population from one decade to the next decade for 3 consecutive decades were a 10% increase, a 20% increase, and a 10% decrease. About what percent was the increase in the city's population over the 3 decades?

A. 10%
B. 20%
C. 25%
D. 30%
E. 70%

And now we're back to growth factors and decay factors.

So, a 10% increase is a growth factor of 1 + 0.1 = 1.1. A 20% increase then would be 1 + 0.2 = 1.2.

A 10% decrease is a decay factor of 1 − 0.1 = 0.9.

Applying the two growth factors and one decay factor as presented in this problem, we get (1.1)(1.2)(0.9) = 1.188. The amount greater than one is the percent of increase written in decimal form. In this case it's 0.188, which is 18.8%. Therefore, the closest answer is 20%. **B**.

26.

A smartphone has a regular price of $68.69 before taxes. It goes on sale at 20% below the regular price. Before taxes are added, what is the sale price of the smartphone?

A. $11.99
B. $29.98
C. $39.95
D. $47.96
E. $54.95

Here's another ACT problem where you can use the **decay factor** to answer quickly and easily. 20% below the regular price is the same as applying a decay factor of (1 – 0.2) = 0.8 to the regular price. So, (0.8)(68.69) = 54.95. **E.** 10 seconds.

27.

A local golfing league established its handicap for golfers who have an average of 80 or more as 75% of the difference between 80 and the golfer's average score. If H represents the handicap of such a golfer and A represents his or her average score, which of the following equations gives H in terms of A ?

A. $H = 155 - A$

B. $H = A - 155$

C. $H = 80 - \frac{A}{0.75}$

D. $H = 80 - 0.75A$

E. $H = 0.75(A - 80)$

The handicap H should be a positive number, so we want the difference between the golfer's average A and a score of 80, which is A – 80. Then we need to take 75% of that, which is 0.75(A – 80). **E.**

28.

A shirt has a sale price of $24.50 which is 30% off the original price. How much less than the original price is the sale price?

A. $ 0.38
B. $ 1.52
C. $ 6.08
D. $ 7.60
E. $10.50

30% off is a decay factor of 1 – 0.3 = 0.7. If we call x the original price, then,

0.7x = 24.50. So, x = 24.50/0.7 = $35.

Then, the answer to the question is the difference between the 2 prices. 35 – 24.50 = $10.50. **E.**

29.

The sum of 2 and 150% of 1 has the same value as which of the following calculations?

A. 100% of 2
B. 150% of 2
C. 300% of 2
D. 350% of 1
E. 400% of 1

150% is equal to 1.5 as a decimal number. So, 150% of 1 is just (1.5)(1) = 1.5. The sum of 2 and 1.5 is 3.5. 350% of 1 = (3.5)(1) = 3.5. So, **D**.

30.

The diameter of one circle is 10 inches long. The diameter of a second circle is 25% longer than the diameter of the first circle. To the nearest square inch, how much larger is the area of the second circle than the area of the first circle?

F. 7
G. 28
H. 44
J. 64
K. 254

The radius of the given circle is 10/2 = 5. Now, understanding that a 25% increase is the same as a growth factor of (1 + 0.25) = 1.25, we apply it immediately to get (1.25)(5) = 6.25 for the radius of the second circle. The difference of the areas will tell us how much larger the area of the second circle is than the area of the first circle. So, using πr^2 for the area of a circle, $\pi(6.25)^2 - \pi(5)^2 = 44.18$ which is closest to choice **H**.

That completes our review of typical percentage word problems likely to appear on the SAT or ACT. Keep reviewing these until the concepts covered really sink in, especially growth factors and decay factors. Once you master using them you'll see easily and quickly you can solve these type of word problems that used to cause so much confusion and frustration.

Probability

Probability word problems occur very frequently on both the SAT and ACT. These problems usually are accompanied with a graph, chart or table of some type that provides a group of data. Often, most of the values provided won't be relevant. It will be your job to determine which data are relevant to the problem and which are not. Other problems do not include any charts, graphs, or tables. You will just need to read the problem and interpret it correctly with the given values. With practice you'll get the hang of it. So, let's begin.

1.

Number of Hours of TV Watched Per Week

	None	1 to 4	5 or more	Total
Group X	8	20	22	50
Group Y	2	12	36	50
Total	10	32	58	100

The data in the table above were produced by a social researcher studying the TV watching habits of people in a town. Group X consisted of 50 people who are college graduates earning over $100,000 per year, and Group Y consisted of 50 people who are high school graduates earning less than $50,000 per year. If a person is chosen at random from those who watched at least 1 hour of TV per week, what is the probability the person belonged to Group Y?

A) $\dfrac{48}{100}$

B) $\dfrac{90}{100}$

C) $\dfrac{48}{90}$

D) $\frac{48}{50}$

Believe it or not, this problem only requires you to know **two** numbers! As with all probability problems, we need to know the **group** from which we are taking data. That group number **always** goes in the **denominator** of the solution. In this case, the relevant group are **those who watch at least 1 hour of TV.** How many people belong to that group? Now, look at the table. They consist of people in the 1 to 4 group **and** the 5 or more group. That's a total of 32 + 58 = **90** people. The correct answer **must** have that number in the denominator or a reduced form of it. As you can see, only choice **C** has the correct denominator. Done!

If there were other choices that had a denominator of 90, you would then have to calculate the numerator, which would represent the number of people among the 90 who specifically belong to Group Y. As you can see from the table, that would be 12 + 36 = 48. So, once again, the answer would be C, 48/90.

2.

Results on the Medical Board Exam for Medical School Graduates

	Passed Board Exam	Did Not Pass Board Exam
Took review course	56	42
Did not take review course	15	32

The table above summarizes the results of 145 medical school graduates who took the medical board exam. If one of the surveyed graduates who passed the board exam is chosen at random for an interview, what is the probability that the person chosen did <u>not</u> take the review course?

A) $\frac{56}{71}$

B) $\dfrac{15}{71}$

C) $\dfrac{42}{145}$

D) $\dfrac{15}{145}$

Remember, the **denominator** of every probability problem is the **group** from which the random data is chosen. In this problem, it's the group of graduates who **passed the bar exam.** That group is 56 + 15 = **71** graduates. So, eliminate C and D immediately. Then, we are only interested in a person who **did not take the review course.** According to the table, there are **15** of those. So, choice **B** is the answer. If you are confused which group belongs in the numerator and which in the denominator, remember that the denominator group is **always larger** than the numerator.

3.

| | Age | | Total |
Gender	Under 30	30 or older	
Male	20	8	28
Female	17	5	22
Total	37	13	50

The table above shows the distribution of age and gender for 50 people who entered a raffle. If the raffle winner will be selected at random, what is the probability that the winner will be either a male under 30 or a female age 30 or older?

A) $\dfrac{11}{25}$

B) $\dfrac{27}{50}$

C) $\dfrac{1}{2}$

D) $\dfrac{33}{50}$

Once again, the key to answering these type of probability problems quickly is to focus on the relevant numbers and **ignore all the others.** Often students feel confused and overwhelmed when confronted with so much information, although this is a relatively simple table. Even the more cluttered ones boil down to a few relevant numbers.

Here we are only interested in males under age 30, of which there are **20**, and females 30 or older, of which there are **5**. The only other relevant number is the number of people in the contest, of which there are **50**.

This is an **or** type of probability problem, in which they are asking for the probability of one situation **or** another. In that case, we **add** the probabilities to get

20/50 + 5/50 = 25/50 = 1/2   Choice **C**.

Notice, there were **9** different numbers presented in this problem, but only **3** were relevant.

4.

	Driver's Test	
Gender	Pass	Fail
Female		
Male		
Total	174	42

The incomplete table above summarizes the number students who passed and the number of students who failed the driver's test among seniors at Piedmont High School. There are 3 times as many females who passed as there are females who failed, and

101

there are 5 times as many males who passed as there are male who failed. If there are a total of 42 students who failed and 174 students who passed, which of the following is closest to the probability that a student who passed selected at random is a female?

A) 0.310

B) 0.250

C) 0.430

D) 0.510

This one may seem complicated, but there's a shortcut to doing a problem like this. Using the choices we can insert values in the table to see if they all add up. For choice A the probability that a student who passed the driver's test is female is given as **0.310**. How many students is that? It's just 0.310(174) which is about **54**. Let's put that where it belongs in the table and see if we can fill in the rest of the boxes.

	Driver's Test	
Gender	Pass	Fail
Female	**54**	18
Male	120	24
Total	174	42

They all work! Here's why. They tell us there are 3 times as many female students who pass as ones who failed. So, that means 54/3 = 18 belongs in the Female/Fail box. Then there must be 24 male students who failed to add up to 42 students who failed. And since there are 5 times as many males who pass than those who failed,

24x5 = 120. And 120 plus 54 equals 174. So, it all works out. Choice **A** is correct. No system of equations necessary!

5.

Type of Lawyer	Type of Practice		Total
	Private	Law Firm	
Bankruptcy	238	175	413
Immigration	307	223	530
Total	545	398	943

In a survey, 943 bankruptcy and immigration attorneys indicated the type of practice they belong to. The results are summarized in the table above. If one of the lawyers is selected at random, which of the following is closest to the probability that the selected lawyer is an immigration lawyer who belongs to a law firm?

A) 0.236

B) 0.421

C) 0.560

D) 0.563

Here again, there are only **two** numbers we need to determine. First, the group **from which the data is selected**. And, by now you know that number always goes in the **denominator**. In this case, it's the group of all the lawyers in the survey, which are **943**. Then we need to know the **specific** data about which we are to determine the probability. In this case, it is "an immigration lawyer who belongs to a law firm". That number is given on the table as **223**.

Then, the probability is 223/943 = 0.236 Choice **A**.

You should start to notice that problems like the one above can be solved in a few seconds when we focus on the right values.

6.

Ice Cream and Topping Selections

		Flavor	
		Strawberry	Pistachio
Topping	Whipped Cream	8	2
	Sprinkles	4	4

The table above shows the flavors of ice cream and the toppings chosen by the people at a party. Each person chose one flavor of ice cream and one topping. Of the people who chose strawberry ice cream, what fraction chose sprinkles as a topping?

A) $\frac{1}{2}$

B) $\frac{1}{3}$

C) $\frac{2}{9}$

D) $\frac{2}{3}$

By now, these types of problems should be simple for you. But here the question is asked a bit differently. "What **fraction**" means basically the same thing as what is the probability, since probability is the ratio of two numbers, which is also a fraction.

So, as always, we want to identify the **denominator** first, which is the **group from which the data is taken.** And remember, it's **always greater** than the specific data group they are asking about. In this case, the denominator is the group of **people who chose strawberry ice cream.** That number is 8 + 4 = 12. Then we want the number of people who chose **sprinkles** as a topping. That number is 4. So, the answer is 4/12 = 1/3. **B.**

Again, with practice, you'll be able to answer these type of questions in seconds flat.

7.

Feeding Information for Tropical Fish

	Fed only dry food	Fed both live and dry food	Total
Fresh	20	8	28
Salt	12	17	29
Total	32	25	57

The table above shows the kind of foods that are fed to the freshwater and saltwater tropical fish at a local pet store. What fraction of the freshwater fish are fed dry food only?

A) $\frac{12}{29}$

B) $\frac{5}{7}$

C) $\frac{5}{8}$

D) $\frac{20}{57}$

Here's another problem that uses term "fraction" instead of "probability". And now we know that it's solved exactly the same way.

The group from which the data is taken is in the **denominator**, and the specific data from that group goes in the numerator.

We're taking data from the freshwater fish, of which there are **28**. And we want specifically the number of them that are fed only dry food, of which there are **20**. So, the fraction is 20/28. But we must reduce it to find the correct answer. 20/28 reduces to 5/7. Choice **B.** Next.

8.

Number of Players by Score and Trials

	5 out of 5	4 out of 5	3 out of 5	2 out of 5	1 out of 5	0 out of 5	Total
Trial 1	3	4	1	1	1	0	10
Trial 2	3	3	2	1	1	0	10
Trial 3	3	3	1	1	1	1	10
Total	9	10	4	3	3	1	30

The same 10 basketball players, during 3 different free throw trials, were given 5 tries to score a basket. Each player received 1 point for each successful free throw. The number players receiving a given score during each trial is shown in the table above.

No player received the same score during two different trials. If a player is selected at random, what is the probability that the selected player received a score of 5 during Trial 2 or Trial 3, given that the player received a score of 5 during one of the three trials?

A) 1/3

B) 2/3

C) 2/5

D) 3/5

Focus on the last part of the last sentence: **given that the player received a score of 5 during one of the three trials.** That means we're only concerned with the **first column** where players received a score of 5, and we can ignore the rest of the data!

Then, **3** contestants received a score of 5 during trial 2, and **3** players received a score of 5 during trial 3. There are a total of **9** players who scored a 5 during all three trials, so that's the main group we're choosing from, and it will, therefore, be in the denominator.

Whenever you are asked for one probability **or** another, you must **add** the probabilities provided they don't both happen at the same time. In this case they don't, so 3/9 + 3/9 = 1/3 + 1/3 = 2/3. **B**. Done.

9.

Number of Dogs with Fleas

	Fleas	No Fleas	Total
Injection	22	78	100
Flea Collar	28	72	100
Total	50	150	200

The table shows the results of a study that tested the efficacy of a new flea medication injection for dogs. A random sample of 200 dogs received either the injection or a traditional flea collar each day during a 2-week period, and the researchers reported how many of the dogs had fleas during that time period. What proportion of the dogs that received the new injection were observed to still have fleas?

A) $\dfrac{11}{18}$

B) $\dfrac{11}{50}$

C) $\dfrac{9}{50}$

D) $\dfrac{11}{100}$

This is another probability problem, but we don't see the word probability anywhere. This time they are using the word **proportion.** Now add that to the list of synonyms for probability. Before, we saw the word **fraction**. Now we see the word proportion. They **all** mean the same thing with these types of problems. So, all the rules apply, as before.

First, identify the group **from which the data is taken.** In this problem it's taken from "dogs that received the new injection". That number is **100.** And that always goes in the **denominator.** Then we look for the specific data they're asking about. Those dogs that "were observed to still have fleas". That number, from the table, is **22.** Then, like in all the other problems, the probability/fraction/proportion = 22/100 = 11/50. Choice **B.**

10.

Movie Goer Purchases at a Theater

	Beverage purchased	Beverage not purchased	Total
Popcorn purchased	50	25	75
Popcorn not purchased	20	15	35
Total	70	40	110

On Saturday, a local movie theater sold 110 tickets. The table above summarizes whether or not a movie goer purchased popcorn, a beverage, both, or neither. Based on the data in the table, what is the probability that the movie goer selected at random did not purchase popcorn?

A) $\frac{25}{40}$

B) $\frac{50}{75}$

C) $\dfrac{20}{70}$

D) $\dfrac{35}{110}$

This one is appear fairly straightforward and uses the term probability, so we should know what to do. Again, with these types of probability problems, it usually boils down to a couple of numbers.

The last sentence tells us all we need to know. We're looking for the number of people who did **not** purchase popcorn, out of all the customers. We can see from the table that number is **35** out of **110** customers. So, the answer is **D**. Done.

11.

	IQ Score			
Age group	<100	100-120	121-140	>140
25-50	5	32	21	12
51-75	10	30	11	x

The IQ (Intelligence Quotient) of people is sometimes analyzed according to age group. The theory is that as we get older our cognitive abilities and speed of mental responses tend to decline. The table above shows the distribution of IQ scores and ages for a random group of people. If one of these people in the 51-75 year old age group is chosen at random, the probability that the person has an IQ between 121 and 140 is $\dfrac{1}{5}$. What is the value of x ?

Since no choices are given, this would be a *grid-in* question on the SAT. Therefore, you must calculate the answer yourself without the benefit of using given choices.

109

This problem is not really much different than all the other probability problems we've seen so far. The difference here is that it introduces a variable x in the data. But it's approached the exact same way.

The group **from which the data is taken** are people who are ages 51 to 75. There are 10 + 30 + 11 + x of those, or **51 + x**. That figure belongs in the **denominator.** The **specific** data asked for is a person whose IQ is in the 121-140 category.

According to the table, in the 51-75 row, there are **11** of those. And the question **tells** us that probability is 1/5. So,

$$11/(51 + x) = 1/5$$

A simple cross multiplication gives us 51 + x = 55, so x = **4.** Done.

12.

Survey Results

Answer	Percent
Never	43.3%
Rarely	27.8%
Often	22.7%
Always	6.2%

The table above shows the result of a survey of workers in an office who use a PC who were asked how often they would play video games on their PC during their breaks. Based on the table, which of the following is closest to the probability that an office worker answered "Always", given that the office worker did not answer "Never"?

A) 0.11

B) 0.19

C) 0.22

D) 0.37

Whenever you see the word **given** in a probability problem, that is the part that goes in the **denominator.** In this case, it's given that the tablet user did **not** answer "Never". Well, that's just the percentages of all the other answers: 27.8 + 22.7 + 6.2 = **56.7.** Next, we just need to know the percentage of tablet users that answered "Always", which from the table is 6.2%.

So, the probability is just 6.2/56.7 = 0.109 which is closest to choice **A.** Done.

13.

During a presidential election, a high school held its own mock election. Students had the option to vote for Candidate A, Candidate B, or several other candidates. They could also choose to spoil their ballot. The table below displays a summary of the election results.

	Candidate A	Candidate B	Other	Total
10th grade	0.32	0.58	0.10	1.00
11th grade	0.50	0.42	0.08	1.00
12th grade	0.63	0.32	0.05	1.00
Total	0.48	0.44	0.08	1.00

614 students voted for Candidate A. Approximately how many students attend the school?

Here we have a problem where the terms "probability, fraction, or proportion" are nowhere to be found. Can this still be considered a probability problem?

YES, because it you think about it, the values given in the table represent the probabilities that students in the various grades voted for a certain candidate.

Then, we could say that 0.48 or **48%** of all the students voted for Candidate A, based on the total value given in the Candidate A column on the table.

111

We now know how to determine probabilities, so it's no different here.

If 614 students voted for Candidate A, then that number over the total number of students in the school tells us the proportion or probability that they voted for candidate A, which we already know is 48%.

The question is asking us to find the total number of students who attend the school, so, if we call **x** the total number of students, the equation is simple:

$$\frac{614}{x} = 0.48$$

Solving for x:

0.48x = 614

x = 614/0.48 = **1279**.

This problem had no choices, so it would be a grid-in problem on the test, most likely on Section 4, since a calculator is required.

14.

The 2013 U.S. Census recorded the highest educational attainment of all adults aged 25 years or older in county *T*, one of the most educated parts of the country. The results are given in the two-way table below.

	Men	Women	Total
High School Diploma	7,535	7,234	14,769
Bachelor's Degree	17,170	23,455	40,625
Master's Degree	45,105	41,078	86,183
Professional Degree	23,501	23,405	46,906
Doctoral Degree	16,232	15,817	32,049
Total	109,543	110,989	220,532

According to the data presented in the table above, if you were to choose a person at random out of the entire population aged 25 years or older in county *T*, what is the approximate probability that the person you chose is a man with a doctoral degree (given as a percent)?

A) 2%

B) 7%

C) 28%

D) 51%

This one is much more straightforward. We have all the information we need in the table and they're asking for a probability.

The probability, in this case, is of a man with a doctoral degree. That probability is among all adults aged 25 or older in county T. So, the number of men with doctoral degrees will be in the numerator, and the total number of adults aged 25 or older will be in the denominator.

Using the values given in the table, the fraction is 16,232/220,532 = about 0.07 or 7%. Choice **B**.

15.

The table below shows the relative investment in alternative energy sources in the United States by type. One column shows the relative investment in 2007 of $75 million total invested in alternative energy. The other column shows the projected relative investment in 2017 given current trends. The total projected investment in alternative energy in 2017 is $254 million.

United States Investment in Alternative Energy Sources

	Actual 2007 Investment	Projected 2017 Investment
Biofuels	0.31	0.34
Wind	0.40	0.32
Solar	0.27	0.30
Fuel Cells	0.02	0.04
Total	1.00	1.00

Based on the information in the table, if an investment was made in alternative energy in 2007, what is the probability that the money was invested in wind resources?

A) $\dfrac{1}{25}$

B) $\dfrac{3}{10}$

C) $\dfrac{2}{5}$

D) $\dfrac{3}{5}$

The most time consuming aspect of problems like these is reading and interpreting them.

Surprisingly, if we go straight to the question, and skip reading the beginning paragraph, we can answer it almost immediately.

The question directs us to go straight to the table and focus on the first column, which are investments made in 2007. Specifically, they are asking about wind resources.

We see a value there of 0.40. If you look at the total, you see 1.00, which means that 0.40 is just 40% of the total investment.

That's another way of saying that there is a 40% probability that an investment in alternative energy sources made in 2007 was in wind.

Looking at the choices, we see they are all fractions. So, then we just need to convert 0.40 into a fraction.

Since 0.40 = 4/10, we can reduce that to 2/5. Choice **C**.

16.

	Candidate A	Candidate B	Undecided	Total
Democrat	24	56	70	150
Republican	117	70	50	237
Independent	15	18	80	113
Total	156	144	200	500

The table above illustrates the results of a political poll. Five hundred voters were first asked whether they were registered as Democrat, Republican, or Independent. The voters were then asked whether they planned to vote for Candidate A, for Candidate B, or were Undecided. What percent of the registered Democrats plan to vote for Candidate A ? (Disregard the percent symbol when gridding your answer.)

Going straight to the question, the problem asks what percent of the registered Democrats plan to vote for Candidate A. That's another way of asking what is the probability that among Democrats, what is the probability they will vote for Candidate A?

Then, as always, the probability is determined by finding the main group of data from which the specific data is taken from, and placing it in the denominator, while the specific data always goes in the numerator.

The main group is the total number of Democrat voters, which the table tells us is 150.

Specifically, those who plan to vote for Candidate A, are 24.

Then, the probability or percentage of registered Democrats who plan to vote for Candidate A is simply 24/150 = 0.16 = **16%**.

17.

A jar contains only red, white, and blue marbles. It contains twice as many red marbles as white marbles and three times as many white marbles as blue marbles. If a marble is chosen at random, what is the probability that it is not red?

A) $\frac{1}{5}$

B) $\frac{2}{5}$

C) $\frac{3}{5}$

D) $\frac{4}{5}$

This one will take more analysis then some others, but it shouldn't be too difficult to figure out.

They are asking for the probability of <u>not</u> red. The marbles that are not red are white and blue. So, it's the same asking for the probability of choosing white and blue marbles at random.

But we don't have any numbers, so where do we begin? We begin with the *relationships* between the marbles.

There are twice as many red marbles as white marbles. Using descriptive variables where R represents the number of red marbes, W the number white marbes, and B the number of blue marbles, our first equation is:

$$R = 2W$$

They also tell us there are three times as many white marbles as blue marbles, so:

$$W = 3B$$

The total number of marbles are R + W + B, and the number of not red are W + B.

Then, in terms of the variables, the probability of not red is:

$$\frac{W + B}{R + W + B}$$

How do we get a numerical value out of that? The answer is *substitution*.

We can put everything in terms of B, since W = 3B and R = 2W = 2(3B) = 6B.

Then, by substitution, the probability becomes:

$$\frac{3B+B}{6B+3B+B} = \frac{4B}{10B} = \frac{4}{10} = \frac{2}{5}$$

Choice **B**.

Even though this problem was a little trickier to solve, the basic set up to determine the probability was the same as all the others.

18.

OPINION POLL ON PROPOSAL 81A

Age of Voter	Approve	Disapprove	No Opinion	Total
18 to 39	918	204	502	1,624
40 to 64	1,040	502	102	1,644
65 and older	604	420	115	1,139
Total	2,562	1,126	719	4,407

Based on the information given in the table above, of those surveyed who expressed an opinion on Proposal 81A, approximately what was the probability that the voter was under 40 years of age?

A) 30%

B) 38%

C) 45%

D) 63%

19.

Daphnia are a type of water flea commonly found in lakes. Females can reproduce asexually, and they will either produce a male or a female embryo depending on the stress level of their environment. If, in a stressful environment, a female has a 75% chance to reproduce asexually, and the odds of a male being born are 2:1, what is the probability that a female in this environment will asexually produce a male?

A) 0.5

B) 0.6

C) 0.7

D) 1.0

This problem has no charts or tables, but it's still asking for the probability of something. In this case, that a female water flea will asexually produce a male.

As with all word problems, knowledge of a particular field of study is not necessary in order to answer the question.

The key to answering this question is to correctly interpret what is meant by the statement, "...the odds of a male being born are 2:1." That simply means that there are two males born for every one female.

With that understanding, the problem is easy to solve, because now we know there for every 3 water fleas born, 2 should be male. So, the *probability* of a male water flea being born is **2/3**.

This problem is a bit different from the others in that in introduces a second probability: the probability that a female with reproduce asexually. And, that probability (or chance) is given as 75%.

Then we must apply that probability to the probability of a male being born in order to answer the question completely.

So, (.75)(2/3) = 0.5. Choice **A**.

20.

An anthropologist surveyed a random sample of residents in two states to find out whether they had been born in their state of residence, in another state, or in another country. Her data are shown in the table below.

Birthplaces of Rhode Island and California Residents (hundreds of residents)			
	In state of residence	In another U.S. state	In another country
Rhode Island	776	23	64
California	630	161	72

What can the anthropologist reasonably conclude from her data?

119

A) Residents of California are more likely to leave the state than residents of Rhode Island.

B) Residents of California are more likely not to have been born in-state than residents of Rhode Island.

C) Residents of California are more likely to travel internationally than residents of Rhode Island.

D) Residents of California are more likely to have been born in another country or in another U.S. state than to have been born in-state.

This is another probability problem that doesn't explicity state itself as such. But you can deduce it from the choices.

For instance, looking at choice B) Residents of California are more likely not to have been born in-state than residents of Rhode Island. In order to determine if that's true you would need to find the probability of a resident in each state to have been born in another state or another country. The data needed to find those probabilities are given in the table.

For Rhode Island, if we add up all the values representing the number of residents in that state from the sample, we get 776 + 23 + 64 = 863 (in hundreds).

For California, we get 630 + 161 + 72 = 863 also.

Since we're interested in those not born in-state, the probability would be (23 + 64)/863 = 87/863 = approximately **0.10** for Rhode Island, and (161 + 72)/863 = 233/863 = **0.27** for California.

Since the California probability is clearly higher than the Rhode Island, choice **B** is true and must be the correct answer.

Notice that you could have eliminated choices A and C right away since the data has nothing to do with residents leaving or traveling from the states.

21.

The Khan family is planning to build a 4-room cottage which consists of 2 bedrooms (BR), a living room (LR), and a bathroom. Shown below are the rectangular floor plan (left figure) and a side view of the cabin (right figure). In the side view, the roof forms an isosceles triangle ($\triangle ABC$), the walls are perpendicular to the level floor ($\overline{ED}$), $\overline{AC} \parallel \overline{ED}$, F is the midpoint of $\overline{AC}$, and $\overline{BF} \perp \overline{AC}$.

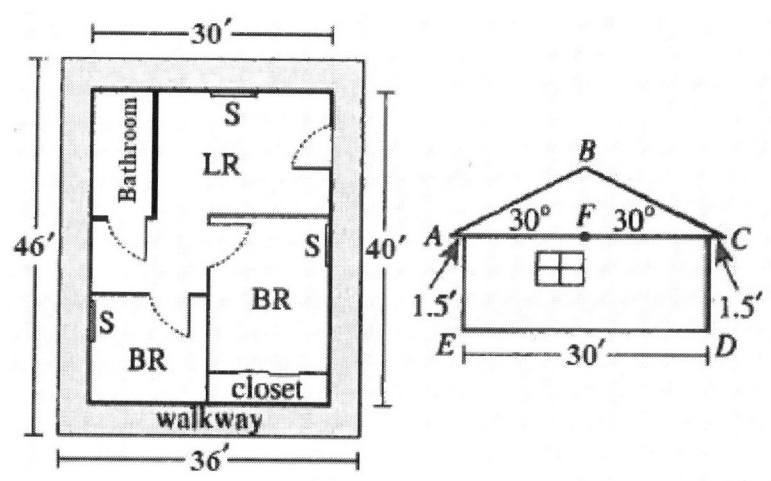

During the week the Khans plan to roof the cottage, there is a 30% chance of rain each day.

Mr Khan plans to roof the cottage on 2 consecutive days. Assuming that the chance of rain is independent of the day, what is the probability that it will rain both days?

A. 0.09
B. 0.18
C. 0.36
D. 0.40
E. 0.60

This question is obviously from an ACT test since it has 5 choices. This is a multi-question problem, which are very commonly found on the ACT. Only the question that deals with probability is presented here.

The only information relevant to solve this problem is found under the diagram: **"During the week the Khans plan to roof the cottage, there is a 30% chance of rain each day."**

But, we're looking for the probability that it will rain <u>two days in a row</u>. When we calculate probabilities involving one event **and** another event occuring, we **multiply** the probabilities. So, (0.30)(0.30) = 0.09. Choice **A**. Done.

Note that sometimes the occurrence of one event impacts the probability of another event. In that case it's not as straightforward as simply multiplying the probabilities.

22.

A marble will be randomly selected from a bag of solid-colored marbles. The probability of selecting a white marble is $\frac{7}{13}$. The probability of selecting a red marble is $\frac{2}{13}$. What is the probability of selecting a red marble *or* a white marble?

A. $\frac{1}{13}$

B. $\frac{9}{13}$

C. $\frac{9}{26}$

D. $\frac{14}{26}$

E. $\frac{14}{169}$

As you can see, ACT problems are very similar to SAT problems. So, they're solved the same way.

As long as two events are **independent**, meaning the outcome of one does not effect the outcome of the other, then we just **add** the probabilities when we are asked about the probability of one **or** the other occuring. Then, the answer is **B**.

Remember, don't waste time reading the whole thing. Focus on the probabilities and the word **or**.

Note: If they had asked for the probability of selecting a red **and** a white marble, then we would **multiply** the probabilities, in which case E would have been the answer.

23.

The graph below shows the number of doctors who were present on Thursday from each of the 5 groups at a medical conference. What is the probability that a doctor selected at random from the conference is in Group 4 ?

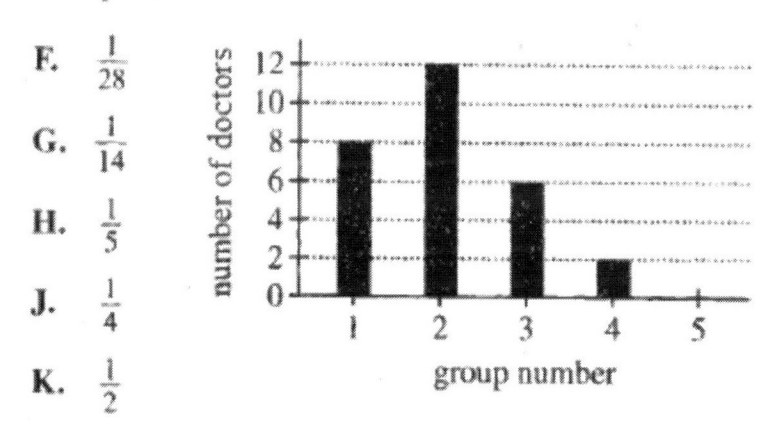

F. $\frac{1}{28}$

G. $\frac{1}{14}$

H. $\frac{1}{5}$

J. $\frac{1}{4}$

K. $\frac{1}{2}$

Here we only need to focus on two things: The number of doctors in group 4 and the **total** number of doctors present at the medical conference on Thursday. Those numbers are readily available. Looking at the bar graph, the number of doctors in group 4 were **2**. And the total number of doctors present that day is determined by adding up all the bar heights on the graph, 8 + 12+ 6 + 2 = **28**. Then, the probability is 2/28 = 1/14. Choice **G**.

As usual, with these type of probability problems the **larger** group from which the data is taken is **always** in the denominator, and the smaller group about which the question is being asked is always in the numerator.

123

24.

To graduate as an archeologist, a student must correctly order 4 artifacts by age, from youngest to oldest. The student knows which one is the oldest artifact, but randomly guesses at the order of the other 3 artifacts. What is the probability the student will get all 4 in the correct order?

F. $\dfrac{1}{16}$

G. $\dfrac{1}{6}$

H. $\dfrac{1}{5}$

J. $\dfrac{1}{3}$

K. $\dfrac{1}{2}$

A problem like this is more likely to appear on an ACT exam than an SAT. In general, ACT word problems tend to be a little more involved than SAT word problems. But I must emphasize the words in general, because the SAT certainly has its share of more difficult word problems too.

An easier way to solve this is to set up a simple diagram:

$$\underline{}\ \underline{}\ \underline{}\ \underline{X}$$

The X in the last space represents the position of the oldest artifact on the list. Then, let A = the youngest artifact, B = the second youngest, and C = the third youngest on the list. So, the correct order on the diagram would be $\underline{A}\ \underline{B}\ \underline{C}\ \underline{X}$.

Since the student is randomly guessing, they could arrange the first three spaces as A B C or A C B or B A C or B C A or C A B or C B A. That's **six** possible orders, with only **one** correct order, A B C.

So, the probability is one out of six, or 1/6. Choice **G**.

25.

A betting game is played using an open box with a rectangular bottom measuring 5 inches by 12 inches. A square with side lengths of 3 inches is painted on the bottom of the box. The game is played by flipping a small coin into the open box. If the coin comes to rest in the painted square, the player wins a prize. Assuming a coin dropped into the box comes to rest at a random spot on the bottom of the box, which of the following is closest to the probability that the coin comes to rest in the painted square?

A. 0.05
B. 0.10
C. 0.15
D. 0.31
E. 0.67

Here, we only need to determine the probability of a coin landing on the square shape inside the rectangular shape, as shown below:

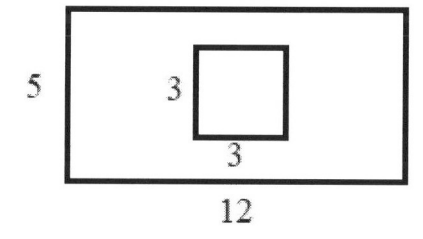

That probability is just the area of the square divided by the area of the rectangle. So, (3)(3) / (5)(12) = 9/60 = 0.15.   Choice **C**.

26.

Skylar will use a bag of 20 solid-colored marbles for a game in which each player randomly draws marbles from the bag. The number of marbles of each color is shown in the table below.

Color	Number
Blue	6
Red	5
Black	4
White	3
Green	2

Skylar will randomly draw 2 marbles from the bag, one after the other, without replacing the first marble. What is the probability that Skylar will draw a white marble first and a black marble second?

A. $\frac{1}{75}$

B. $\frac{3}{100}$

C. $\frac{3}{95}$

D. $\frac{39}{145}$

E. $\frac{2}{5}$

This one is very fast and simple if you'll just pay attention to the phrase **without replacing**. That means that there are only 19 marbles left after Skylar draws the first white marble. The probability of drawing a white marble is 3/20, and then the probability of drawing a black marble after that is 4/**19**. When we are asked for the combined probability of one event occuring **and** then another, we must **multiply** the probabilities. Therefore, (3/20)(4/19) = 12/380 = 3/95. **C.**

27.

A math class has 12 sophomores and 5 juniors. The teacher will randomly select 2 students, one at a time, to represent the class in a committee at the school. Given that the first student selected is a junior, what is the probability that the second student selected will be a sophomore?

A. $\frac{12}{17}$

B. $\frac{3}{4}$

C. $\frac{4}{17}$

D. $\frac{1}{2}$

E. $\frac{2}{15}$

There are a total of 12 + 5 = 17 students in the math class. If the first student selected for the committee is a junior, that leaves 16 students to choose from for the second pick. Among those 16 there are 12 sophomores. Then, the probability is $\frac{12}{16} = \frac{3}{4}$.

Choice **B**.

28.

One morning at a donut shop, each customer ordered either a regular or sugar-free donut, and each ordered it either with coffee or without coffee. The number of customers who ordered each type of donut with or without coffee is listed in the table below.

Order	Regular	Sugar-free	Total
With coffee	15	7	22
Without coffee	8	5	13
Total	23	12	35

A customer will be randomly selected from all 35 customers for a prize. What is the probability that the selected customer will have ordered a regular donut without coffee?

A. $\frac{1}{6}$

B. $\frac{8}{23}$

C. $\frac{8}{35}$

D. $\frac{1}{2}$

E. $\frac{5}{8}$

With probability problems like these, go directly to the question to find the numbers you need to answer the problem quickly.

In this case, the group from which a customer will be selected is **all** the customers. That number is **35**. And the particular customer selected is one who ordered a regular donut without coffee, of which there are **8** as shown on the table. Then the answer immediately is $\frac{8}{35}$. Choice **C**. Done.

Don't waste time reading the whole problem. Just focus on the question and find the needed numbers on the table. Be careful to reduce the fraction, if possible, to find the right choice.

29.

The probability of Steve being chosen to play in the lineup for his soccer team is $\frac{1}{11}$. What are the odds in favor of Steve being chosen to play?

128

The probability of Steve being chosen to play in the lineup for his soccer team is $\frac{1}{11}$. What are the odds in favor of Steve being chosen to play?

(Note: The *odds* in favor of an event are defined as the ratio of the probability that the event will happen to the probability that the event will NOT happen.)

F. $\frac{1}{8}$

G. $\frac{1}{9}$

H. $\frac{1}{10}$

J. $\frac{8}{1}$

K. $\frac{9}{1}$

This one should only take a few seconds after reading the problem, since you need to understand the definition of *odds*, which is given. Then, the probability that the event will happen is 1/11, and the probability that that it will NOT happen is 10/11. So, the ratio is (1/11) / (10/11) = 1/10. Choice **H**.

30.

The table below shows the letter grades 60 students earned on the final exam in American Literature. The highest possible grade is A; the lowest possible grade is F.

Final exam grade	Number of students
A	10
B	14
C	18
D	10
F	8

A student from this group will be chosen at random. What is the probability that the student's final exam grade is C or higher?

A. 0.3
B. 0.4
C. 0.6
D. 0.7
E. 0.9

Solve in 10 seconds by immediately tallying the number of students who got an A, B, or C. That would be 10 + 14 + 18 = 42. Then, the probability is 42/60 = 0.7. **D**.

That concludes this chapter on probability type word problems. If you reviewed all 30 examples, you should have a good idea of what to expect to see on the SAT or ACT when asked to determine the probability of something based on information on a chart, graph, or table. There were also examples of problems that only contained the necessary information in the question itself. Either way, you should now be fairly efficient at solving these types of problems.

Of course, there is always the possibility of seeing a probability problem unlike any presented here. That's up to the creators of the SAT and ACT to decide. But, at least you'll have a fighting chance to solve it if you understand the explanations that have been shown in this chapter.

Linear Relationships

The majority of word problems on the SAT and ACT deal with linear relationships in one form or another. You saw this already in the very first chapter.

In this chapter we're going to look at examples of linear word problems that don't require setting up systems of equations, but still must be properly interpreted to answer correctly.

1.
Sam works for an appliance repair company. Every week he is assigned a pallet of appliances that need to be repaired. The equation A = 112 − 25d represents the number of appliances he has left to repair at the end of each day, where A is the number of appliances left and d is the number of days he has worked that week. What is the meaning of the value 112 in this equation?

A) Sam repairs appliances at a rate of 112 per week

B) Sam starts the week with 112 appliances to repair

C) Sam repairs appliances at a rate of 112 per day

D) Sam will complete the repairs within 112 days

This is a very typical type of linear word problem that appears often on the SAT. There's a key to answering it quickly and accurately. It's hidden right in plain sight. But first you need to recognize what the equation given in the problem really is.

It's a simple linear equation written in **slope/intercept form**. Let's review.

The most common equation of a straight line is what is known as the slope/intercept equation.

$$y = mx + b$$

Most of you, I assume, have seen this before. But let's review it anyway. The x and the y just represent the x and y coordinates of any point on the given line. The letter m is called the slope of the line, which basically means the angle the line is oriented in (more on the mathematics of the slope later). And the letter b is called the y-intercept or the **starting value of the line.** If that were all you knew about the equation of a line, it would be enough to answer this question.

But you may be wondering how exactly A = 112 − 25d is the linear equation I just described. Well, let's rearrange the given equation and define the given variables and values.

$$A = -25d + 112$$

Now it should be looking more familiar. Instead of y we have A, and instead of x we have d. That's totally ok, because x and y can be replaced with any letters in the alphabet. "A" in this case represents the number of phones left to fix, and d represents the number of days worked that week. The -25 would be the slope. But we'll skip the significance of that for now because the question is asking about the 112. That should look familiar. It's the y-intercept, isn't it? And it's also known as the **starting value.** Do you see the word **start** in any of the choices? It should jump right out in choice **B**, which is the correct answer.

2.

A home remodeling company estimates the price of a job, in dollars, using the expression $100 + 25ch$, where c is the number of carpenters who will be working and h is the total number of hours the job will take using c carpenters. Which of the following is the best interpretation of the number 25 in the expression?

A) The company charges $25 per hour for each carpenter.

B) A minimum of 25 carpenters will work on each job.

C) The price of every job increases by $25 every hour.

D) Each carpenter works 25 hours per job.

Before you cringe, consider this. The expression they're showing is just the basic y = mx + b form of a line. In this case it's y = 25ch + 100. So m, which is the slope or **rate of change,** is 25. And rate of change is always a number **per** something.

That "something" is whatever the 25 is attached to. In this case it's "ch", which is the number of carpenter-hours. Choice **A.** Done.

Don't let "ch" or any double-variable throw you off. Stay focused on the y = mx + b equation. Remember, that is the **main** equation you will see and use on the SAT for **all** linear relationships.

The test is not designed for any higher math than the typical high school math courses through Algebra 2. Once you have established that a relationship is linear (often they will even tell you that it is) immediately think of y = mx + b, and identify which variables belong to the values stated in the problem.

3.
$$d = 25w + 200$$

Jack made an initial deposit to a savings account. Each week thereafter he deposited a fixed amount to the account. The equation above models the amount d, in dollars, that Jack has deposited after w weekly deposits. According to the model, how many dollars was in Jack's initial deposit? (Disregard the $ sign when gridding your answer.)

The given equation is just another y = mx + b type of linear equation. Just recall that the y-intercept is also called the **starting** value or the **initial** value, or any synonym of those words! Therefore, the answer here is **200**. Next.

4.

The line $y = px + 3$, where p is a constant, is graphed in the xy-plane. If the line contains the point (r, s), where $r \neq 0$ and $s \neq 0$, what is the slope of the line in terms of r and s?

A) $\dfrac{s-3}{r}$

B) $\dfrac{r-3}{s}$

C) $\dfrac{3-s}{r}$

D) $\dfrac{3-r}{s}$

First recognize that the given equation is in the y = mx + b form, once again. So the slope m = p and the y-intercept b = 3. Then, the shortcut here is to immediately substitute x and y for r and s because (r,s) represents an ordered pair in the (x,y) plane.

Then, s = pr + 3 , and we know the slope is p. So just solve for p.

pr = s – 3, then divide by r to get p = (s – 3) / r. Choice **A**.

5.

The average number of dogs per shelter in a certain city from 2008 to 2018 can be modeled by the equation $y = 0.78x + 83.4$, where x represents the number of years since 2008, and y represents the average number of dogs per shelter. Which of the following best describes the meaning of the number 0.78 in the equation?

A) The total number of dogs per shelter in 2008

B) The average number of dogs per shelter in 2008

C) The estimated increase in the average number of dogs per shelter each year since 2008

D) The estimated difference between the average dogs per shelter in 2018 and in 2000

Here again we see the y = mx + b form of a linear equation. That tells us right away which number represents the **slope** and which represents the **y-intercept.** So we know that 0.78 is the slope. But we also know that the slope is the **rate of change**, which is the change in the y value **per** change in the x value. The y value in this case is defined as the **average number of dogs per shelter.** The x value is defined as the **number of years since 2008.** So then, choice **C** most closely describes that rate of change.

6.
The cost of using a telephone in a motel room is $0.30 per minute. Which of the following equations represents the total cost d, in dollars, for h <u>hours</u> of phone use?

A) $d = 0.30h + 6$

B) $d = 0.30(60h)$

C) $d = \dfrac{60h}{0.30}$

D) $d = \dfrac{0.30h}{60}$

Here the **rate** is given in the first sentence, which we know is the m value in the y = mx + b equation. But there is no b here because there is no initial or starting charge indicated. Therefore, we can eliminate choice A right away. Now, notice if x represented minutes then the equation would simply be d = 0.30x. But they want the cost in terms of h **hours.** Since there are 60 minutes in each hour, x = 60h. So, by substitution, c = 0.30(60h). Choice **B.** Next.

7.

The weight of laboratory mice, in ounces, is a linear function of the amount of fat each mouse consumes in a day, in grams, and is given by W(g) = 0.2g + 6.3. Which of the following statements is the best interpretation of the number 6.3 in this context?

A) The weight of a mouse, in ounces, at 0 grams of fat intake per day.

B) The weight of a mouse, in ounces, at 0.2 grams of fat intake per day.

C) The increase in weight of a mouse, in ounces, that corresponds to an increase of 1 gram of fat.

D) The increase in the weight of a mouse, in ounces, that corresponds to an increase of 0.2 grams of fat.

Once again we have y = mx + b presented with different variables. But by now we know what each variable represents. In this case, the 0.2 is the slope m, and the 6.3 is the y-intercept b.

Here they are asking about the y-intercept 6.3. And once again we have a few ways of interpreting it, either as the y-intercept or the starting or initial value or any word that is synonymous with those words. As the y-intercept it is the y value when x = 0. In this case, **g** is the x value. So, immediately we can choose **A** as the correct answer because g represents the daily grams of fat and when g = 0, then W(g) = 6.3.

8.

At a diner, c cups of coffee are made by adding s scoops of ground coffee to a coffee pot filled with hot water. If $s = 0.5c + 1$, how many additional scoops of ground coffee are needed to make each additional cup of coffee?

A) None

B) A half

C) One

D) One and a half

Again, we have a linear equation. For **most** linear word problems they are looking for either the slope m or the y-intercept b. Can you guess which one it is for this problem? If you guessed the slope, you'd be right! That's because the slope is also the **rate of change** or the ratio of the change in the y variable to the change in the x variable. The way the question is worded, it can only be the m part of the y = mx + b equation of a line. In this case, m is the number in front of the c variable. That number is 0.5, or a half. **B.**

9.

The Home Owners Association (HOA) of a certain condominium community plans to expand the total number of homes on its property by a total of n new homes built per year. There were p homes on the property at the beginning of this year. Which function best models the total number of homes, y, the HOA plans to have x years from now?

A) $y = nx + p$
B) $y = nx - p$
C) $y = p(n)^x$
D) $y = n(p)^x$

Since you know what m and b stand for in the y = mx + b form of a linear equation, then this one is easy.

We are told the **rate** of new home construction is *n* homes per year. So, that will be our m. Then it says there were *p* homes at the **beginning** of this year. The word beginning is synonymous with **start** or **initial**. So, that's our b. Then the equation is y = nx + p. Choice **A**.

10.

Top Wheels Investment		
Car Model	Purchase Price (dollars)	Monthly lease price (dollars)
Turbo XL	34,000	350
Safari 4WD	42,000	433
Road Hog Sedan	29,500	304
Sprite Convertible	23,000	237
Sportster RX	32,500	335

The Top Wheels car dealership invested in five different models of cars listed in the table above. The table shows the amount, in dollars, the dealership paid for each model and the corresponding monthly lease price, in dollars, the dealership charges for each of the five models.

The relationship between the monthly lease price, *r*, in dollars, and the car's purchase price *p*, in thousands of dollars, can be represented by a linear function.

Which of the following functions represents the relationship?

A) $r(p) = 6.5p - 4.3$

B) $r(p) = 7.3p + 2.5$

C) $r(p) = 9.5p + 10.3$

D) $r(p) = 10.3p - 2.6$

Here again, they are **telling us that the function is linear.** That means we can use the y = mx + b equation to see what's happening. In fact, all the choices are in that form! So then, it's just a matter of seeing if m or b is what we need. Since it would be more complicated to determine the y-intercept in this case, let's try finding the slope m since it's just the ratio of r : p because r is the y variable and p is the x variable in y = mx + b! Then choose **any** purchase price (**in thousands**) and lease price, and then divide them. Remember, we're **not** looking for exact values, just reasonable ones. How about the Safari 4WD? Why not. r/p = 433/42 = **10.3.** Do you see any equation with the m value of 10.3? Well, it's **D**, of course. Done. No need to know anything else.

As a side note, in general, the slope is the ratio of the y and x values only if they are directly proportional. Like in this case, the lease price is directly proportional to the purchase price. There is no lease price for a car that has no purchase price, so the -2.6 in the equation in choice D is meaningless because if the purchase price of the car were $0, the lease price would NOT be -$2.6 which would make absolutely no sense. If the relationship is not directly proportional then you must use **the change** in two y values divided by **the change** in two x values to determine the slope of the line.

11.

Susan wants to purchase tickets from a vendor to watch a theatrical performance. The vendor charges a one-time service fee for processing the purchase of the tickets. The equation $T = 12n + 8$ represents the total amount T, in dollars, Susan will pay for n tickets. What does the 8 represent in the equation?

A) The price of one ticket, in dollars

B) The amount of the service fee, in dollars

C) The total amount, in dollars, Susan will pay for one ticket

D) The total amount, in dollars, Susan will pay for any number of tickets

By now you should have a good idea of what a linear equation looks like, especially the y = mx + b form. And now immediately you know that b in this case equals 8.

As we have seen, b means several things. First it is the y-intercept, which is the value of the function where x = 0. The variable n in this problem is really the x value.

So then what does n = 0 mean? Well, they tell us that n represents **the number of tickets.**

Now, logically, if Susan purchases **no** tickets, then she would not be buying anything from the vendor. But 3 of the choices all have n = 1 or another number of tickets, which **can't** be correct. So, choice **B** is the only possible answer.

12.
$$y = 29.99 + 1.80x$$

The equation above models the total cost y, in dollars, that a company charges a customer to rent a car for one day and drive the car x miles. The total cost consists of a flat fee plus a charge per mile driven. When the equation is graphed in the xy-plane, what does the y-intercept of the graph represent in terms of the model?

A) A flat fee of $29.99

B) A charge per mile of $1.80

C) A charge per mile of $29.99

D) Total daily charges of $31.79

Right away we know the y-intercept is 29.99 based on the given equation. Remember, order doesn't matter. y = 29.99 + 1.80x is the same as y = 1.80x + 29.99, which is the standard y = mx + b form. Since the **initial** value of the total cost is $29.99 before any miles have been driven, then it must be the flat fee. Choice **A.**

13.
Gold mining in a certain area dropped from 5 million ounces in 2010 to 2.1 million ounces in 2018. Assuming that the gold production decreased at a constant rate, which of the following linear functions f best models the production, in millions of ounces, t years after the year 2010?

A) $f(t) = \frac{29}{80}t + 5$

B) $f(t) = \frac{21}{80}t + 5$

C) $f(t) = -\frac{29}{80}t + 5$

D) $f(t) = -\frac{21}{80}t + 5$

This problem might seem a little daunting, but it's really quite simple. Whenever you see the term **constant rate** you should automatically assume you're dealing with a **linear** relationship. And you know, by now, that **rate** is another meaning for the **slope**. They're telling us that the oil and gas production **decreased** at a constant rate. That

141

tells us immediately that **the slope must be negative.** Then we can eliminate choices A and B right away. Remember, the slope is the change in y over the change in x. The y variable in this case is ounces of gold produced which decreased from 5 million to 2.1 million. That's a change of **2.9.** Stop!!! Then the only choice it **can** be is **C**, because C and D both have the same denominator for the slope and the only difference between them is the numerator which has to be some multiple of 2.9.

So, the simple elements of the linear equation y = mx + b and a little logic made this seemingly hard problem not bad at all. Notice, once you determined the slope had to be negative, then you didn't need to go any further after you calculated the difference between 5 and 2.1.

14.

A new car wash starts off with 3 employees but expects to expand rapidly hiring 2 new employees each quarter (every 3 months) for the first 2 years. If an equation is written in the form $y = ax + b$ to represent the number of employees, y, employed by the company x quarters after the car wash opened, what is the value of b ?

A gift. You are now becoming an expert at identifying and analyzing the y = mx + b form of a linear equation. So, you know immediately that b represents the y-intercept or the **starting** value. Then you can answer this one right away from the very first sentence. **3**. Next.

15.

Between 1990 and 2008, data were collected every three years on the amount of garbage added annually to landfills throughout the United States, in billions of pounds. The graph below shows the data and a line of best fit. The equation of the line of best fit is $y = 4.53x + 31.47$, where *x* us the number of years since 1990 and *y* is the amount of garbage added annually, in billions of pounds.

Accumulation of Garbage Dumped at Landfills

[Graph: x-axis "Number of Years since 1990" from 0 to 20; y-axis "Amount of Garbage (billions of pounds)" from 0 to 120, showing scattered points with a line of best fit increasing from about 30 to about 115.]

Which of the following is the best interpretation of the number 4.53 in the context of the problem?

A) The amount of garbage, in billions of pounds, dumped in US landfills during the year 1990.

B) The number of years it took the United States to add 1 billion pounds of garbage to its landfills.

C) The average annual increase in garbage, in billions of pounds, added to US landfills from 1990 to 2008.

D) The average annual increase in garbage, in billions of pounds, added to US landfills per year in the US from 1990 to 2008.

As intimidating as this problem may seem, it's just a basic y = mx + b problem! Now, any time you see that, you should relax and feel confident that you can handle it. They give us the following equation

$$y = 4.53x + 31.47$$

143

So, immediately we know 4.53 is the slope or rate of change, and 31.47 is the y-intercept or starting value.

The question asks for the meaning of 4.53, so we're almost there already since we know it's the slope or rate of change. And we know that means the change in the y value **per** the change in the x value. The y value in this problem is the amount of garbage, in billions of pounds, added to the landfills and the x value is the years since 1990. Given those facts, **D** is the best description.

16.

Which of the following statements is true about the graph of the equation $3y - 4x = -5$ in the xy-plane?

A) It has a negative slope and a positive y-intercept.
B) It has a negative slope and a negative y-intercept.
C) It has a positive slope and a positive y-intercept.
D) It has a positive slope and a negative y-intercept.

Here you should immediately put the equation into a form that gives you the most useful information. And, of course, that is the y = mx + b form. Doing that yields

$$y = 4/3x - 5/3$$

Then we know immediately that the slope is positive and the y-intercept is negative. **D.**

17.

The front of a roller-coaster car is at the bottom of a hill and is 10 feet above the ground. If the front of the roller-coaster car rises at a constant rate of 5 feet per second, which of the following equations gives the height h, in feet, of the front of the roller-coaster car s seconds after it starts up the hill?

A) $h = 5s + 10$

B) $h = 10s + \dfrac{150}{5}$

C) $h = 5s + \dfrac{150}{10}$

D) $h = 10s + 5$

There's that term again, **constant rate.** That should alert us immediately to the fact that we are dealing with a **linear** relationship, most commonly represented by y = mx + b. And if you look at the choices, that's exactly what we're dealing with!

Now, there's a super-fast shortcut for this one if you just understand what the **first sentence** is telling you. Before the car even **starts** up the hill it is already **10 ft** above the ground. That must be the **y-intercept.**

The **only** choice with a y-intercept of 10 is choice **A**. Done!

18.

A man purchases a boat valued at $65,000. The value of the boat depreciates by the same amount each year so that after 10 years the value will be $28,000. Which of the following equations gives the value, v, of the boat, in dollars, t years after it was purchased for $0 \leq t \leq 10$?

A) $v = 28,000 - 3,700t$

B) $v = 65,000 - 3,700t$

C) $v = 65,000 + 3,700t$

D) $v = 65,000 - 28,000t$

Here's where your practice of seeing so many linear relationship problems using y = mx + b really pays off. By now you are not fooled at all by the choices which are **all** in the y = mx + b, the only difference being that the mx and the b terms are in reverse order...which makes **no difference!**

So, immediately we know that b = 65,000. That eliminates choice A. The next thing we should notice is the phrase **depreciates by the same amount.** That's the same as saying **decreasing at a constant rate.** And you know we have seen THAT phrase before. So, by now, we know they are talking about **the slope of a line.** And more specifically, a **negative slope.** That eliminates choice C.

So, we're down to choices B or D. But you know it can't be D because if it depreciated $28,000 for 10 years, that would be $280,000 which is **more** than the original amount, which is impossible. So, the answer must be **B.** It's not even necessary to calculate the slope!

Although the explanation may seem long, the actual resolution of the problem will go much quicker if you understand the points made here.

19.
A hot air balloon, initially 5 feet above the ground, begins to gain altitude at a rate of 3 feet per second. Which of the following functions represents the hot air balloon's altitude above the ground y, in feet, t seconds after the hot air balloon begins to gain altitude?

A) $y = 5 + 3$

B) $y = 5 + 3t$

C) $y = 5 - 3t$

D) $y = 5t + 3$

Again, we're not fooled by the reverse order of the y = mx + b equation. And we know that 3 feet per second is the **rate** which is the same as the **slope** which is the "m" part of the equation. And t in this case is the same as the x variable. That means **B** is the only possible answer. Next.

20.

A phone plan charges a flat fee of $20 per month for the first 200 minutes of talk time, plus $0.10 for each additional minute. Which of the following graphs represents the cost, y, of x minutes of talk time?

A)

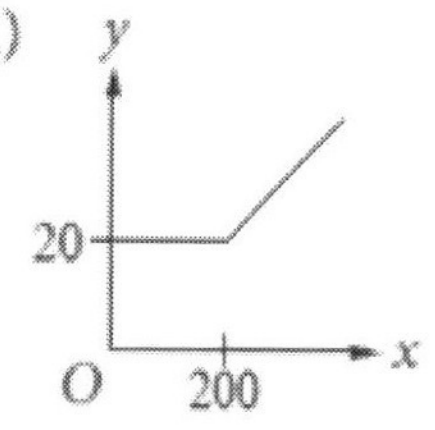

B)

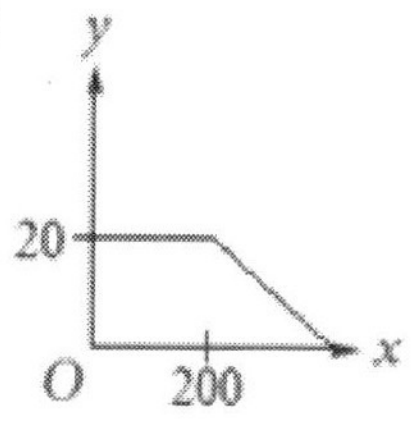

C)

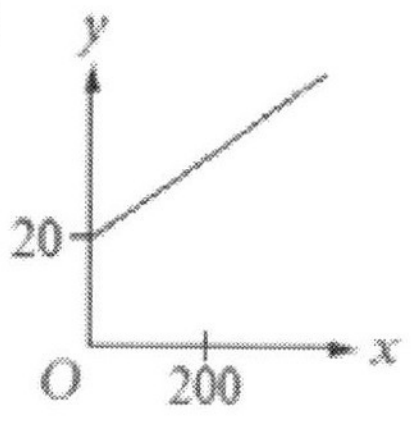

D)

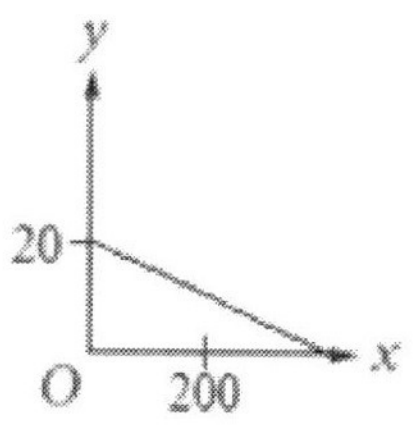

Here a **flat** fee represents a **flat** line up to the 200 mark. That eliminates C and D immediately. Then, the cost goes **up** from there, leaving **A** as the only plausible choice. Next.

21.

To produce aluminum softball bats, it costs the Recreation Equipment Supply Company $5,000 for overhead, plus $3 per softball bat produced. What is the maximum number of bats that can be produced by the company for $20,000 ?

A. 1,750
B. 3,502
C. 5,000
D. 5,750
E. 7,500

Here's an ACT problem. But, as you can see, it could have easily appeared on the SAT too, with one less answer choice.

If you can write the linear equation that represents the given information immediately, then you'll be able to solve this problem in a few seconds. The equation should be y = 3x + 5000 because they tell us it costs $3 **per** bat, so that must be the "m" in the basic y = mx + b equation for any linear relationship. Also, there is a one time overhead cost of $5,000, no matter how many bats are produced. So, that must be the "b", which is the initial amount. And, the variables x and y represent the number of bats and the total cost respectively. So, for $20,000, we can calculate: 20,000 = 3x + 5000. Then, 3x = 15,000, and x = 15000/3 = 5000 bats. **C**.

22.

A water tank that initially contained 200 gallons of water is leaking water at a constant rate of 3 gallons per minute. For the amount of time the tank has water, which of the following function models gives the number of gallons, G, in the tank t minutes after the leak started?

A. $G(t) = 196 - t$

B. $G(t) = 200 - 3t$

C. $G(t) = 200t - 3$

D. $G(t) = 200t - 3t^2$

E. $G(t) = 200\left(\frac{3}{4}\right)^t$

Whenever you see the term "constant rate" you should know that you are dealing with a **linear** relationship. As such, it can be represented mathematically as y = mx + b. By now you know that "b" is the y-intercept, or initial value. The first sentence of this problem tells us that the water tank **initially** contained 200 gallons of water, so that's our b term. The slope is also known as the **rate**, and it is given as 3 gallons per minute. But, it is **negative** because it's causing the amount of water to go **down**. Then, the linear equation becomes y = -3x + 200. Rearranging that to 200 – 3x, and substituting G(t) for y, we get the equation in choice **B**.

23.

Francis programs his calculator to evaluate a linear function, but he doesn't say what the function is. When 6 is entered, the calculator displays the value 3. When 16 is entered, the calculator displays the value 7. Which of the following expressions explains what the calculator will display when any number, n, is entered?

F. $\frac{2}{5}n$

149

G. $\frac{5}{2}n$

H. $n - 3$

J. $n - 9$

K. $\frac{5}{2}n - \frac{21}{2}$

As is often the case on the ACT, their word problems tend to be a little more confusing than those on the SAT. But again, that's only a general observation.

Believe it or not, you can answer this one very quickly. First notice the term **linear function**. You should then realize immediately it must be of the form **y = mx + b.** Now, just substitute values, recognizing that when they say **entered** it simply means the **input**, and when they say **displays** it simply means the **output**. Then it all falls into place:

3 = m(6) + b

7 = m(16) + b

You now have a simple system of linear equations which are easy to solve:

    7 = 16m + b

- 3 = 6m + b

    4 = 10m

Notice that the y-intercept (b) cancels, and you're left with an easy solution for the slope (m), which is 4/10 = 2/5.

The **only** choice with a slope of 2/5 is **F**. Done!

24.

The shipping rate for customers of Ship Quick consists of a fee per box and a price per pound for each box. The table below gives the fee and the price per pound for customers shipping boxes of various weights.

Weight of box (pounds)	Fee	Price per pound
Less than 10	$ 5.00	$1.00
10–25	$10.00	$0.65
More than 25	$20.00	$0.30

Gregg wants Ship Quick to ship 1 box that weighs 15 pounds. What is the shipping rate for this box?

F. $ 9.75
G. $16.50
H. $19.75
J. $20.00
K. $24.50

Reading the question under the table, we can see that this problem only involves the information in the second row of the table, since Gregg wants to ship a 15 pound box.

We can discern, by now, that since the fee is a set amount, it must be the **b** value in the y = mx + b equation. The **m** value would be the price per pound.

For the variables in the equation, **x** is the weight of the box in pounds, and **y** is the resulting shipping rate (rate in this case means the charge, not rate of change).

Then, substituting the values from the table, we get y = 0.65(15) + 10 = $19.75. **H.**

25.

Students studying motion observed a cart rolling at a constant rate along a straight line. The table below gives the distance, d feet, the cart was from a reference point at 1-second intervals from $t = 0$ seconds to $t = 5$ seconds.

t	0	1	2	3	4	5
d	14	20	26	32	38	44

Which of the following equations represents this relationship between *d* and *t* ?

A. $d = t + 14$
B. $d = 6t + 8$
C. $d = 6t + 14$
D. $d = 14t + 6$
E. $d = 34t$

Here, the terms <u>constant rate</u> and <u>straight line</u> reveal that we are dealing with a linear relationship.

And, of course, that means our basic equation y = mx + b comes into play. Just by looking at the choices we see that **d** is the y variable and **t** is the x variable.

So, the basic linear equation here is d = mt + b. But, what is m and what is b?

Well, we can see from the table that as t goes up by 1, d goes up by 6. That means, the rate of change or slope must be **6**.

The y-intercept b always occurs where x = 0, since it is <u>on</u> the y-axis. The table shows that when t = 0, d = 14. So, b = **14**.

Then, putting it all together, d = 6t + 14. Choice **C**.

26.

A dog eats 7 cans of food in 3 days. At this rate, how many cans of food does the dog eat in 3 + *d* days?

F. $\frac{7}{3} + d$

G. $\frac{7}{3} + \frac{d}{3}$

H. $\frac{7}{3} + \frac{7}{3d}$

J. $7 + \frac{d}{3}$

K. $7 + \frac{7d}{3}$

Again, an ACT question that's seemingly not so straightforward.

But you should still be able to at least determine that there is a linear relationship between the number of days and the cans of dog food consumed.

Then, y = mx + b can be used here. However, in this case, b would be 0 since there is no information about any starting number of cans of food.

Then, the equation reduces to just y = mx. Graphically, that's just a straight line through the origin.

Our y would be the number of cans of dog food, and x would be the number of days. What about m? That's our *rate*, remember? They tell us the dog eats 7 cans in 3 days. That's a rate of 7 cans per 3 days, which means m = 7/3.

27.

A house painter charges $24.00 per hour for a painting job that requires more than 5 hours to complete. For any job requiring 5 hours or less, the house painter charges a flat fee of $100. If n represents the number of hours the job requires, which of the following expressions gives the charge, in dollars, for a job requiring more than 5 hours to complete?
F. 124.0
G. $-24n + 100$
H. $24n - 100$
J. $24n$
K. $24n + 100$

Here's another linear word problem that requires a bit more thinking than usual.

There are two linear relationships described in this problem. The first one is under the condition that the house painter requires more than 5 hours to complete the job.

If n represents the number of hours, then that relationship can be given by the equation **y = 24n**, since the painter's rate of pay is $24 per hour and there is no additional starting fee.

The other condition is when the painter works for 5 hours or less. In that situation, the painter charges a flat fee of $100. That equation would be **y = 24n + 100**.

153

Since the question asks for the expression for a job requiring more than 5 hours to complete, the answer is 24n, choice **J**.

28.

> For every cent increase in price of a pound of apples, the grocery store sells 25 fewer pounds per day. The grocery store normally sells 800 pounds of apples per day at $1.09 per pound. Which of the following expressions represents the number of pounds of apples sold per day if the cost is increased by $3x$ cents per pound of apples?
> F. $(1.09 + 3x)(800 - 75x)$
> G. $800 - 25x$
> H. $800 - 75(1.09)x$
> J. $800 + 75x$
> K. $800 - 75x$

In this problem we have <u>decreasing rate</u> of 25 pounds of apple per day, for every cent increase in the price of a pound of apples. So, in terms of <u>cost</u>, the amount of apples sold decreases by <u>25 pounds per cent</u>.

A decreasing rate is graphically represented by a <u>negative</u> slope. In this case, the slope, m, would be m = -25.

If we start with 800 pounds of apples and we decrease by 25 pounds per cent, the linear equation is y = -25x + 800.

But if we increase the price by 3x, then we must substitute 3x for x to get:
Y = -25(3x) + 800 = -75x + 800, which is equivalent to choice **K**.

Notice that the $1.09 per pound information was not really relevant. That throws many students off because they assume they must use all the data that's given. While that is usually true, it's not always the case, as in this problem.

This one was a little tricky, so review it until it clicks or move on if it doesn't. Remember, on the ACT or the SAT, it's not worth racking your brains out on a problem that confuses you and causes you to waste a lot of time.

29.

John Jones has decided to go into the business of producing and selling boats. In order to begin this venture, he must invest $10 million in a boat production plant. The cost to produce each boat will be $7,000, and the selling price will be $20,000. Accounting for the cost of the production plant, which of the following expressions represents the profit, in dollars, that John will realize when x boats are produced and sold?

- A. $13,000x - 10,000,000$
- B. $27,000x - 10,000,000$
- C. $9,973,000x$
- D. $20,000x$
- E. $13,000x$

In this problem we must break down the information into parts and set up a linear equation that represents the profit.

Immediately, we know that $10 million invested means money spent, and therefore must be subtracted from any sales before a profit can be realized.

So, right away, we should realize that only choices A or B are possible.

Then, the cost to produce each boat must be subtracted from the selling price for the same reason. Therefore each boat sold has a profit of 20,000 – 7,000 = $13,000.

Putting it all together, the final profit is then 13,000x – 10,000,000. Choice **A**.

30.

Gloria's washing machine is broken. Since her machine is pretty old, she doesn't want to spend more than $100 for repairs. A service call will cost $35 and the labor will be an additional $20 per hour. There are no other charges. What is the maximum number of hours that the repair person can work without the total cost exceeding $100?

- F) 2.5
- G) 2.75
- H) 3.0

155

J) 3.25
K) 5.0

Even though this is technically an inequality problem, it can be treated as an equality because fractions of an hour are permitted.

Then, based on the given information, we can set up up the equation as

y = 20x + 35. Since the maximum Gloria wants to spend is $100, we can substitute that value for y.

Then, 100 = 20x + 35

Solving for x, which is the number of hours, we get

20x = 65. Therefore, x = 3.25. Choice **J**.

And with that, we have completed 30 linear relationship word problems.

Hopefully, you have been able to follow the solutions presented without too much difficulty and will be better prepared to answer similar questions that you may see on the SAT or ACT.

Review this chapter carefully until you feel confident that you can handle these types of problems that turn up frequently on the test. It would also be a good idea to supplement what you have learned here with other similar word problems that you might find from other sources available in books and on the internet.

Measures of Central Tendency

Mean, median, mode, range, and standard deviation are all terms associated with measures of central tendency. Although you may not have heard that phrase before, you most probably have heard the aforementioned terms associated with it.

Quite a few problems on the SAT and ACT deal with these measures of central tendency. They range from very easy to very challenging in terms of difficulty.

In this chapter we'll review many of the most common and a few not so common examples of in this category.

1.

Shoulder Height of German Shepherd						
20	21	21	22	22	22	23
23	24	24	24	24	25	25
26	26	27	27	28	28	35

The table above lists the shoulder heights, to the nearest inch, of a random sample of 21 German Shepherd dogs. The outlier measurement of 35 inches is an error. Of the mean, median, and range of the values listed, which will change the most if the 35-inch measurement is removed from the data?

A) Mean

B) Median

C) Range

D) They will all change by the same amount.

Answering this problem requires knowing definitions. The mean is the same as the average, the median is just the middle value in an ordered list of values from least to greatest, and the range is the difference between the greatest and smallest value. So, if they remove the **greatest** value, 35, from the list, which do you think will change the most? Of course, it's the range. Choice **C**. Done.

If you're unclear about mean, median, and mode it would be a good idea to review those definitions until you're pretty sure about their meanings because the SAT and ACT are almost sure to ask one or two questions concerning them.

2.

The weights, in pounds, for 17 babies in a maternity ward were reported, and the mean, median, range, and standard deviation for the data were found. The baby with the lowest reported weight was found to actually weigh 1 pound less than its reported weight. What value remains unchanged if the four values are reported using the corrected weight?

A) Mean

B) Median

C) Range

D) Standard deviation

In this problem, you should immediately eliminate choice A because if one of the baby's weight changes than the average weight of the babies would change too. Next, remember that medium is the middle value of a list of **ordered** values, from least to greatest. So, if the least value is actually less than reported, it is **still** the least value and the order of the list wouldn't change. So, **B**. Next.

3.

| List A | 3 | 4 | 5 | 8 | 8 | 10 |
| List B | 1 | 3 | 5 | 9 | 10 | 10 |

The table above shows two lists of numbers. Which of the following is a true statement comparing list A and list B ?

A) The means are the same, and the standard deviations are different.

B) The means are the same, and the standard deviations are the same.

C) The means are different, and the standard deviations are different.

D) The means are different, and the standard deviations are the same.

Here we are introduced to the term <u>standard deviation</u>. Roughly speaking, the standard deviation represents how far away the individual values that make up the data are from the mean. So, for example, if the average (mean) age of the people in 2 different communities is 32, but the first community has a lot of babies and elderly people, then it's standard deviation would be greater than the other community which is comprised mainly of people between 25 and 35 years of age.

Then, if we take the average of the lists, we that it is 6.33 for both. So, we can eliminate choices C and D right away.

Then, we should be able to realize that there are more values that are further away from the mean (average) in the list B than list A. So, the answer is **A**.

4.

A Pet Food company chose 200 families at random from each of two towns and asked each family how many pets they have. The results are shown in the following table:

Family Pets Survey

Number of Pets	Town A	Town B
0	80	50
1	70	60
2	30	40
3	10	30
4	10	20

There are a total of 1,800 families in Town A and 2,600 families in Town B.

What is the median number of pets for all the families surveyed?

A) 0

B) 1

C) 2

D) 3

This problem may appear to be more daunting than the others, but if you follow the definitions, then it's not so bad.

As stated previously, the **median** is the **middle number** in an ordered list from least to greatest.

So, in this problem, what is the middle of 200? It's **100**. Technically it's between the 100th and 101st number in a list of 200 numbers, but 100 is fine here.

You can see from the table that the first 80 families from Town A and the first 50 families from Town B all have **0** pets. And the next 70 families from Town A and the next 60 families from Town B have **1** pet. Then, the 100th family from each town falls into the category of having **1** pet. Choice **B**.

Review that one as often as necessary until it sinks in, because both the SAT and ACT will throw at you problems that require more than just basic understanding.

5.

Number of States with 10 or More Congressional Districts in 2010

Congressional Districts	Frequency
10	1
11	1
12	1
13	1
14	2
16	1
18	2
27	2
36	1
53	1

In 2010, there were 13 states with 10 or more congressional districts, as shown in the table above. Based on the table, what was the median number of congressional districts for the 13 states?

A) 12

B) 14

C) 16

D) 18

Here's a similar problem to the previous one.

Since we're dealing with 13 states, the median position is the **7th**. Now, just count where the 7th position is on the list in the table which is already in order. The first 4 have 10, 11, 12, and 13 congressional districts respectively. The next 2 have 14, and then the next, which is in the **7th** position, has 16. So, the answer is **C**. Done.

6.

Ages of 20 People Enrolled in an Adult Education Class

Age	Frequency
33	5
35	4
38	4
42	3
45	2
50	1
60	1

The table above shows the distribution of ages of 20 people enrolled in an adult education class. Which of the following gives the correct order of the mean, median, and mode of the ages?

A) mode < median < mean
B) mode < mean < median
C) median < mode < mean
D) mean < mode < median

For a problem like this it may be best to use your graphing calculator. I have a TI-83 Plus, but all of the newer models do the same thing. Just follow the steps outlined in your particular owner's manual. With the TI-83, the steps are:

[STAT] → 1: Edit → L1 (populate this list with the **Age** values from the table) → L2 (populate this list with the **Frequency** values from the table) → [STAT] → CALC → 1: 1-Var Stats → L₁, L₂ → ENTER.

This will reveal the mean, $\bar{x}$, as about **39** and the median, Med, as **38**. For the mode you can just see which age occurs most frequently, which in this case is **33**. Therefore, the answer is choice **A**.

7.
> The maximum value of a data set consisting of 33 positive integers is 79. A new data set consisting of 34 positive integers is created by including 90 in the original data set. Which of the following measures must be 11 greater for the new data set than for the original data set?
>
> A) The mean
> B) The median
> C) The range
> D) The standard deviation

Whenever you see the terms **maximum or minimum** in a question with a set of data, it usually means you're dealing with the **range**, because the range is just the difference between the maximum and minimum values of the data. Since the new maximum is 90 and the old maximum was 79, the range must increase by 90 – 79 = 11, which is exactly what the problem states. Therefore, **C**.

8.
> In the 1990s, the park rangers at Yellowstone National Park implemented a program aimed at increasing the dwindling coyote population in Montana. Results of studies of the coyote population in the park are shown in the scatterplot below.

Coyote Population in Yellowstone Park

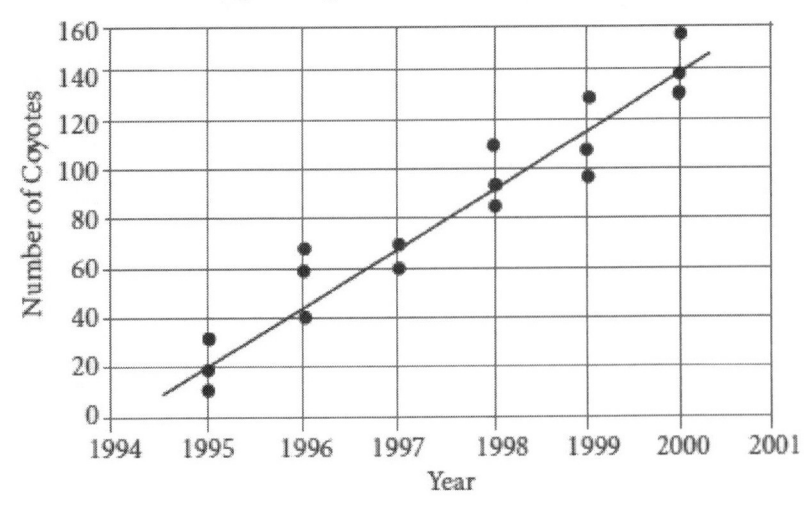

According to the data in the scatterplot, which of the following best represents the percent increase between the median of the results of the studies from 1995 and the median of the results of the studies from 1996?

A) 50%

B) 100%

C) 150%

D) 200%

This problem requires finding medians and percent increase, so we'll be using what we learned in the chapter on percentages to get the final answer.

But first, let's determine the medians of the coyote population from 1995 and 1996.

Looking at the graph, we see three data points at 1995 in <u>ascending order</u>. Then, right away, we know the middle point must be the median, which looks like about **20**. It doesn't need to be exact since the question is asking for the best among the choices.

For 1996, the middle point looks right about at **60**.

Remembering from the chapter on percentages that the percentage increase of two values is the new value minus the old value over the old value times 100, we get

$\frac{60-20}{20}$ x 100 = 200%. Choice **D**.

9.

John Croxley, the mayor of Black Rock, NY, is counting the number of restaurants that have opened in his town per month for the last seven months. He compiles the seven numbers into Set F, which contains the elements 4, 5, 11, 13, 16, 18, and x. If both the median and average (arithmetic mean) of Set F equal 11, what must be the value of x, the unknown number of restaurants that opened in Mayor Croxley's town last month?

A) 9
B) 10
C) 11
D) 12

In this problem, knowing that the median of Set F is 11 only tells us that x must be *less than or equal to* 11 in order for 11 to be the middle number in the set.

However, knowing that the <u>mean</u> is 11 allows us to set up an equation that can be solved for x:

$$\frac{4+5+11+13+16+18+x}{7} = 11$$

Then,

67 + x = 77

And, so x = 10. Choice **B**.

10.

Set R consists of all the one-digit prime numbers. Set S contains all of the elements of Set R, as well as an additional positive integer, x.

Michael wants to change the value of *x* so that the mean of Set S is equal to the median of Set S and for Set S to have no mode. What value of *x* would accomplish his goal?

Let's start by specifying the sets. If Set R consists of all one-digit prime numbers, then the numbers are 2, 3, 5, and 7.

So, Set S must be 2, 3, 5, 7, and x.

Then, the mean of Set S is $\frac{2+3+5+7+x}{5} = \frac{17+x}{5}$.

The media of Set S will depend on what x is. If it is greater than 5, then 5 will be the median. If it is less 3, then 3 will be the median.

However, if 3 is the median, then $\frac{17+x}{5}$ = 3, and then 17 + x = 15, and so x = -2, which can't be because the problem states that x is a positive number.

So, the median must be 5, in which case $\frac{17+x}{5}$ = 5, and the 17 + x = 25, and so x = **8**.

This would be a grid-in answer, since no choices are given.

Obviously, this problem required more thinking than a typical central tendency problem. So, you could expect to see it near the end of the exam.

The tables below show the points scored by two different basketball players, Jay and Ed. Ed's average (arithmetic mean) for 4 games is 2 less than Jay's average for 5 games.

Use these date for Question 11 and Question 12.

Jay's points	Ed's points
20	15
16	21
25	17
15	
14	

11. How many points did Ed score during the fourth game?

A. 12
B. 11
C. 10
D. 9
E. 8

First we need to find out what Jay's mean score is by adding all his scores and dividing by 5:

$$\frac{20 + 16 + 25 + 15 + 14}{5} = 18$$

We are told that Ed's average is 2 less than Jay's, which means Ed's average is 16.

Then, if we call x Ed's 4th score, we can set an equation to solve for x:

$$\frac{15 + 21 + 17 + x}{4} = 16$$

Continuing to solve for x:

53 + x = 64, then x = 11. Choice **B**.

12.

> Say that Ed scored 16 points in the fourth game. What should be added to Jay's median score to equal the median of Ed's scores?

F. 0.5
G. 1.0
H. 1.5
J. 2.0
K. 2.5

If Ed scored 16 points in the fourth game, then to determine his median score, we first put Ed's scores in order from lowest to highest:

15, 16, 17, 21

Then Ed's median score is exactly between 16 and 17, which is 16.5.

Putting Jay's scores in order from lowest to highest we get:

14, 15, 16, 20, 25

Then Jay's median score is the middle number, 16.

So, **0.5** should be added to Jay's median score to equal the median of Ed's scores.

So, choice **A**.

13.

> a, b, and c are all positive integers such that $a + b + c = 150$, and none of these values are equal to each other. What is the smallest possible value for the median of a, b, and c?

A. 5
B. 4
C. 3
D. 2
E. 1

Here again, we notice that this ACT type question is not quite as straightforward as you might expect on the SAT. But again, I warn you, sometimes the reverse is true.

Anyway, let's try to solve it. We'll have to use some logic and pay careful attention to the information given.

We're told that a, b, and c are all positive integers. That means that the smallest any of the numbers can be is 1, because, although 0 is an integer, it is neither positive nor negative.

But we want the smallest value for the median, which is the middle number. Since the numbers a, b, and c must be arranged from lowest to highest, the lowest first number should be 1, and the next lowest number should be 2, which is also the median.

Then, the arrangement is 1, **2**, 147 since all the numbers must add up to 150.

Therefore, the answer is **C**.

Hopefully you followed that, because it just used simple logic and an understanding of what the median is.

14.

Pre: STUDENT PERFORMANCE ON TWO SCIENCE TESTS

STUDENT	Test I Score	Test II Score
A	70	90
B	85	80
C	85	70
D	90	70
E	85	85

The chart above shows the scores on two tests for five students in a science class. If John's score was equal to the mode for Test I and equal to the median for Test II, then which of the five students represents John's scores?

F. A

G. B

H. C

J. D

K. E

Let's take it one part at a time. First, we need to find the mode for Test I. Remember mode is the number that appears most frequently. For Test I, clearly it's the number **85**.

Next, let's find the median for Test II. We should know by now how to do that. First, we put the scores in ascending order. Then, identify the middle one.

70, 70, **80**, 85, 90

So, the question becomes, which student got an 85 on Test I and 80 on Test II.

Clearly, that's student B. Choice **H**.

15.
The number n is to be added to the list $\{3, 4, 5, 6, 10, 12\}$. If n is an integer, which of the following could be the median of the new list of seven numbers?

I) 5

II) 5.5

III) 6

A) I only

B) II and III only

C) I and III only

D) I and II only

E) I, II, and III

Again, let's use some logic. If another number is added to the list, we will have an *odd* number of numbers. That means, there will be a distinct middle value which is the median when the numbers are arranged in ascending order.

If n is greater than 5, let's say 7, then the list would be:

3, 4, 5, **6**, 7, 10, 12   And, as you can see, 6 would be the median.

If n is less than 5, let's say 2, then the list would be:

2, 3, 4, **5**, 6, 10, 12   Then, clearly, 5 would be the median.

So, **D** is the answer.

This problem helps us to realize that any list with an <u>odd</u> number of numbers will have a distinct median in the middle, with an even number of numbers to the left and right of the median. Any list with an <u>even</u> number of numbers will have a <u>median in between</u> two distinct numbers, which is determined by taking the average of the two numbers.

16.
> The average (arithmetic mean) of seven integers is 11. If each of these integers is less than 20, then what is the least possible value of any one of these integers?
>
> (A) –113
>
> (B) –77
>
> (C) –37
>
> (D) –22
>
> (E) 0

Remember that the mean or average is the sum of the number divided by the number of numbers. Here, the number of numbers is 7 and the mean is 11. That means the <u>sum of the numbers</u> must be (7)(11) = **77**.

If we want <u>one</u> of the numbers to be the <u>least possible</u>, then the others must be the greatest. Think about that if the logic eludes you.

171

But, all of the integers must be less than 20, according to the problem. So, the greatest all the other integers can be is **19**.

If we call x the least possible integer, then:

x + 19 + 19 + 19 + 19 + 19 + 19 = 77

x + 114 = 77, so x = -37. Choice **C**.

Although this one may have seemed a little tricky, if you follow the steps in the solution you should realize that it is quite doable and not that hard. Review it until it sinks in.

17.

184	176	181	157	168
154	148	165	190	162

A group of patients is recruited for a clinical trial. Their heights, recorded in centimeters, are listed in the table above. Two more patients are recruited to the study. After these patients join, the mean height is 169 cm. Which of the following could be the heights of the two new patients?

A) 146 cm and 177 cm

B) 150 cm and 188 cm

C) 165 cm and 177 cm

D) 157 cm and 186 cm

As you can see, some central tendency SAT questions can be a little challenging too.

But, this one really isn't too bad if you just analyze what they're saying a bit.

The table shows the heights of 10 patients. If two more are recruited to the study then there will be 12. Easy enough.

Then, they tell us that the mean height, after the new patients join, is 169 cm.

Well, that's really all the information we need to answer the question, since we know that the sum of the heights of all the patients is equal to the number of patients times the mean.

In this case, we don't know the heights of the two new patients, but they are revealed in one of the given choices.

If we let x = the sum of the heights of the two new patients, then we can set up the following equation:

184 + 176 + 181 + 157 + 168 + 154 + 148 + 165 + 190 + 162 + X = (12)(169)

1685 + X = 2028

X = 343

Now that we know the sum of the heights of the two new patients is 343 cm, we just need to check the choices to see which one adds up to 343.

And, you'll see that 157 + 186 = 343. Choice **D**.

18.
The table shows the test scores from ten students in Mr. Smith's science class.

91	80	77	65	91
95	100	75	85	92

Which of the following statements is true?

A) the range is greater than the mean
B) the mode is greater than the median
C) the median and the mean are equal
D) the median and the mode are equal

The easiest value to find first is the mode, which is the number that occurs most frequently. That would be **91**.

The range is just the difference between the highest and the lowest number. That would be 100 − 65 = **35**.

For the median, we arrange the numbers from lowest to highest and determine the middle value:

$$65, 75, 77, 80, \boxed{85, 91,} 91, 92, 95, 100$$

$$\frac{85 + 91}{2} = 88$$

And finally, the mean:

$$\frac{91 + 80 + 77 + 65 + 91 + 95 + 100 + 75 + 85 + 92}{10} = \mathbf{85.1}$$

Then, among the choices, only **B** is true.

19.
The principal at Make Believe Academy wants to determine how frequently the senior class eats lunch at the cafeteria on campus. The principal sent out a survey to 35 seniors asking, "How many times this week have they eaten in the Cafeteria?" The histogram below summarizes the results of the seniors surveyed.

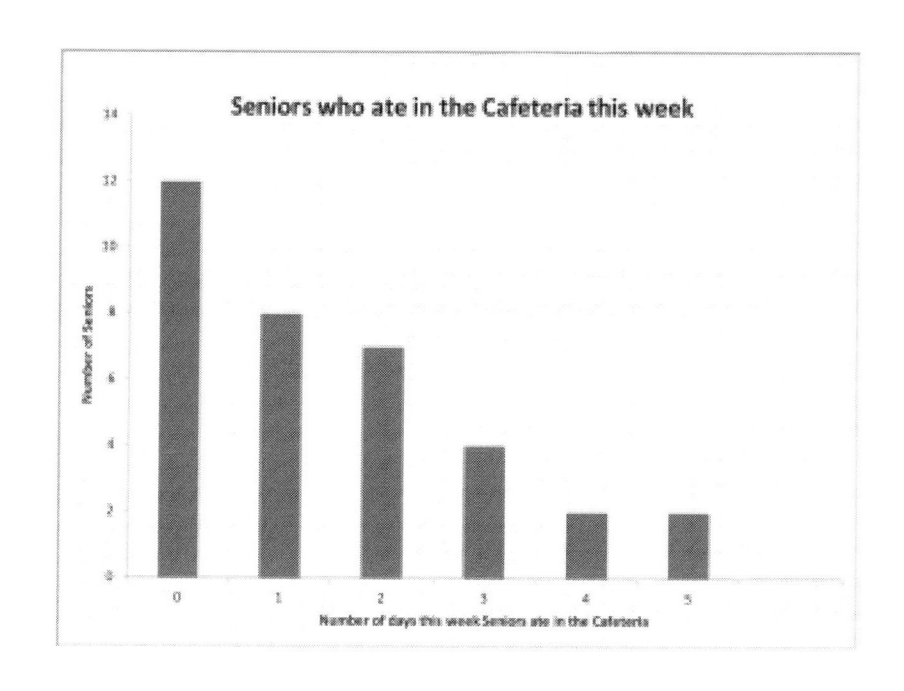

What is the mean for the number of seniors who ate in the cafeteria this week?
A. 2.49
B. 1.49
C. 1.89
D. 1.39
E. 2.29

This type of histogram is called a *frequency distribution*, because the data is grouped by repeating values and distributed across a spectrum of values.

Then to find the mean we must multiply the specific number of days in the week that seniors ate in the cafeteria by the number of seniors who ate that many days there, add up all those values, and then divide by the total number of seniors.

So, the mean would be:

$$\frac{(0)(12) + (1)(8) + (2)(7) + (3)(4) + (4)(2) + (5)(2)}{35} = \frac{52}{35} = 1.49$$

Choice **B**.

20.

Referring to the same histogram in the previous question, what is the median for the number of seniors who ate in the cafeteria this week?

A. 4
B. 3
C. 1
D. 0
E. 5

Remember, the median is the middle number of an ordered list of ascending values.

This list is connected to the number of seniors, of which there are 35. That means the middle value is connected to the 18th senior.

Well, we can see from the histogram that the first 12 seniors ate at the cafeteria 0 times.

If we continue to the next 6 seniors which takes us to the 18th senior, we see that they belong to the histogram bar with a value of **1**.

Then, the answer is **C**.

21.

The average of 7 distinct scores has the same value as the median of the 7 scores. The sum of the 7 scores is 357. What is the sum of the 6 scores that are NOT the median?

By now we are fully familiar with the fact that the average or mean is **the sum of the numbers divided by the number of numbers.** In this case, they tell us that the sum of the numbers (scores) is 357. So, then we just need to divide by the number of scores, which is 7. Therefore, 357/7 = 51.

They also tell us that the median has the same value as the average. Therefore the median is 51 too. Then, NOT the median means removing the 51 from the sum. So, 357 – 51 = 306. Choice **A**. Next.

22.

> The list of numbers 42, 37, 36, *X*, *Y*, 16 has a median of 31. The mode of the list of numbers is 16. To the nearest whole number, what is the mean of the list?
> A. 20
> B. 25
> C. 26
> D. 27
> E. 30

What in the world? But, don't despair, it's not as complicated as it looks. Remember that the median is **always** the middle number of a list of number in **ascending order.** Look at what the problem is presenting. It's a list in descending order. So, let's just turn it around to get

16, Y, X, 36, 37, 42

Ok, now what? They tell us the median is 31. That means X must be **26** because 31 is exactly between 26 and 36. But what is Y? It must be **16** because they tell us the **mode**, which is the number which appears most often, is 16.

So, the list of numbers must be 42, 37, 36, 31, 16, 16. Now just take the average by adding them up and dividing by 6 to get 29.67. The nearest whole number is **30.** Choice **E.**

A problem like this would be rated as difficult from the ACT company itself. So, it would be wise to skip it on the test and return to it later if you have the time. If you do have the time later, then just relax and apply what you know about mean and median and follow what the problem is asking closely, writing down everything you know as you go along. If it still doesn't click, don't worry about. It's still only worth one point and you shouldn't sweat it too much. Remember, there are a lot of fish to fry on the test. Don't let one problem mess up your psychological confidence.

23.

In a data set of 10 distinct values, the single smallest value is replaced with a much smaller value to form a new data set. Which of the following statements is true about the values of the mean and median for the new data set as compared to the mean and median of the original data set?

F. The mean will decrease; the median will stay the same.
G. The mean will stay the same; the median will decrease.
H. The mean and median will both stay the same.
J. The mean and median will both decrease.
K. Using the given information, the means and medians of the 2 data sets cannot be compared.

This one is very similar to a previous problem you saw already where the largest value was replace with a much larger value in a set of data. In this case, it's the smaller value, but it's still an **outlier**. Remember, an outlier doesn't change the median, but it does change the **mean** because it significantly changes the sum of the numbers. So, the answer is **F**.

24.

The first 7 terms in an arithmetic sequence are listed below. What is the difference between the mean and the median of the 7 terms?

$$\frac{1}{3}, \frac{2}{3}, 1, \frac{4}{3}, \frac{5}{3}, 2, \frac{7}{3}$$

F. 0

G. $\frac{3}{7}$

H. $\frac{2}{3}$

J. 2

K. 7

You can answer this one **immediately** if you remember that for **any arithmetic sequence** the mean and median are the **same value**. Then the difference is always **zero**! **F.** How's that for a shortcut?

25.

Set A and Set B each consist of 5 distinct numbers. The 2 sets contain identical numbers with the exception of the number with the greatest value in each set. The number with the greatest value in Set B is greater than the number with the greatest value in Set A. The value of which of the following measures *must* be greater for Set B than for Set A ?

A. Mean only
B. Median only
C. Mode only
D. Mean and median only
E. Mean, median, and mode

If the only number that is different is the greatest value in each set, then the **order** of the numbers from least to greatest doesn't change. So, the **median** of both sets must be the same since all the numbers are the same except for the last number. But, the **sum** of the numbers in set B is greater since its greatest number is greater than set

179

A's. Therefore, it's **mean** must be greater since the mean is just the average of the numbers. So, the answer is **A**.

Note that the **range** of set B would also be greater, although it was not given as a choice.

26.

> What is the product of the mean and the median of the first 5 prime numbers?
>
> (Note: 2 is the first prime number.)
>
> A. 27
> B. 28
> C. 39
> D. 41
> E. 42

Again, the mean is just the average, which is (2 + 3 + 5 + 7 + 11) / 5 = 28/5. The median is the middle number of the five numbers arranged from lowest to highest, which, in this case is 5.

Then, the product of the mean and median is (28/5)(5) = 28. **B**.

27.

> Conrad has plotted 5 points in the standard (*x,y*) coordinate plane below. He then plots a new point as follows: the *x*-coordinate of the new point is the mean of the *x*-coordinates of the 5 points already plotted; the *y*-coordinate of the new point is the mean of the *y*-coordinates of the 5 points already plotted. Which of the following ordered pairs gives the coordinates of Conrad's new point?

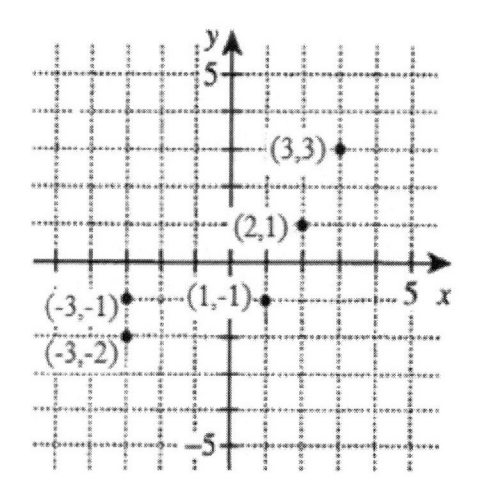

A. (−2,−2)
B. (−1,−1)
C. (0, 0)
D. (1, 1)
E. (2, 2)

Since we know the mean is just the average of all the x-coordinates, then

$\frac{1+2-3+3-3}{5} = \frac{0}{5}$, which is 0. And, the average of all the y-coordinates is

$\frac{-1+1-2+3-1}{5} = \frac{0}{5} = 0$.

Then, the new point is (0,0). Choice **C**.

28.

The mean age of the 6 people in a room is 35 years. One of the 6 people, whose age is 45 years, leaves the room. What is the mean age of the 5 people remaining in the room?

A. 14
B. 20
C. 25
D. 33
E. 35

By now, a problem like this should be easy to solve.

If the mean (average) age of 6 people is 35 years, then the **sum** of their ages is (6)(35) = 210 years. If one 45 year old leaves, then the sum drops to 210 – 45 = 165. Now, there are 5 people left. The average then becomes 165/5 = 33. **D.**

29.

What is the sum of 3 consecutive odd integers whose mean is 13 ?
A. 39
B. 75
C. 81
D. 87
E. 93

Remember, that, by definition, the mean (average) of any group of numbers is the sum of those numbers divided by the number of numbers in the group. Then, by the same fact, the **sum** of those numbers must equal the product of the average times the number of numbers. Then, it doesn't matter if the numbers are 3 consecutive odd integers, 3 consecutive even integers, 3 non-integers, or 3 numbers of **any kind!** The sum of the numbers, in this problem, must be (3)(13) = 39. **A.** Done!

30.

The table below gives some statistics based on the points Samantha earned on each of her first 3 math exams.

Statistic	Points
Median	80
Range	13
Maximum	91

If it can be determined, what is the mean number of points Samantha earned on her first 3 math exams?

F. 79
G. 80
H. 83
J. 85
K. Cannot be determined from the given information

If Samantha earned 91 points on her highest test, and the range of her tests was 13, then her lowest score must be 91 – 13 = 78. We now know the points on all of her tests. So, the mean, which is her **average** score, is just (78 + 80 + 91)/3 = 249/3 = 83. **H**.

And that concludes this chapter on measures of central tendency word problems. It's hard to predict how many, if any, will be on your particular test. But, as always, it's better to be prepared then sorry. If you do encounter one or two, or more, they will most likely be in the form of the examples presented, more or less. If you remember the basic definitions of mean, median, mode, and range, you should do just fine.

Quadratic Relationships

Up until now, we've only dealt with linear relationships in word problems. And, for sure, the vast majority of word problems will be of the linear variety on both the SAT and ACT. However, there can be, and often is, a significant number of word problems that will test your understanding of quadratic relationships.

In this chapter, we'll review these types of problems and the best approaches to solving them.

1.
$$h = -5.8t^2 + 50t$$

The equation above represents the approximate height, h, in feet, of a model rocket t seconds after it is launched vertically upward from the ground with an initial velocity of 50 feet per second. After approximately how many seconds will the rocket hit the ground ?

A) 5.8

B) 50

C) 7.6

D) 8.6

If you paid attention in your Algebra II class, you recognize the equation above immediately as a *quadratic equation*.

The standard form of a quadratic equation is y, or f(x), = Ax² + Bx + C.

In the given problem, the C term is missing. That's totally fine. It's still a quadratic equation. The only requirement for an equation to be quadratic is that the highest power of the given variables is 2.

Another way of looking at the fact that the C term is missing is say that C = 0.

That's significant, because the graph of <u>any</u> quadratic expression is a <u>parabola</u>.

The C term is the <u>y-intercept</u>. So, in this case, if the y-intercept is zero, the curve starts at the origin, which means when t = 0, then h = 0.

Here, h represents the height. So, when h = 0 the rocket is on the ground. It starts on the ground at t = 0, which makes perfect sense.

But the question asks when it will hit the ground again. That means we have to solve for t when h = 0. So, the equation to solve is:

-5.8t² + 50t = 0

Factoring out a common t we get:

t(-5.8t + 50) = 0

We already know that h = 0 when t = 0, so we need to solve for the other value of t:

-5.8t + 50 = 0

-5.8t = -50

t = -50/-5.8 = 8.6. **D**.

2.
$$y = x^2 - 7x + 12$$

The equation above represents a parabola in the *xy*-plane. Which of the following equivalent forms of the equation displays the *x*-intercepts of the parabola as constants or coefficients.

A) $y - 12 = x^2 - 7x$

B) $y + 3 = (x - 4)^2$

C) $y = x(x - 7) + 12$

D) $y = (x - 3)(x - 4)$

Pay attention to the term **x-intercepts**. That means the same thing as the **roots** (technically the real roots, because roots can also be imaginary).

The form of a quadratic equation that reveals the roots is the **factored form, y = (x – root1)(x – root2).** With that fact alone you can see that the answer is **D.**

No need to even factor the given quadratic yourself because they're not asking for the solution.

3.
$$y = 2$$
$$y = ax^2 + b$$

In the system of equations above, a and b are constants. For which of the following values of a and b does the system of equations have exactly two real solutions?

A) $a = -2, b = 2$
B) $a = -2, b = 3$
C) $a = 2, b = 3$
D) $a = 4, b = 3$

For problems like this it's helpful to learn how to draw simple parabolas very quickly.

Let's see how to draw $y = ax^2 + b$. There are two thing the "a" tells us: how wide or narrow the parabola is, and whether it opens up or down. In this problem **we don't care** how wide or narrow the parabola is. We only care about how it opens. A **positive** number means the parabola opens upward, like a cup. A **negative** number means it opens downward, like a hill. The "b" here is very important. It tells how high above or below the x-axis the vertex of the parabola is. These facts are illustrated below:

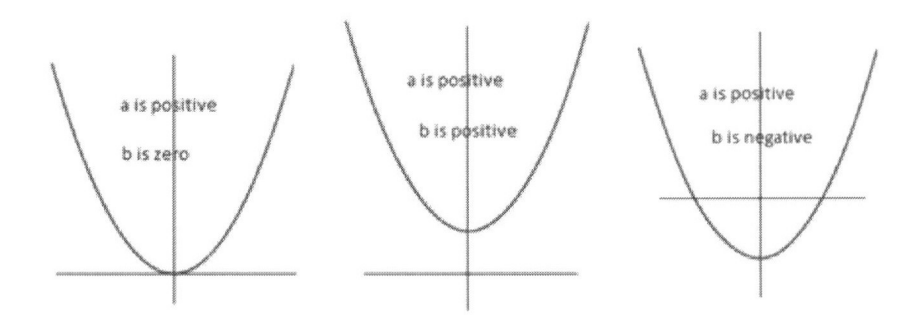

a is positive, b is zero

a is positive, b is positive

a is positive, b is negative

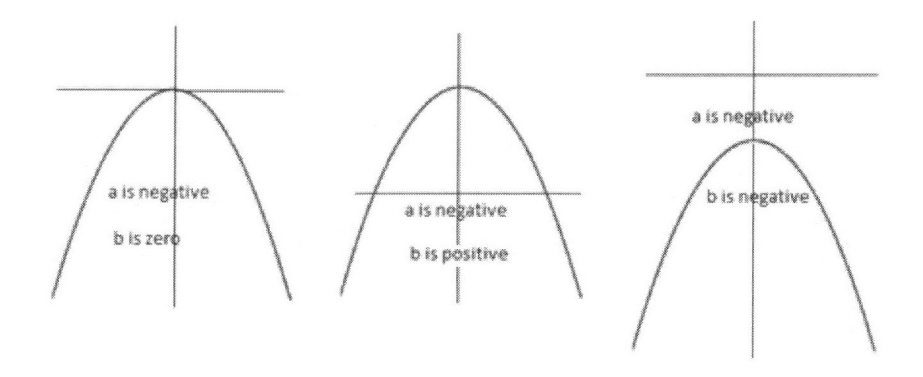

Next, let's understand what y = 2 looks like. It's just a straight horizontal line at a height of 2 on the y-axis. There are two solutions since that horizontal line crosses the parabola twice. Like this:

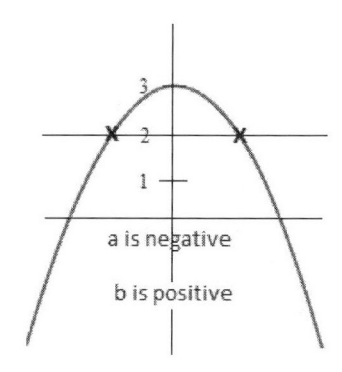

Therefore, the answer is choice **B**.

Bear in mind, the b in this problem is **not** the same as the b in the standard form of a quadratic function, which is f(x) = ax^2 + bx + c. (We'll discuss this later). This problem does not present an x term where b normally is the coefficient. The b coefficient in a typical quadratic function would shift the parabola right or left, not up or down as seen in this problem. In this problem the b coefficient behaves much like the c coefficient in the typical quadratic function.

4.
$$y = a(x-3)(x+5)$$

In the quadratic equation above, a is a nonzero constant. The graph of the equation in the xy-plane is a parabola with vertex (b, c). Which of the following is equal to c ?

A) $-16a$
B) $-12a$
C) $-10a$
D) $-8a$

Here, they are giving us the **factored form** of the quadratic equation. How convenient, because now we know the **roots** must be 3 and -5 because the factors always reveal the roots since plugging the roots into the factors makes the whole equation equal zero.

So then how does that provide us with a shortcut? Well, remember, the x –coordinate of the **vertex** always lies exactly between the two roots. That means b has to be exactly between 3 and -5. You find that by adding the two roots and dividing by 2. So b = (3 – 5) / 2 = -2/2 = -1.

But the question asks for c. But c is just the y value of the vertex, so we can plug -1 back into the original equation to get c = a(**-1** – 3)(**-1** + 5) = a(-4)(4) = -16a. Choice **A**.

Reviewing, to answer a problem like this quickly, immediately identify the roots and thereby very quickly determine the x and then y value of the vertex, which, in this case was the c and d values.

5.
$$f(x) = (x+5)(x-3)$$

Which of the following is an equivalent form of the function f above in which the minimum value of f appears as a constant or coefficient?

A) $f(x) = x^2 - 15$

B) $f(x) = x^2 + 2x - 15$

C) $f(x) = (x-1)^2 - 16$

D) $f(x) = (x+1)^2 - 16$

As stated previously, every quadratic equation represents a parabola. And the word **minimum** is just another way of saying the **vertex** (while the word **maximum** would be used to describe the vertex of an upside-down parabola).

Recall, a quadratic expressed in vertex form is $f(x) = a(x - h)^2 + k$, where (h,k) are the coordinates of the vertex.

Also recall that the x-coordinate of the vertex is **always exactly between the two roots.** In this problem we immediately know that the roots are -5 and 3 from the given factors (x + 5) and (x – 3). Exactly midway between -5 and 3 is **-1.** But here's where you must be careful. The vertex form of the quadratic is $f(x) = a(x - $ **-1**$)^2 + k$, which is really $a(x +$ **1**$)^2 + k$. And that can only be choice **D.** It was not even necessary to calculate k because of the given choices. So why waste time?

6.
A homeowner is designing a rectangular deck in his back yard. The length of the deck is to be 8 feet longer than the width. If the area of the deck will be 240 square feet, what will be the length, in feet, of the deck?

A) 12

B) 15

C) 20

189

D) 25

A problem like this may not immediately jump out as being a quadratic relationship, but when you translate the English into mathematical equations you'll see that is.

Given that the length of the deck is to be 8 feet longer than the width, we can set up our first equation:

$$L = W + 8$$

So far, no hint that is anything other than a linear relationship until we are told that the area of the deck will be 240 square feet. Then, knowing that the area of any rectangular shape is just the length times the width, our second equation is:

$$LW = 240$$

Now we have a choice. We can substitute the length for W + 8 from the first equation and solve for the width, or substitute the width for L – 8 based on the first equation and solve for the length. Since the question asks for the length, we'll do the latter:

$$L(L - 8) = 240$$

Then, distributing, we have our quadratic equation:

$$L^2 - 8L = 240$$

Subtracting the 240 in order to put that equation into standard form we can then solve for L:

$$L^2 - 8L - 240 = 0$$

There are 3 main methods for solving for the roots (solutions) of a quadratic equation: *factoring, using the quadratic formula, or completing the squares*.

We'll use factoring for this one because it won't be too difficult to figure out, but you should familiarize yourself with the quadratic formula and completing the squares if you're not sure about how to use those other alternative methods.

With factoring we have to ask ourselves what factors of -240 add up to the coefficient of the middle term, -8.

It might help to set up a table to answer that, or you could use your graphing calculator. Depending on the model, your owner's manual will describe the steps required to do it, or you can look it up over the internet.

Assuming you've done all that, you should determine that the factored form is (L – 20)(L + 12) = 0. You can FOIL that to prove it's correct.

Then, the solutions are L = 20 and L = - 8.

We can immediately discard the – 8 since the length can't be a negative number. We call that an *extraneous solution*.

So, the answer is 20. Choice **C**.

7.

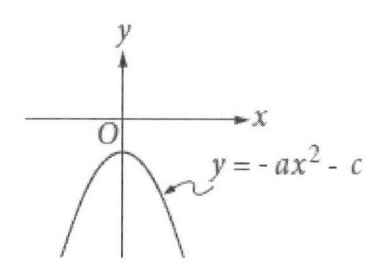

$y = -ax^2 - c$

The vertex of the parabola in the *xy*-plane above is $(0, -c)$. Which of the following is true about the parabola with the equation $y = a(x - b)^2 + c$?

A) The vertex is (b, c) and the graph opens upward.

B) The vertex is (b, c) and the graph opens downward.

C) The vertex is $(-b, c)$ and the graph opens upward.

D) The vertex is $(-b, c)$ and the graph opens downward.

Remember the **vertex form** of a quadratic equation is f(x) or y = a(x – h)² + k, where (h,k) are the coordinates of the vertex.

So **right away** we know the vertex is at (b, c). That eliminates choices C and D. Then we see that "a" is **positive**, and that means the parabola opens **upward**. So, the answer is **A**.

8.
$$3x^2 - 6x = t$$

In the equation above, t is a constant. If the equation has no real solutions, which of the following could be the value of t ?

A) -4

B) -1

C)   1

D)   3

The fastest way to solve this one is to identify the type of parabola this equation would represent if it were equal to **zero.** We always set quadratics equal to zero to find the roots, remember? So,

$$3x^2 - 6x = 0$$

$$3x(x - 2) = 0$$

$$x = 0 \text{ and } x = 2$$

Then the x-coordinate of the **vertex** lies exactly between 0 and 2, which is 1. And therefore, the y-coordinate is found by plugging 1 into the original expression to get $3(1^2) - 6(1) =$ **- 3.**

That means the parabola is right-side up with a **minimum** value at **y = - 3.**

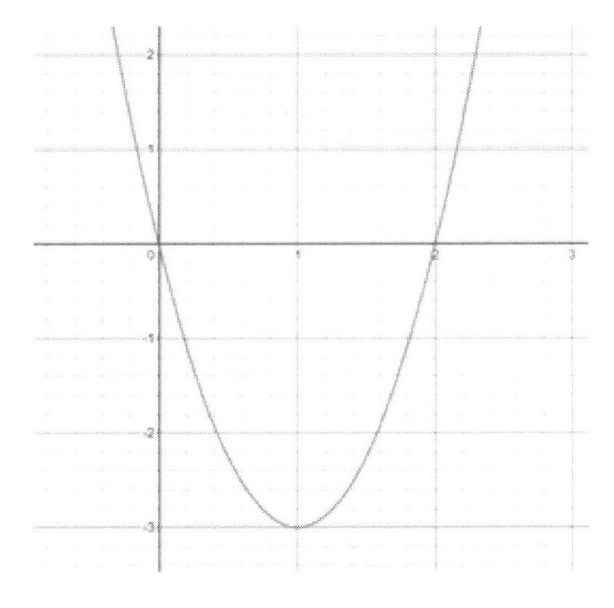

Now, t is a constant which represents a **straight horizontal line** that crosses the y-axis at whatever value t is. If this line **intersects** the parabola then there are solutions to the given equation.

But, apparently, any value of t **below** the parabola's minimum of − 3 would not intersect, and therefore have **no real solutions.** So, choice **A** is the answer.

If you understand this explanation, you'll be able to quickly solve a problem like this. So, review it until it clicks.

9.

The function f is defined by $f(x) = (x+5)(x+1)$. The graph of f in the xy-plane is a parabola. Which of the following intervals contains the x-coordinate of the vertex of the graph of f ?

A) $-4 < x < -2$

B) $-3 < x < 1$

C) $1 < x < 3$

D) $3 < x < 5$

Once again, remember that the x - coordinate of the vertex always lies exactly between the two roots of the quadratic function.

That means the x-coordinate of the vertex here must be at **x = -3**, since we know the roots are -5 and -1 from the given factors.

Now, just look at the choices. Which choice includes -3 as an answer for x? That would be **A**.

But, be careful. Even though choice B shows -3, it is NOT included as a value for x because of the < sign.

193

10.

In the xy-plane, a line that has the equation $y = c$ for some constant c intersects a parabola at exactly one point. If the parabola has the equation $y = -2x^2 + 6x$, what is the value of c ?

As we have seen in a previous problem that when a variable is a constant, it represents **a straight line** on a graph. More specifically, if y = a constant, it represents a straight **horizontal** line.

Now, look at the given quadratic equation. We should know immediately that it is an **upside down parabola**, since the leading coefficient is negative. Ok, now think logically. Where is the **only place** a straight horizontal line will touch a parabola at a single point? You should realize that it is at the **vertex!**

You could determine the vertex by finding the roots and then the x-coordinate midway between them, and then plugging that value into the equation to get the y value, **or use your graphing calculator.** Depending on your particular brand the steps may be different but they are **all** easy to do, and you should get something like this:

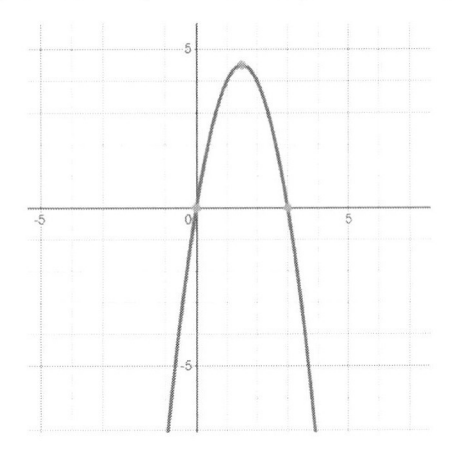

It's quite easy to see from this graph that the y value of the vertex is at **4.5**. Done.

No choices were given, so the answer would be a grid-in on the test.

11.

A car is traveling at x feet per second. The driver sees a red light ahead, and after 1.5 seconds reaction time, the driver applies the brake. After the brake is applied, the car takes $\frac{x}{24}$ seconds to stop, during which time the average speed of the car is $\frac{x}{2}$ feet per second. If the car travels 165 feet from the time the driver saw the red light to the time it comes to a complete stop, which of the following equations can be used to find the value of x?

A) $x^2 + 48x - 3,960 = 0$
B) $x^2 + 48x - 7,920 = 0$
C) $x^2 + 72x - 3,960 = 0$
D) $x^2 + 72x - 7,920 = 0$

Judging from the choices, we know right away we're dealing with a quadratic relationship. But how to set it up?

The fractions may seem intimidating but this question is really just a Speed x Time = Distance problem.

The time it takes the car to stop, after the brake is applied, is given as x/24 seconds.

The speed is given as x/2 feet per second. And the distance the car travels before coming to a stop is 165 feet.

However, the time from when the driver sees the red light to applying the brakes is 1.5 seconds while traveling at a speed of x feet per second.

So, putting it all together, we have (x/2)(x/24) + (x)(1.5) = 165

Then, x²/48 + 1.5x = 165.

So, there's our quadratic equation. It's a bit ugly, so let's try to clean it up.

If we multiply everything by 48 we'll get rid of the 48 in the denominator. That gives us: x² + 72x = 7,920.

And, just putting that into standard form, we get x² + 72x – 7,920 = 0. Choice **D**.

12.

The product of the ages of Sally and Joey now is 175 more than the product of their ages 5 years prior. If Sally is 20 years older than Joey, how old is Joey?

A) 8

B) 10

C) 12

D) 15

Again, it's not immediately apparent that we're dealing with a quadratic relationship, but we'll soon find out as we set up the equations.

Let's use descriptive variable to make sure we know who's who. So, S is Sally and J is Joey.

If the product of the ages of Sally and Joey is now 175 more than the product of their ages 5 years prior, then the translation of that statement into a math equation is:

$$(S)(J) = (S - 5)(J - 5) + 175$$

Since we have 2 unknown variables, we'll need another equation. And, since Sally is 20 years older than Joey, that equation would simply be:

$$S = J + 20$$

Substituting that into the first equation we get:

$(J + 20)(J) = (J + 20 - 5)(J - 5) + 175$

Continuing to solve for J:

$J^2 + 20J = (J + 15)(J - 5) + 175$

$J^2 + 20J = J^2 - 5J + 15J - 75 + 175$

$10J = 100$

$J = 10$. Choice **B**.

In this one, the J^2's cancelled out, so you didn't even have to solve a quadratic equation.

13.

Doug went to a conference in a city 120 km away. On the way back, due to road construction, he had to drive 10 km/hr slower, which resulted in the return trip taking 2 hours longer. How fast did he drive on the way to the conference.

A) 30

B) 40

C) 50

D) 60

You'll soon see this is another quadratic relationship as you set up the equations.

And, it's another Speed x Time = Distance problem. Let's stick with S for the speed and T for the time.

Then, going to the conference, ST = 120. That doesn't get us very far, but it's a start.

Next, they tell us that on the way back, Doug drove 10 km/hr slower, resulting in the trip taking 2 hours longer.

Now, here's a critical part that you must realize. Even though Doug had to drive slower and it took more time on the way back, the <u>distance</u> did not change! Usually, coming and going to any destination is the same distance unless you take some kind of detour, which was not stated in this problem.

Then, our second equation should be (S – 10)(T + 2) = 120. And, substituting T for 120/S from the first equation, we get:

$$(S - 10)(120/S + 2) = 120$$

FOILing and solving for S:

120 + 2S – 1200/S – 20 = 120

Multiplying everything by S to get rid of the S in the denominator, we get:

$120S + 2S^2 - 1200 - 20S = 120S$

$2S^2 - 20S - 1200 = 0$, then divide everything by 2 to get:

$S^2 - 10S - 600 = 0$

And, that's our quadratic equation to solve. Continuing...

(S – 30)(S + 20) = 0

S = 30, and S = -20, which we can discard since we're looking for the positive (forward) speed.

Then, **A** is the answer.

Although this may have seemed long and tedious, with practice you'll be able to solve it pretty quickly.

14.

If the length of each side of a square is increased by 6, the area is multiplied by 16. Find the length of one side of the original square.

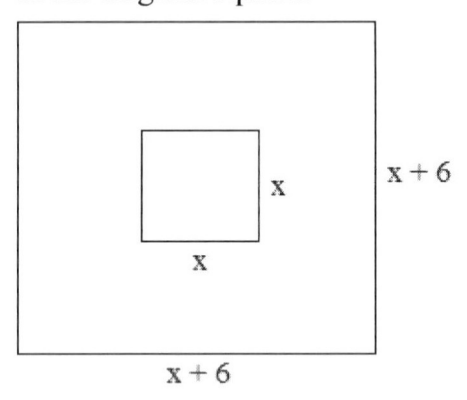

This would be a grid-in problem since no choices are given.

The diagram shows us the original square and the new, larger square after the length of each side of the original square is increased by 6.

The area of the original square is simply x^2, so the new area would be $16x^2$ based on the information given.

Then, $(x + 6)(x + 6) = 16x^2$

Continuing to FOIL and solving for x:

$x^2 + 6x + 6x + 36 = 16x^2$

$15x^2 - 12x - 36 = 0$, dividing everything by 3 we get:

$5x^2 - 4x - 12 = 0$

$(5x + 6)(x - 2) = 0$

x = 2 is the only solution that yields a positive result.

15. Tom and Linda want to surround their 60 by 80 cm wedding photo with matting of equal width. The resulting photo and matting is to be covered by a 1 m² sheet of expensive archival glass. What is the width of the matting? (round to the nearest tenth of a centimeter).

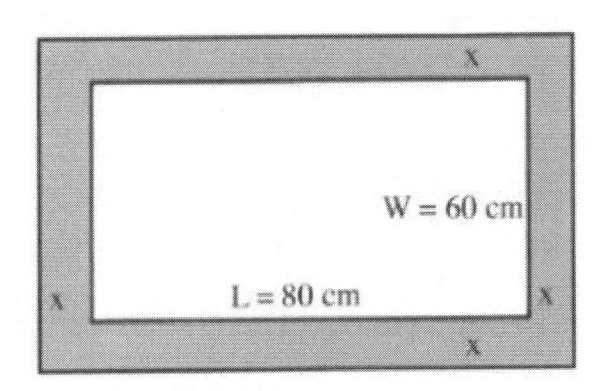

The illustration helps to clarify what the problem is asking for. From the drawing we can set up the necessary equation, bearing in mind the width of the matting, x, is added to both sides of the length and width. Then,

$$(80 + 2x)(60 + 2x) = 10{,}000$$

Remember, the units are in centimeters. That's why the area under the glass is 10,000 cm², instead of 1, since 1m² = (1m)(1m) = (100cm)(100cm) = 10,000 cm².

Continuing to FOIL and solve:

$4800 + 160x + 120x + 4x^2 = 10{,}000$

To eliminate the leading coefficient infront of the x^2 we should divide by 4:

1200 + 40x + 30x + x² = 2500

x² + 70x − 1300 = 0

Here, you can use your graphing calculator to find the roots, or the quadratic equation. Let's go with the quadratic equation for instructional purposes:

$$x = \frac{-b \pm \sqrt{b^2 - 4ac}}{2a}, \quad \text{where } a = 1, b = 70 \text{ and } c = -1300$$

Substituting the values in yields:

$$x = \frac{-70 \pm \sqrt{70^2 - 4(1)(-1300)}}{2(1)} \qquad x = \frac{-70 \pm 10\sqrt{101}}{2}$$

$$x = -35 + 5\sqrt{101} \qquad x = -35 - 5\sqrt{101} \text{ (rejected)}$$

x = about **15.2** cm. That would be the grid-in answer.

16.
Tim is an avid skateboarder, and is doing a crazy trick yet again. He has decided to do a sweet 720 off a ramp on a platform and into a moving pillow truck. The top of the truck is at the same height as the platform. His current height (in feet) is modeled by the following equation:

$$y = -0.1x^2 + 2.5x + 15$$

How high does Tim get off the platform before plummeting down into the pillow truck? (to the nearest foot)

Here again, it would help to draw out a graphical representation of the situation:

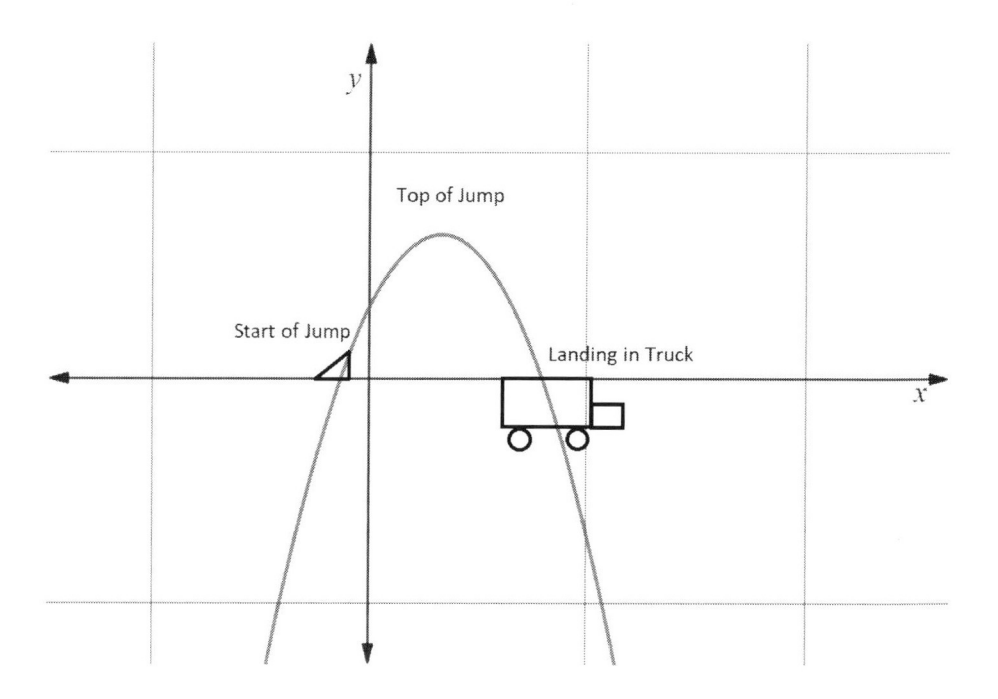

Let's reconsider the given equation, so that we can facilitate finding the real roots (x-intercepts) and thereby the location of the vertex.

We are given $y = -0.1x^2 + 2.5x + 15$. Not a very pleasant equation to deal with. Let's clean it up and simplify it by first putting it standard form and then getting rid of the -0.1 leading coefficient by multiplying everything by -10:

-0.1x² + 2.5x + 15 = 0, then multiply by -10 to get

x² − 25x − 150 = 0 Now that's much better, and much easier to factor:

(x − 30)(x + 5) = 0

Then, the real roots, or x − intercepts are at x = 30 and x = -5.

Do you remember how to find the location of the vertex once we know the roots? Isn't it exactly between the 2 roots?

Then, the location of the vertex is at (30 − 5) / 2 = **12.5** on the x-axis.

To find the y- value, which is the height of Tim's jump, we just plug 12.5 into the given equation:

-0.1(12.5)² + 2.5(12.5) + 15 = 30.625 which is **31** feet to the nearest foot. Grid-in 31.

Another way to find the x-coordinate of the vertex is to use the formula **–b/2a** which determines the *line of symmetry*. Every parabola is symmetrical about an imaginary vertical line that goes directly through the vertex. That line is called the line of symmetry.

Using that formula in the given problem, we can find the location of the vertex even faster.

Based on the given equation, -b/2a = -2.5/(2(-0.1)) = 12.5. We get the same result as before. Then, we only need to plug that value into the given equation to get the answer.

17.

You are given the following system of equations:

$$y = x^2$$
$$mx + ny = -p$$

where $m, n,$ and P are integers. For which of the following will there be more than one (x,y) solution, with real-number coordinates, for the system?

F. $m^2 + 4np > 0$
G. $n^2 - 4mp > 0$
H. $m^2 - 4np < 0$
J. $n^2 - 4mp < 0$
K. $n^2 + 4mp < 0$

Again, a complicated looking problem that really isn't. You must remember this: the number and type of roots of any quadratic function can be determined from the **discriminant**. What's the discriminant? It's the part of the **quadratic equation** that is inside the square root:

$$b^2 - 4ac$$

If that expression is **negative**, then we are dealing with **imaginary** roots. If it is **positive**, then the roots are **real**.

How does that help us here? Well, if we substitute the first equation into the second we get mx + nx² = -p. Now, rearranging that, we get nx² + mx + p = 0. Hey, that's just the standard form of a quadratic function. Now we're getting someplace because now we know what the a, b, and c terms are of the discriminant. They are a = n, b = m, and c = p.

Now, substituting back into the discrimant we get **m² – 4np.** And, since we want real roots (solutions), that expression must be **positive**, which is another way of saying greater than zero.

Then, the answer is **H**.

While this explanation may seem a bit complicated, once you understand how the discriminant works, a problem like this can be solved in a few seconds.

18.

Which of the following most precisely describes the roots of the equation $3x^2 + 5x + 2 = 0$?

F. 1 rational (double) root
G. 1 irrational (double) root
H. 2 rational roots
J. 2 irrational roots
K. 2 complex roots (with nonzero imaginary parts)

Here's another example where the discriminant comes into play.

Remember that you can know the characterists of the roots of **any** quadratic function by analyzing the **discriminant: b² – 4ac**, like we saw in a previous problem.

Remember, $b^2 - 4ac$ is the term inside the square root of the quadratic equation.

Then, whenever $b^2 - 4ac$ is positive, you know that the roots must be **real**, and if it is negative, the roots are **imaginary**. Furthermore, if the discriminant is positive and a **perfect square**, then it's roots will be rational. If it is not a perfect square, then the roots will be **irrational**. And finally, if the discriminant is 0, then the there is only **one** rational root. Technically, a quadratic function always has 2 roots, so if the discriminant is 0, it will have a double root with the same value.

Back to the problem, using the discriminant, we have $5^2 - 4(3)(2) = 25 - 24 = 1$, which is a perfect square. Therefore, the answer is **H**.

19.

The length of a car's skid mark in feet as a function of the car's speed in miles per hour is given by l(s) = .046s² - .092s + 0.138 If the length of skid mark is 230 ft, find the speed in miles per hour the car was traveling. (to the nearest mph)

This is another grid-in, so you can't just plug in the choices to see which one produces 230 as the result.

Then, we must set up the equation and solve:
.046s² - .092s + 0.138 = 230
.046s² - .092s - 229.862 = 0

Since we don't need to find the vertex, we can just use the quadratic formula and solve:

$$\frac{-(-0.092) \pm \sqrt{(-0.092)^2 - 4(.046)(-229.862)}}{2(.046)}$$

If you don't make any careless mistakes plugging in the numbers, you should get about **72** mph, for the positive solution.

For problems like the previous one, careless mistakes can be the biggest problem.

20.

The profit from selling local ballet tickets depends on the ticket price. Using past receipts, the profit can be modeled by the function $p = -15x^2 + 600x + 60$, where x is the price of each ticket. What is the **maximum profit** that can be made?

A) $5,820

B) $6,020

C) $7,040

D) $8,500

204

The negative leading coefficient tells us that this quadratic will look like an upside down parabola with a maximum value at the vertex.

Since we are looking for the maximum value of the profit, we can use the line of symmetry formula to quickly calculate the location of the vertex.

So, -b/2a = -600/2(-15) = -600/-30 = 20.

Then, we just have to plug that into the given function to determine the maximum profit.

So, p(20) = -15(20)^2 + 600(20) + 60 = 6060. Choice **B**.

That concludes the quadratic word problem examples in this chapter. Study them well so that you can quickly and efficiently answer any similar problem on the test. There were not as many examples as in previous chapters because quadratic relationship word problems don't turn up as often as the others. However, the creators of the SAT and ACT can change that at any time. So, be prepared!

Proportions

Word problems that can be answered using proportions occur relatively frequently on both the SAT and ACT. The key to solving them is first recognizing proportional relationships when you see them. We'll be looking at a good number of examples of problems that test your ability to recognize and utilize proportions to solve various word problems.

1.
The amount of money an insurance salesman earns is directly proportional to the number of people he calls. The salesman earns $150 for every 10 calls he makes. How much money will he earn when he calls 35 people?

   A) $425

   B) $525

   C) $650

   D) $750

They key to answering proportion problems is that you make certain you are comparing the exact same things. In this case we're comparing the amount of money a salesman earns in relation to the number of people he calls.

If we call the amount of money he earns when he calls 35 people, x, then the set up is very simple:

$$\frac{150}{10} = \frac{x}{35}$$

Notice, if we put the money earned in the numerator and the number of people called in the denominator of one ratio, then we **must** do the same with the other ratio.

Solving by cross multiplying we get:

10x = (150)(35)

Then, dividing by 10, x = (15)(35) = 525. Choice **B**. Simple enough, right?

2.
Natalie jogs 50 meters in 14.5 seconds. If she jogs at this same rate, which of the following is closest to the distance she will jog in 5 minutes?

A) 350 meters

B) 550 meters

C) 930 meters

D) 1030 meters

This one looks simple too, but be careful! Here, we're relating <u>meters to seconds</u>. That means both ratios must be in those units.

That means, we must convert minutes into seconds in order to answer correctly.

So, 5 minutes = (5)(60) = 300 seconds. And, now we can set up the proper proportion using x for the distance Natalie jogs in 5 minutes.

$$\frac{50}{14.5} = \frac{x}{300}$$

Again, cross multiplying:

14.5x = (50)(300)

Then, x = 15000/14.5 = 1034. So, the closest answer is **D**.

3.
Gold is the most corrosion resistant substance known to man. A coating of gold on an integrated circuit is

so thin that a sheet weighing one ounce can cover up to 5 basketball courts. If a basketball court has an area of approximately 522 square yards, about how many square yards could 21 ounces of gold cover ?

A) 25,000

B) 35,000

C) 45,000

D) 55,000

Since one ounce of gold can cover 5 basketball courts and each basketball court has an area of 522 square yards, then one ounce of gold can cover (5)(522) = 2610 square yards.

Now we can set up the proportion that will tell us how many square yards 21 ounces of gold can cover:

$$\frac{2610}{1} = \frac{x}{21}$$

And, very quickly, we can solve for x = (2610)(21) = 54,810 or about 55,000. **D**.

4.

Planet	Acceleration due to gravity $\left(\frac{m}{sec^2}\right)$
Mercury	3.6
Venus	8.9
Earth	9.8
Mars	3.8
Jupiter	26.0
Saturn	11.1
Uranus	10.7
Neptune	14.1

The chart above shows approximations of the acceleration due to gravity in meters per second squared $\left(\dfrac{m}{sec^2}\right)$ for the eight planets in our solar system.

An object on Earth has a weight of 150 newtons. On which planet would the same object have an approximate weight of 170 newtons?

A) Venus
B) Saturn
C) Uranus
D) Neptune

Here, we just use the information provided in the chart to set up the needed proportion. In this case we are equating the gravity to weight ratio on earth to the gravity to weight ratio on another planet. Once we determine the gravity, x, on the unknown planet we'll use the chart to determine which planet it is.

$$\frac{9.8}{150} = \frac{x}{170}$$

Solving for x:

150x = (9.8)(170) = 1666

Then x = 1666/150 = **11.1**, which, according to the chart, corresponds to the gravity on Saturn. **C**.

5.
A square field measures 100 feet by 100 feet. Ten people each mark off a randomly selected region of the field; each region is square and has side lengths of 10 feet, and no two regions overlap. The people use metal detectors to find coins buried

in the ground to a depth of 5 inches beneath the ground's surface in each region. The results are shown in the table below.

Region	Number of coins	Region	Number of coins
A	17	F	13
B	12	G	9
C	8	H	11
D	15	I	7
E	5	J	14

Which of the following is a reasonable approximation of the number of coins to a depth of 5 inches beneath the ground's surface in the entire field?

A)   111

B)   1,110

C)   11,100

D)   111,100

Believe it or not, this is just another proportion problem.

The table tells you how many coins there are in 10 regions, A through J, and that each have the same area of 10 x 10 = 100 square feet. So, the total area of those regions is **100 x 10 = 1000 square feet,** right? How many coins? Just add them up. 17 + 12 + 8 +... etc. = **111 coins**.

Now the question becomes, if there are 111 coins in 1000 square feet, about how many coins should there be in **100 x 100 = 10,000 square feet**, which is the entire field? That's answered with the following proportion:

$$\frac{111}{1000} = \frac{x}{10,000}$$

Then, x = (111)(10,000)/1000 = 1,100. **B.** Now do you believe it?

6.

To make an Italian restaurant's signature lasagna the chef needs 4 ounces of ricotta cheese for each serving. How many pounds of ricotta cheese are needed to make 35 servings of lasagna?
(1 pound = 16 ounces)

A) 7.50

B) 8.75

C) 9.35

D) 10.50

Once again, be careful to compare the same units. In this case, we should set up the proportion by relating ounces to the number of servings. At the end, we will convert to pounds.

$$\frac{4}{1} = \frac{x}{35}$$

Solving for x we get (4)(35) = 140 ounces. Since there are 16 ounces in a pound, the number of pounds are 140/16 = 8.75. **B**.

7.

If 100 US dimes were stacked on top of each other in a column, the column would be approximately $5\frac{3}{8}$ inches tall. At this rate, which of the following is closest to the number of one-cent coins it would take to make a 11-inch-tall column?

A) 150
B) 200
C) 250
D) 300

We know this is a proportion because it relates the height of the coin stack to the number of coins and compares it to another stack with a different height.

Then, the set up is the same as any other proportion, except that it would probably be best to convert the mixed number to a whole number with a decimal. If we call the new number of coins x, the equation becomes:

$$\frac{100}{5.375} = \frac{x}{11}$$

Continuing to solve for x:

x = (100)(11)/5.375 = 204.65. Then, the closest choice is **B**.

By now you should be really getting the hang of this. Let's continue...

8.
Priya is planning to send her favorite dry rub recipe to a friend who lives in France. Before sending the recipe, Priya wants to convert the American customary units in the instructions into metric units so that her friend will easily be able to understand the measurements. If the recipe calls for a ratio of four ounces of paprika to every seven ounces of chili powder, and if Priya's friend is planning to make a large batch of dry rub with 91 total ounces of chili powder, approximately how many total grams of paprika and chili powder will the recipe require? (1 ounce = 28.3 grams)

A) 4,047 grams
B) 4,521 grams
C) 4,925 grams
D) 5,149 grams

As is often the case, long word problems tend to intimidate students and cause them to skip the whole thing, hoping to come back later to try to solve it. That later time often never arrives because they get preoccupied with other challenging problems and run out of time, and a doable problem like this one is wasted or desperately guessed on.

But the meat of this problem doesn't really start until the middle where the ratio of paprika to chili is given and you need to determine the new amount of paprika, given a different amount chili. We should be pretty efficient at doing that by now:

$$\frac{4}{7} = \frac{P}{91}$$

As you probably guess, P in this case would be the new amount of paprika need to make 91 ounces of chili. That won't solve the whole problem, but it's an important part.

So, solving for P we get P = (4)(91)/7 = 52 oz.

But the question asks for the total grams of paprika and chili powder the recipe requires.

So far we know Priya will need 52 oz of paprika and 91 oz of chili, which adds up to 143 oz.

Now, all that is needed is to convert ounces to grams, which is easily done since they tell us that 1 ounce = 28.3 grams. So, (143)(28.3) = 4046.9 grams. Choice **A**.

So, this was basically just a proportion problem with a few extra simple steps.

9.

Officer Blake drives his squad car 1 mile per minute while patrolling local highways during his shift. If he has driven 480 miles by the end of his shift, how many total hours did he drive his car at the above rate?

A) 8
B) 12
C) 16
D) 20

Here's another proportion problem that just requires a simple unit conversion at the end to solve.

For this proportion we are relating miles to minutes. We know Officer Blake drives 1 mile in 1 minute, and we need to determine how many hours it takes him to drive 480 miles. But first we must determine the number of minutes based on the proportion:

$$\frac{1\ minute}{1\ mile} = \frac{x\ minutes}{480\ miles}$$

I included the units this time in the equation so that you can clearly see how they match.

Then, x obviously is 480 minutes.

Now, it's just a matter of changing 480 minutes into 480/60 = 8 hours. **A.**

10.

The number of hours Robert spends in his game room is proportional to the number of hours he spends playing *Call of Destiny IV: Modern Battlefield*. If he plays *Call of Destiny IV* for 6 hours, he will spend 8 hours in his game room. How many hours will Robert spend in his game room if he plays *Call of Destiny IV* for only 3 hours?

This one is interesting in that it relates hours to hours. Usually, proportions relate different units. However, even though the units are the same, the problem relates the hours Robert spends playing a video game to the number of hours he spends in his game room. That allows us to set up a proportion, like we have done on all the other problems.

$$\frac{8 \text{ hours in game room}}{6 \text{ hours playing video game}} = \frac{x \text{ hours in game room}}{3 \text{ hours playing video game}}$$

Even though it's easy enough to solve this proportion mathematically, you can immediately determine that the number of hours he will spend in his game room is **half** of 8, since the time he spends playing the video game is **half** of what he spent previously. So, the answer is **4**. This problem was a grid-in.

11.
A dog eats 9 treats in 4 days. At this rate, how many treats does the dog eat in 4+x days?

A) $\frac{9}{4} + \frac{9x}{4}$

B) $\frac{9}{4} + 4x$

C) $9 + \frac{9x}{4}$

D) $\frac{9}{4} + \frac{x}{4}$

E) $9 + \frac{x}{4}$

In this problem we have a proportion that has a variable included in the days. So we must use a different variable to find the number of treats it represents.

First let's establish that we are relating dog treats to days. They tell us that a dog eats 9 dog treats in 4 days. They want to know how many treats the dog eats in 4 + x days.

The set up is still the same as before, with exception of the additional given variable x. So let's use the variable t for the new number of treats. So,

$$\frac{9}{4} = \frac{t}{4+x}$$

Now, we'll solve for t in terms of x by cross multiplying, as usual:

4t = 9(4 + x)

4t = 36 + 9x

t = (36 + 9x)/4 = 9 + (9/4)x, which is choice **C**.

12.

A solution has 30 ml of solution X and 50 ml of solution Y. If you wanted a solution containing 240 ml of solution Y, how much total solution would you need?

A) 504 ml

B) 158 ml

C) 144 ml

D) 384 ml

This is another problem that doesn't appear to be a proportion type problem, but it is.

Notice that the ratio of the X solution to the Y solution is 30:50 or **3:5**.

We know that a proportion is just two ratios that are equal to each other. But what is the second ratio here? It is the amount of X solution needed for a solution containing 240ml of Y solution. So, the proportion is:

$$\frac{3}{5} = \frac{x}{240}$$

216

Then, solving for x:

x = (3)(240)/5 = 144ml of X solution

But the question asks for the total solution needed, which is simply X + Y or 144 + 240 = 384ml. Choice **D**.

13.
> A bucket holds 4 quarts of popcorn. If 1/3 cup of corn kernels makes 2 quarts of popcorn, how many buckets can be filled with the popcorn made from 4 cups of kernels?
>
> A) 96
>
> B) 24
>
> C) 6
>
> D) 3

This problem is fairly straightforward, but you must be careful about what they're asking for.

We can set up a proportion relating cups of kernels to quarts of popcorn. We'll let x be the number of quarters produced by 4 cups of kernels:

$$\frac{1/3}{2} = \frac{4}{x}$$

Then, solving for x:

(1/3)x = (4)(2)

x = 3(8) = 24 quarts of popcorn.

But they're asking for the number of <u>buckets</u>. Since each bucket holds 4 quarts of popcorn, 24/4 = 6 buckets. **C**.

14.

A recipe for making 10 loaves of bread requires 24 cups of flour and 4 tablespoons of baking powder. If the proportions in this recipe are to be used to make 3 loaves of bread, how many cups of flour will be needed? (Do not round your answer)

A) 72

B) 2.7

C) 30

D) 7.2

Here's an example of a proportion problem where some of the information is irrelevant. Do you see where it is?

Notice that the question is asking for the number of cups of flour need to make 3 loaves of bread.

So, it's relating loaves of bread to cups of flour. We didn't need to know that the recipe also requires 4 tablespoons of baking powder. So, we can ignore that fact.

Then, just relating cups to loaves, we can set up the following proportion:

$$\frac{24}{10} = \frac{x}{3}$$

Solving for x:

x = (24)(3)/10 = 7.2. Choice **D**.

15.

In a poll of 500 registered voters, 300 voters favored a proposal to increase funding for local schools. Suppose the poll is indicative of how the 22,000 registered voters will vote on the proposal. Which of the following values is closest to how many of the 22,000 registered voters will be expected to vote in favor of the proposal?

A. 13,200
B. 14,830
C. 21,840
D. 22,000
E. 32,640

Here they are relating the number of voters who voted in favor of a certain proposal to the total number of voters. Although this problem falls under the category of statistics since it is surveying a sample of voters, it is solved just as you would any other proportion problem.

We can create the first ratio as the number of voters in the poll who voted in favor of the proposal to the number of registered voters polled, and equate that to the ratio of the total number of voters overall who voted in favor of the proposal to the total number of registered voters.

Since the first ratio is 300/500, we can reduce that to 3/5. So, the proportion is:

$$\frac{3}{5} = \frac{x}{22,000}$$

Solving for x, as usual:

x = (3)(22,000)/5 = 13,200. **A**.

16.

A bag contains 11 red marbles, 13 yellow marbles, and 8 green marbles. How many additional red marbles must be added to the 32 marbles already in the bag so that the probability of randomly drawing a red marble is $\frac{3}{4}$?

A. 16
B. 21
C. 29
D. 34
E. 52

This may not jump out to you as a proportion type problem, but if you set up the necessary relationships you'll see that it is.

We're basically going to set up two ratios and set them equal to each other. As you know by now, that defines a proportion.

The first ratio, and most obvious one, is the one given for the desired probability of drawing a red marble after additional red marbles are added to the bag of marbles. That ratio is 3/4.

The next ratio has to be created from the fact that we're adding a certain number of additional red marbles to the bag. If we call that additional number x, then we will end up with 11 + x red marbles.

But, those additional red marbles increases the <u>total</u> number of marbles in the bag by x also. So, then we will end up with 32 + x marbles in the bag.

Now, we can set up our proportion with the information collected:

$$\frac{3}{4} = \frac{11 + x}{32 + x}$$

Cross multiplying and solving for x:

4(11 + x) = 3(32 + x)

44 + 4x = 96 + 3x

x = 52. **E.**

As you can see, sometimes proportions can be hidden in the problem, and only after you set up the relationships based on the given information you see that a proportion does exist and is the way to solve the problem.

17.

A chemist needs 1 ounce of element X. The only way which the chemist can get element X is to buy compound Y, which contains 10% X. Compound Y costs $3.84 per pound (16 ounces). How much must the chemist pay in order to ensure that she receives 1 ounce of element X?

F. $ .15
G. $ .24
H. $1.50
J. $2.40
K. $3.84

This is another problem with a hidden proportion. Let's see how to find it.

Since the chemist can only get element X from compound Y, he is forced to buy compound Y at $3.84 per pound.

If he buys a pound (16 ounces) he'll get 10% or (0.1)(16) = 1.6 ounces of element X. But, he only needs 1 ounce.

Now do you see the proportion? If we relate cost to ounces we can get two ratios. In the first ratio we know that the chemist has to spend $3.84 to get 1.6 ounces of element X. In the second ratio we're looking for the cost, x, to get 1 ounce of element X. So, the proportion should be:

$$\frac{3.84}{1.6} = \frac{x}{1}$$

Solving for x:

x = 3.84/1.6 = 2.4, which means $2.40. **J.**

18.

There are 76 calories in 10 grams of grated Mozzarella cheese, and 67% of those calories are from fat. When measuring Mozzarella cheese, 5 grams is equal to 1 tablespoon. Which of the following is closest to the number of calories from fat per tablespoon of grated Mozzarella cheese?

F. 3
G. 8
H. 9
J. 13
K. 26

Here's another one that can be reduced to a simple proportion. Since they're asking for the number of calories from fat, and they tell you that 67% of the 76 calories come from fat, you should immediately calculate the approximate number of calories from fat as (.67)(76) = about 51 calories of fat in 10 grams of Mozzarella cheese. Then, we only need to set up a simple proportion:

$$\frac{51}{10} = \frac{x}{5}$$

Cross multiplying and solving for x gives us 25.5 calories, which is closest to **K**.

19.

On a map, $\frac{1}{4}$ inch represents 20 actual miles. Two towns that are $1\frac{3}{4}$ inches apart on this map are how many actual miles apart?

F. 30
G. 45
H. 85
J. 115
K. 140

Since you can use your calculator, the fastest way to go here is to convert the fractions to decimals. So, ¼ = 0.25 and 1 ¾ = 1.75. Now, just set up a proportion and solve:

$$\frac{20}{.25} = \frac{x}{1.75}$$

Then, solving for x:

x = (20)(1.75)/.25 = 140. Choice **K**.

20.

Gianna is converting a 12-foot-by-15-foot room in her house to a craft room. Gianna will install tile herself but will have CC Installations build and install the cabinets. The scale drawing shown below displays the location of the cabinets in the craft room (0.25 inch represents 2 feet).

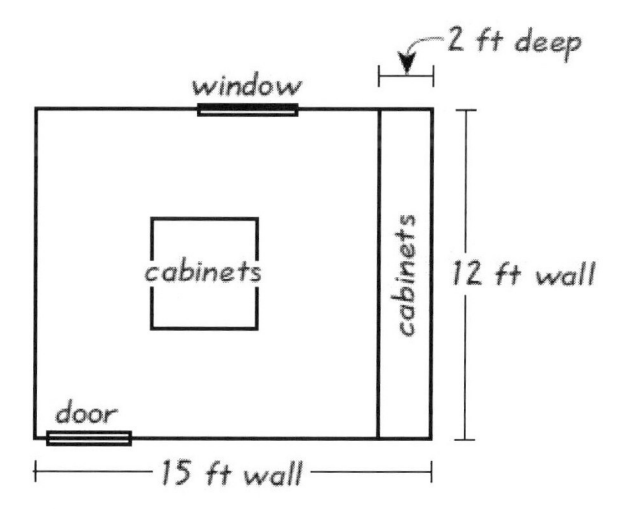

A 15-foot wall is how many inches long in the scale drawing?
A. 1.5
B. 1.875
C. 3
D. 3.375
E. 3.75

This one is a solved using a very straightforward proportion, but you have to read carefully to get the necessary information.

At the end of the first paragraph, in parenthesis, they tell you that 0.25 inches represents 2 feet. Then, if we let x be the number inches in 15 feet, we get the proportion:

$$\frac{0.25}{2} = \frac{x}{15}$$

And solving for x:
x = (0.25)(15)/2 = 1.875. **B**.

That concludes this chapter on Proportions. 20 problems of various types should give you a fairly good idea of what you can expect to see on the SAT or ACT. Depending on the particular test you take, there may be more or less proportion problems than on previous tests. Again, it's better to be prepared than to assume you won't see many.

Geometry

While geometry problems are a very significant part of the both the SAT and ACT, actual word problems requiring geometric calculations occur less frequently. However, they are significant and deserve a thorough review, which we'll do in this chapter.

1.

$$sA = 360$$

The measure A, in degrees, of an exterior angle of a regular polygon is related to the number of sides, s, of the polygon by the formula above. If the measure of an exterior angle of a regular polygon is greater than 40°, what is the greatest number of sides it can have?

A) 7
B) 8
C) 9
D) 10

Even though a formula is given, you'll need to use some common sense here.

Since we're looking for the number of sides, we can re-write the formula as s = 360/A. This shows that s and A are **inversely proportional**, which means that as one goes up the other must go down in value, and vice versa.

Since we want the greatest number of sides, we need the smallest exterior angle A. If we used 40 degrees, then s = 360/40 = 9 sides. But the problem explicitly states that the angle must be greater than 40 degrees. Then, the answer must be the next number down from 9 which is 8. Choice **B**.

2.

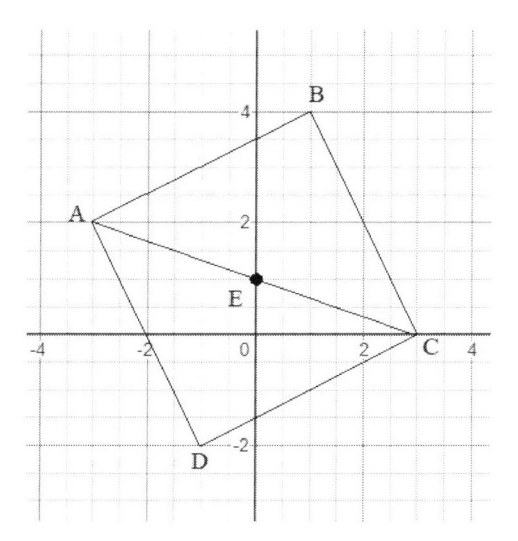

In the *xy*-plane above, ABCD is a square and and point E is the center of the square. The coordinates of points C and E are (3, 0) and (0, 1), respectively. Which of the follow is an equation of a line that passes through points B and D?

A) $y = \dfrac{1}{3}x + 1$

B) $y = 3(x - 1)$

C) $y = 3x + 1$

D) $y = \dfrac{1}{3}x - 1$

The first thing to recognize is that $\overline{AC}$ is a diagonal of the square, and if you draw a line from B to D you get another diagonal which intersects the first diagonal at E.

Why is this important? Because you should know that the diagonals of a square are perpendicular to each other.

From that, you should be able to determine the slope of $\overline{BD}$, since the slopes of perpendicular lines are the negative reciprocals of each other.

We can easily determine the slope of $\overline{AC}$ using *rise/run*, which is 2/-6 = -1/3.

Then the slope of $\overline{BD}$ must be the negative reciprocal of -1/3, which is **3**.

We already know the y-intercept is at 1, so the equation of the line can only be y = 3x + 1. Choice **C**.

3.

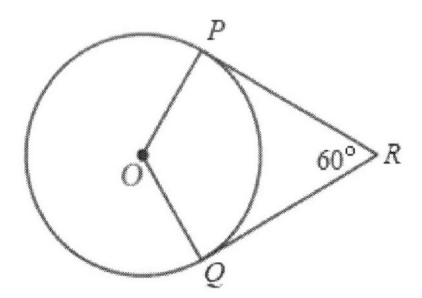

In the figure above, point *O* is the center of the circle, line segments *PR* and *QR* are tangent to the circle at points *P* and *Q*, respectively, and the segments intersect at point *R* as shown. If the circumference of the circle is 66, what is the length of minor arc $\overset{\frown}{PQ}$?

This one is not as complicated as it looks. There are a couple of shortcuts here that will make it a breeze.

Anytime a radius meets a tangent line they form a **90 degree angle.** You must remember this. It can come up numerous times on a single SAT or ACT exam. So, angle P and angle Q must both be 90 degrees.

Another thing you need to know is that the angle opposite an arc in a circle is **directly proportional** to the length of the arc. But what is the measure of angle O? Well, POQR is just a quadrilateral figure because it is a 4-sided polygon. That means all of its angles must add up to 360. Therefore, <P + <O + <Q + <R = 360. We know most of those angles now, so let's just substitute them. 90 + <O + 90 + 60 = 360. That's easy math. So then <O = 360 – 240 = 120 degrees.

But 120 degrees is **one third** the total degrees in a circle. Therefore, the length of the arc is **one third** the circumference! So, 66/3 = **22.** Done.

4.
> In a circle with center O, central angle AOB has a measure of $\frac{3\pi}{2}$ radians. The area of the sector formed by central angle AOB is what fraction of the area of the circle?

Here, just remember that the ratio of the central angle and the degrees or radians of the entire circle is **equal** to the ratio or **fraction** of the sector area and the whole area of the circle.

Then, it's just $3\pi/2 : 2\pi = (3\pi/2) / (2\pi) = $ **3/4**. Done.

5.
> Points A and B lie on a circle with radius 1, and arc $\widehat{AB}$ has length $\frac{\pi}{4}$. What fraction of the circumference of the circle is the length of arc $\widehat{AB}$?

Here we use the fact that **an arc is just a fraction of the circumference.** So, we're practically at the solution already.

We have the length of the arc, now all we need is the circumference. Well, that's easy enough since $C = 2\pi r$. They tell us the radius is 1, so the circumference is just 2π.

Then, the fraction is $\pi/4 \,/\, 2\pi = $ **1/8** Done!

6.

Kerry has a cordless telephone receiver that can operate within a range of 1,000 feet from the telephone's base. Kerry takes the receiver from the base and walks 800 feet due north. From that point she walks due east and stops at the maximum range of the receiver. In which of the following directions can Kerry walk and still be within the range of the receiver?

I. Due north
II. Due south
III. Due west

(A) II only
(B) III only
(C) I and II
(D) I and III
(E) II and III

This one can be solved purely by visual analysis. Refer to the diagram below:

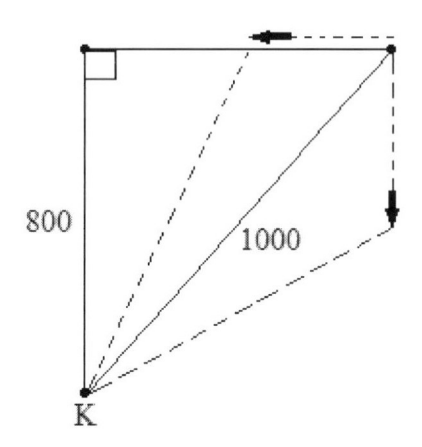

As you can see, Kerry's path follows the legs of right triangle. Then, connecting her initial location to final stop forms the hypotenuse of the right triangle.

So any movement to the left (west) or down (south) would clearly shorten that hypotenuse since the legs of the triangle would become shorter.

Since 1000 feet is the maximum range of the receiver, anything less would be <u>within</u> range.

Then, condition II and III are correct. Choice **E**.

7.
Senai customized her bicycle by exchanging the front wheel for a wheel that had one half the diameter of the back wheel. Now when Senai rides the bicycle, how many revolutions does the front wheel make for each revolution of the back wheel?

(A) 8

(B) 4

(C) 2

(D) 12

To answer this problem you must first realize that the wheels of the bicycle, geometrically, are just circles. Then, understand that functional part of wheel is the outer edge, or the *circumference*.

The formula for circumference is $2\pi r$ or $D\pi$, where r is the radius and D is the diameter.

This problem describes the diameter, so we'll stick with the second formula.

Then, if one diameter is half of the other, its circumference is half also. And the circumference is where "the rubber meets the road" when we're talking about wheels.

So, if the back wheel turns one revolution, the front wheel must turn **2** revolutions to cover the same length (distance). Then, the answer is **C**.

8.

A circular piece of cardboard is cut in half along a diameter. If the diameter is 12 inches, what is the perimeter, in inches, of one of the semicircular pieces?

A) $6\pi + 6$
B) $6\pi + 12$
C) $12\pi + 6$
D) $12\pi + 12$

Again, the circumference of any circle is $D\pi$. In this case, the diameter is 12 inches, so the circumference of the circular piece is 12π. But it's cut in half along the diameter, so the circumference of the semicircular piece is **6π**.

But the question asks for the <u>perimeter</u>, which is the sum of all the sides, including the diameter which is 12 inches long.
Then, the answer must be **B**.

9.

If the perimeter of a rectangle is 10 times the width of the rectangle, then the length of the rectangle is how many times the width?

A) 2
B) 4
C) 6
D) 8

This one can be answered by simply setting up the equations we know.

They tell us that the perimeter (we'll call it P) of a rectangle is 10 times the width of the rectangle. But, we already know the perimeter of <u>any</u> rectangle is:

$$P = 2L + 2W$$

where L is the length and W is the width.

Since the perimeter in this case is 10 times the width, we can re-write the equation as:

10W = 2L + 2W

Then, 2L = 8W

So, L = 8W/2 = **4**W. Choice **B**.

10.

How many cubical blocks, each with edges of length 4 centimeters, are needed to fill a rectangular box that has inside dimensions 20 centimeters by 24 centimeters by 32 centimeters?

A) 38
B) 96
C) 192
D) 240

Whenever they ask how many of a certain object fill or fit inside another object, think volume , which is the space it occupies.

Then, in this case, we have cubical blocks with edge lengths of 4 cm. The volume of any cube is just the edge length cubed. So, each block has a volume of 4^3 = 64 cm^3.

The volume of the rectangular box is calculated by multiplying each dimension. So, its volume is (20)(24)(32) = 15,360 cm^3.

Then, we just need to divide the volume of each cube into the volume of empty box to determine how many cubic blocks will fit. So, 15,360/64 = 240. **D**.

11.

When each side of a given square is lengthened by 2 inches, the area is increased by 40 square inches. What is the length, in inches, of a side of the original square?

(A) 4
(B) 6
(C) 8
(D) 9
(E) 10

We know the area of any square is just the side length squared. So, if we call the original square's side x, then its area is just x^2.

If the side is increased by 2, then the new area would be $(x + 2)^2$.

They tell us that when that happens, the area (original) is increased by 40 square inches. So, with that information, we can set up an equation and solve for x:

$(x + 2)^2 = x^2 + 40$

$(x + 2)(x + 2) = x^2 + 40$

$\cancel{x^2} + 4x + 4 = \cancel{x^2} + 40$

$4x = 36$

$x = 9.$ **D.**

As you can see, if you just write down exactly what the problem is stating, then you can usually come up with the proper equations to solve.

12.

In a plane, lines are drawn through a given point *O* so that the measure of <u>each</u> non-overlapping angle formed about point *O* is 60. How many different lines are there?

- A) Two
- B) Three
- C) Four
- D) Five
- E) Six

It's usually helpful to draw out a geometry word problem whenever feasible.

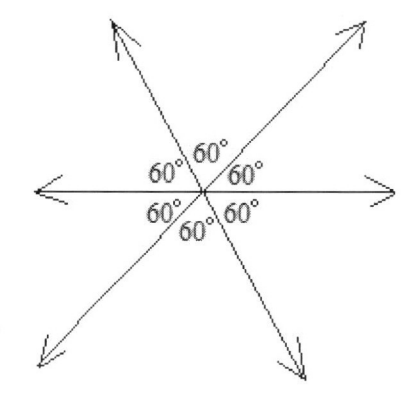

Be careful here! Even though there are 6 non-overlapping angles formed, there are only 3 line which created them. So, the answer is **B**.

13.

How many solid wood cubes, each with a total surface area of 96 square centimeters, can be cut from a solid wood cube with a total surface area of 2,400 square centimeters if no wood is lost in the cutting?

- A) 5
- B) 25

C) 30

D) 80

E) 125

14.

Martha, a planner at the Springboro City Zoo, is developing a proposal for the new Animals of Africa trapezoidal shaped exhibit. The figure below shows her scale drawing of the proposed exhibit with 3 side lengths and the radius of a circular crocodile pit given in inches. In Martha's scale drawing, 1 inch represents 1.5 feet.

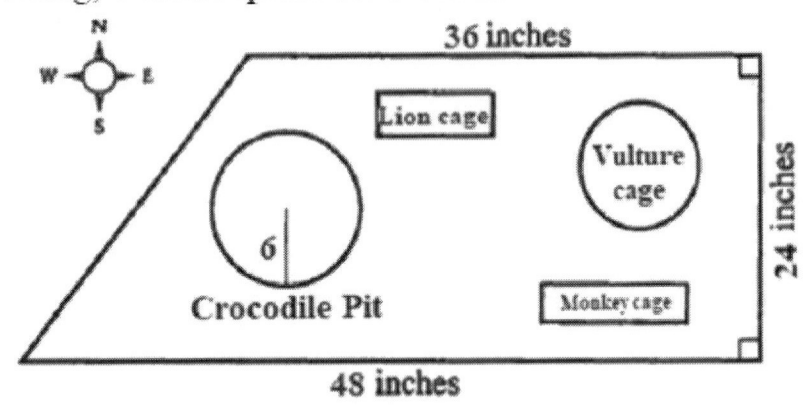

Martha's proposal includes installing a fence on the perimeter of the exhibit. What is the perimeter, in *feet*, of the exhibit?

A. 134.8
B. 142.5
C. 151.7
D. 155.3
E. 162.4

234

We are only missing one side, which is easily obtainable. It's just the hypotenuse of a right triangle. But where is the right triangle? If we draw an altitude from the northwest corner to the base, we should get a figure that looks like this:

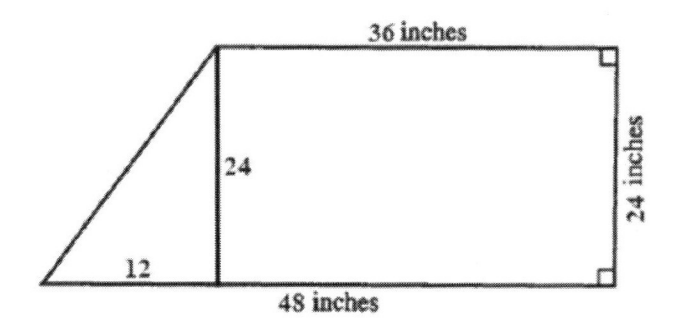

36 inches

24

12

48 inches

24 inches

Do you see it now? Do you see how we calculated the short leg to be 12 since the lower base of the trapezoid is 12 inches longer than the upper base?

Then, we can find the hypotenuse of the right triangle using Pythagorean's formula, which of course is $a^2 + b^2 = c^2$, where a and b are the legs, and c is the hypotenuse.

Then, $12^2 + 24^2 = 720$. So, the hypotenuse is the square root of 720, which is 26.8.

Add that to the other sides and you get 26.8 + 36 + 24 + 48 = 134.8. Choice **A**.

15.

The Khan family is planning to build a 4-room cottage which consists of 2 bedrooms (BR), a living room (LR), and a bathroom. Shown below are the rectangular floor plan (left figure) and a side view of the cabin (right figure). In the side view, the roof forms an isosceles triangle ($\triangle ABC$), the walls are perpendicular to the level floor ($\overline{ED}$), $\overline{AC} \parallel \overline{ED}$, F is the midpoint of $\overline{AC}$, and $\overline{BF} \perp \overline{AC}$.

Refer to the following drawing:

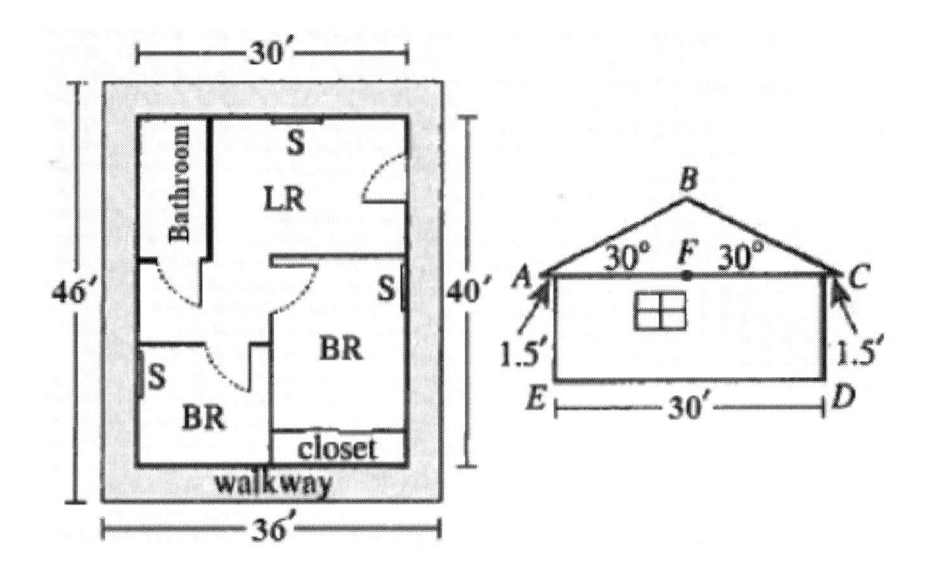

Mr. Khan plans to build a 3-foot-wide walkway around the outside of the cottage, as shown in the floor plan. What will be the area, in square feet, of the top surface of the walkway?

A. 368
B. 456
C. 512
D. 558
E. 612

Ignoring all the clutter, the area of the walkway is just the difference between the outermost rectangle and the inner rectangle.

Then, based on the given dimensions, (46)(66) – (40)(30) = 456. **B**.

The drawing on the right can also be ignored, since it is used to solve another part of this multi-part problem.

16.
Tammy wants to find the volume of a solid round marble.
She fills a rectangular container 6 cm long, 4 cm wide, and

10 cm high with water to a depth of 5 cm. Tammy totally submerges the marble in the water. The height of the water with the submerged marble is 6.8 cm. Which of the following is closest to the volume, in cubic centimeters, of the marble?

A. 30
B. 36
C. 41
D. 43
E. 46

Here, we should focus on the term **cubic centimeters**. Cubic means 3, so we need 3 dimensions to solve. Which 3?

There are two **set** dimensions that don't change, which are the length and width of the of the column of water in the container. The height, however, does. It goes from 5 cm to 6.8 cm after the marble is submerged. And that height difference is **caused** by the marble displacing the water.

That displacement is **exactly** the volume of the marble. Then, (6)(4)(6.8 – 5) = (6)(4)(1.8) = 43.2. So, the closet choice is **D**.

17.

A box in the shape of a cube has an interior side length of 12 inches and is used to ship a right circular cylinder with a radius of 5 inches and a height of 10 inches. The interior of the box not occupied by the cylinder is filled with packing material. Which of the following numerical expressions gives the number of cubic inches of the box filled with the packing material?

F. $6(12)^2 - 2\pi(5)(10) - 2\pi(5)^2$
G. $6(12)^2 - 2\pi(5)(10)$
H. $12^3 - \pi(5)(10)^2$
J. $12^3 - \pi(5)^2(10)$
K. $12^3 - \pi(10)^3$

To solve this one rapidly realize that the space for the packing material is just what's left over after you subtract the volume of the cylinder from the volume of the box.

The volume of **any** cube is its side length cubed. The volume of **any** right circular cylinder is π times the radius of its base squared times its height.

So, plugging in the given values, the answer must be **J**.

18.

Paula is bowling a series of 3 games. She has bowled 2 of 3 games with scores of 147 and 173. The figure below is a top view of the bowling lane. The dimensions for the bowling lane are given in the figure. The *pin deck* is the rectangular area within the bowling lane where the 10 bowling pins are set up.

(Note: The figure is not drawn to scale.)

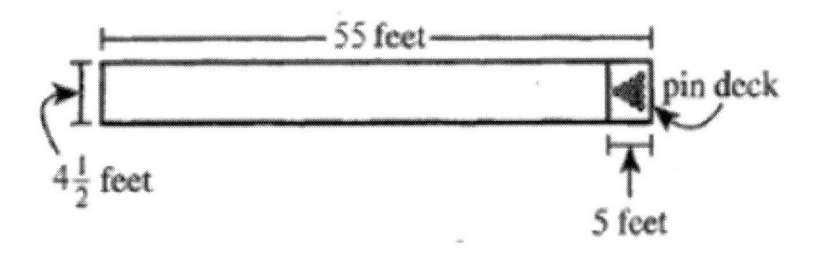

The diameter of each pin at its base is 3.25 in. When all of the pins are set up, which of the following values is closest to the area, in square inches, that is covered by the bases of the pins?

A. 60
B. 83
C. 95
D. 108
E. 123

This is another multi-part problem, but we're only interested in the question dealing with geometry.

Realize that the base of each pin is **circular** (diameter gives this fact away). Then we should know that the area of any circle is just πr^2.

Then the area of the base of each pin is just $\pi(3.25/2)2 = 8.296$. But there are 10 pins, so the total area is 82.96. So, the closest answer is **B.**

19.

A parallelogram has a perimeter of 84 inches, and 1 of its sides measures 12 inches. If it can be determined, what are the lengths, in inches, of the other 3 sides?

A. 12, 12, 48
B. 12, 24, 24
C. 12, 30, 30
D. 12, 40, 40
E. Cannot be determined from the given information

It helps to draw it out:

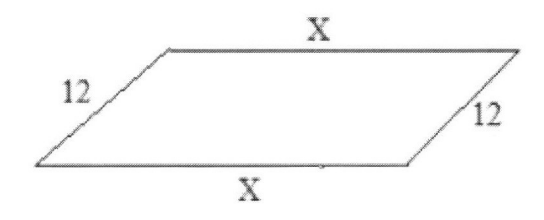

You should know that, since it's a parallelogram, 12 must appear twice. Then, if we call the missing sides x, we have a very simple equation to solve:

12 + 12 + x + x = 84

24 + 2x = 84

2x = 60

x = 30. So, the 3 other sides must be 12, 30, 30. Choice **C.**

20.

In the figure below, a highway rest area (at D) and radar stations (at A and B) lie on a level east-west line; A is 20,000 feet due west of D. An airplane (at C) is shown directly above the rest area, flying due west at a constant speed of 400 feet per second and at a constant altitude of 24,000 feet. The airplane is located at a straight-line distance of 31,241 feet from the radar station at A and 25,000 feet from the radar station at B.

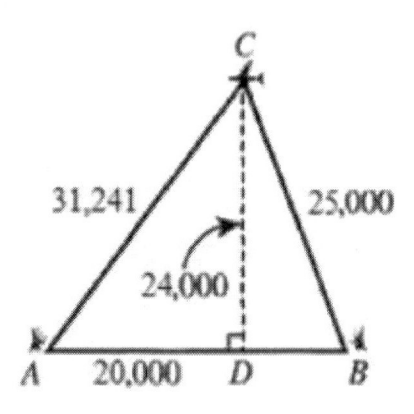

Which of the following values is closest to the distance, in feet, between the 2 radar stations?

F. 22,000
G. 23,000
H. 25,000
J. 27,000
K. 30,000

Here, we only need to focus on triangle CDB. If we temporarily eliminate the zeros, it becomes more clear:

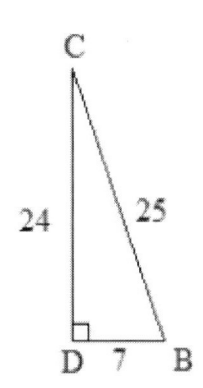

That's a 7-24-25 Pythagorean Triplet. And, if you didn't see that immediately, you could just use Pythagorean's formula to determine that $\overline{DB}$ is 7.

Now, just put the zeros back in and $\overline{DB}$ = 7,000. Then, $\overline{AB}$ = 20,000 + 7,000 = 27,000. Choice **J**.

21.

Tracy made a rectangular poster that is 5 feet long and 4 feet wide. The poster is too large to fit in the available display space, so Tracy is going to make a new poster that will have an area that is 50% of the area of the original poster. The length of Tracy's new poster will be $\frac{4}{5}$ the length of the original poster. How many feet wide will the new poster be?

F. 1 ½
G. 2
H. 2 ½
J. 3 ¼
K. 3 ½

First, we need to determine the area of the **original** poster. That's just (5)(4) = 20 square feet. 50% of that is **10** square feet.

Then, 4/5 the length of the original poster is (4/5)(5) = **4** feet.

Then, since the area of any rectangular shape is just the length times the width, (4)(width) = 10. So, the new width is 10/4 = 5/2 = 2 ½ feet. Choice **H**.

22.

Grace plans to use 32 feet of fencing to enclose a region of his yard for a pen for her pet rabbit. What is the area, in square feet, of the largest rectangular region Grace can enclose?

F. 50
G. 64
H. 72
J. 84
K. 96

Remember this: The largest area enclosed by any rectangular shape is a **square.**

Then, each side of her pen should be 32/4 = 8 feet.

So, the area is must be (8)(8) = 64. **G**.

23.

The intersection of lines l and m forms the 4 angles $\angle A$, $\angle B$, $\angle C$, and $\angle D$. The measure of $\angle B$ is $2\frac{3}{4}$ times the measure of $\angle A$. Which of the following values is closest to the measure of $\angle A$?

A. 36°
B. 48°
C. 55°
D. 68°
E. 72°

Just draw it out to see what you're dealing with:

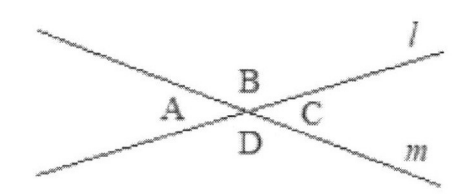

As you can see, angles A and B are **supplementary**, meaning A + B = 180 degrees.

Now, since B is 2 ¾ times the measure of A, we can substitute B for 2.75A.

Then the equation becomes A + 2.75A = 180

3.75A = 180

A = 48. Choice **B**.

24.

Two sides of a triangle are equal in length. The third side is 2 centimeters longer than either of the other 2 sides. Given that the perimeter of the triangle is 95 centimeters, what is the length, in centimeters, of the longest side?

A. 29
B. 30
C. 31
D. 33
E. 34

If in doubt, draw it out:

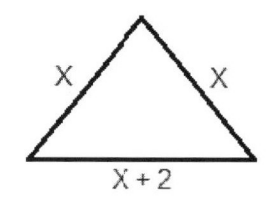

243

Then, x + x + x+2 = 95

3x = 93

x = 31.

Be careful here! That is **not** the solution. They want the **longest** side, which is x + 2, so x + 2 = 33. Choice **D**.

25.

Peter is planning a course for a bike race. The course is in the shape of a right triangle, as shown below. Participants will begin at A, ride directly to B, then directly to C, and directly back to A. Peter wants to put a rest stop at the halfway point on the course. How many miles past B will the rest stop be?

A. 3

B. 6

C. 8

D. 10

E. 13

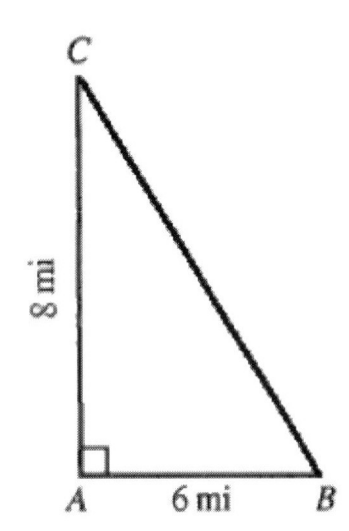

Let's first determine the missing distance from B to C. That's just the hypotenuse of the right triangle, which is easily calculated to be 10. (It's also a 6-8-10 Pythagorean Triplet). Then the total distance of the course is 6 + 10 + 8 = 24 miles. So, the halfway point is at 12 miles from A.

From A to B is 6 miles, then from B to the halfway point must be another 6 miles. Choice **B**.

26.

Carlos has a deck and pool in his backyard. The deck's shape is a rectangle with a semicircle removed and is shown shaded in the figure below. The lengths of the straight sides of the deck are given in feet. Carlos plans to cover the top of the deck with stain. To decide how much stain to purchase, he needs to find the area of the top of the deck. To the nearest square foot, what is the area of the top of the deck?

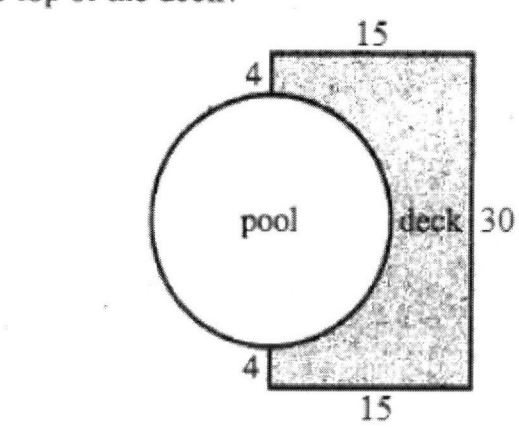

F. 110
G. 226
H. 260
J. 332
K. 414

Basically, we just need to find the area of the rectangle and subtract **half** of the circle area.

So, (15)(30) = 450 square feet for the rectangle.

To get the area of the circle we need to know the radius, which is half the diameter. Clearly, the diameter is 30 – 4 – 4 = 22. So, the radius is 11. Then, (1/2)π(11)2 = 190.

So, the area of the deck is 450 – 190 = 260. Choice **H**.

27.

A 10-inch-by-10-inch square grid shown below is divided into 100 squares, each with a side length of 1 inch. Each vertex of the 2 shaded triangles lies at an intersection of 2 grid lines. What fractional part of the 10-inch-by-10-inch square is shaded?

245

A. $\frac{2}{3}$

B. $\frac{4}{5}$

C. $\frac{4}{9}$

D. $\frac{5}{9}$

E. $\frac{19}{50}$

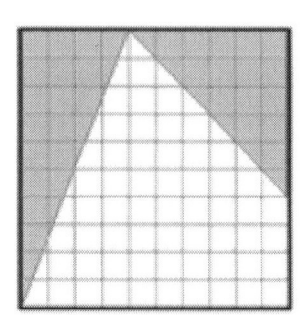

The easiest triangle to calculate the area of is a right triangle, because the base and the height are just the **legs** of the right triangle.

Here we have 2 right triangles shaded in. The area of the one on the left is just (1/2)(4)(10) = 20. The one on the right is just (1/2)(6)(6) = 18.

So, the total area of the shaded region is 20 + 18 = 38.

Then, the shaded part is 38/100 = 19/50 of the square. **E.**

28.

Marie is building a kite. In a drawing of her kite, shown below, $AB = BC$, $AD = DC$, the measure of $\angle ABC$ is 90°, and the measure of $\angle ADC$ is 60°. What is the measure of $\angle BAD$?

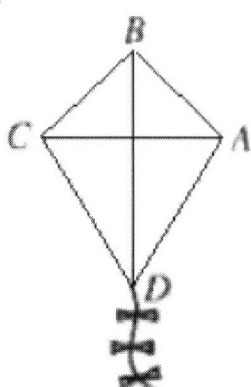

A. 50°
B. 65°
C. 90°
D. 105°
E. 130°

246

The given facts tell us immediately that triangles ABC and ADC are both isosceles. That means their base angles are congruent.

So, <BCA = <BAC = (180 – 90)/2 = 45°. And <ACD = <CAD = (180 – 60)/2 = 60°. Then <BAD = 45 + 60 = 105°. **D**.

Another way to answer this question is to realize that a kite is a quadrilateral polygon. And, as such, all of its interior angles must add up to 360°. Also, a kite has two congruent non-vertex angles. In this case, <BAD and <BCA. If we call those angles x, we can set up a simple equation to solve for x:

2x + 90 + 60 = 360

2x = 210

x = 105. The same result.

29.

A rectangular solid has a volume of 50 cubic units. If the length, width, and height of the solid are each doubled, what will the volume, in cubic units, of the new solid be?

F. 200
G. 400
H. 600
J. 800
K. 2,700

This can be answered very quickly if you just realize that doubling each dimension is the same as multiplying each by 2.

Then, (2)(2)(2) = 8. So, the new solid will be 8 times larger, or (8)(50) = 400. **G**.

30.

The bottom of a man-made pond shown below, has an area of 750 square feet and a perimeter of 156 ft. The man-made pond has a uniform depth of 5 ft of water, and the given lengths are in feet. If it can be determined, what is the volume of water, in cubic feet, that the pond contains?

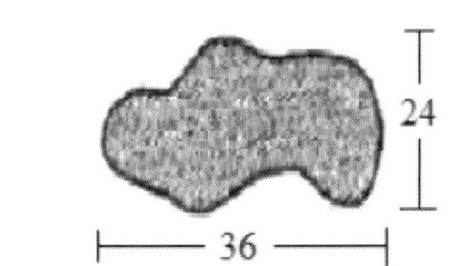

A. 3,150
B. 3,335
C. 3,520
D. 3,720
E. Cannot be determined from the given information

If you're not fooled by the question, this problem is another fast and easy one.

The strange shape of the pond may give you the impression that it won't be easy to determine the volume. But if you remember that the volume of any 3-dimensional shape with a **uniform** height is just **Area of the base x height**, then the problem suddenly becomes almost trivial.

Here, if you realize that the shape shown is just its base, and its area is given in the problem, then the volume is (750)(5) = 3750. **D**.

Knowing the perimeter was totally unnecessary!

Watch out for problems that give you more information than you need. They are designed to test your ability to focus on relevant data.

31.

Each side of square *ABCD* has a length of 40 cm. A certain rectangle whose area is equal to the area of *ABCD* has a width of 25 cm. What is the length, in centimeters, of the rectangle?

- A. 40
- B. 50
- C. 64
- D. 125
- E. 250

We can immediately calculate the area of the square as 40^2 = 1600.

Then, since the area of the rectangle is equal, we can set up the equation (25)(L) = 1600, where L is the length. Solving for L we get L = 64. **C**.

32.

A small circle and a large circle are tangent at *A*, as shown in the figure below. The center, *O*, of the large circle lies on the small circle. The diameter of the large circle is 8 cm. What is the ratio of the area of the small circle to the area of the large circle?

- A. $\frac{1}{4}$
- B. $\frac{1}{3}$
- C. $\frac{1}{2}$
- D. $\frac{\pi}{4}$
- E. $\frac{\pi}{2}$

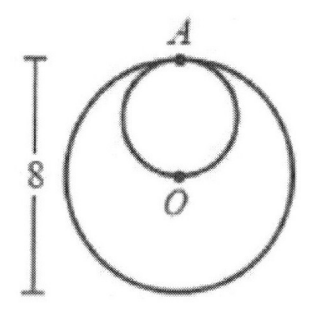

This one can be answered in less than 20 seconds if you immediately calculate the area of both circles.

The area of any circle is πr². So, the area of the large circle is π(4²) = 16π. And, the area of the small circle is π(2²) = 4π.

Then, the ratio of the small to the large is just 4π/16π = 1/4. **A.**

It's interesting to note that **no matter what the diameter of the large circle is**, if the small circle is one half its diameter, then the ratio of the areas will **always** be 1/4. That's because (1/2 r)² = 1/4 r².

So, if you see a problem like this again on the test, you can immediately choose 1/4 as the correct answer, whatever the given value of the diameter, and save even more time.

33.

Squares with sides of length x cm have been removed from each corner of a rectangle measuring 7 cm by 16 cm, resulting in the figure shown below. In terms of x, what is the area, in square centimeters, of the figure?

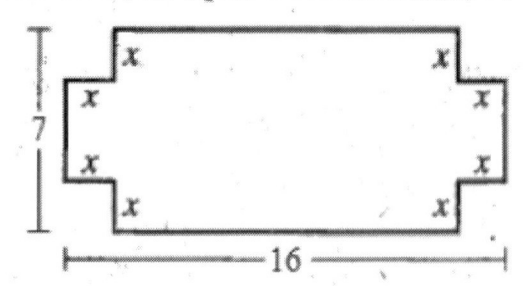

F. $52 - 4x^2$
G. $112 - 4x^2$
H. $112 + 4x^2$
J. $112 - 8x$
K. $112 - 52x + 4x^2$

First calculate the area of the rectangle **without** the 4 cutouts. That's just (7)(16) = 112.

Then, subtract the area of each cutout, (x)(x) = x². There are 4, so the total area of the cutouts is 4x².

So, the answer is 112 − 4x2. **G**.

34.

Philomena has 64 feet of fencing and a 4-foot-wide gate to use to enclose a pig pen. Among the following, a pig pen of which shape and dimensions will have the largest area if only the fencing and the gate are used to enclose it?

A. A square with a side length of 16 feet
B. A square with a side length of 17 feet
C. A rectangle with a length of 14 feet and a width of 16 feet
D. A rectangle with a length of 15 feet and a width of 17 feet
E. A rectangle with a length of 15 feet and a width of 18 feet

Once again, you are being tested on the knowledge that the largest area enclosed by any rectangular shape is a **square**. If you remember that, then this one is solved in a few seconds.

The total fencing length is 64 + 4 = 68 feet. Creating a square out of that length means that each side would be 68/4 = 17 feet. So, **B** is the answer.

35.

In the figure shown below, $\overline{CG} \cong \overline{AE}$, and rectangle *ABCD* has a length of 12 inches and a width of 8 inches. The area of rectangle *EFGD* is 2 times the area of rectangle *ABCD*. What is the length, in inches, of $\overline{CG}$?

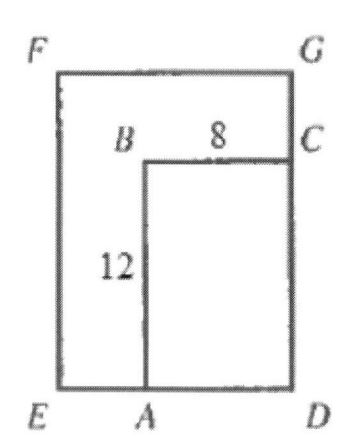

F. 2
G. 2.4
H. 3.5
J. 4
K. 4.8

If we let $\overline{CG}$ = x, then $\overline{AE}$ = x also. And, since rectangle EFGD is 2 times the area of rectangle ABCD, its area must be 2(12)(8) = 192.

Then, we can set up an equation to solve for x:

(x + 12)(x + 8) = 192

x² + 20x + 96 = 192

x² + 20x − 96 = 0

(x + 24)(x − 4) = 0

x = **4** is the only plausible answer, since the measurement can't be negative.

36.

In the figure below, points E, F, G, and H are on the sides of square ABCD. Arc $\overset{\frown}{EH}$ has center at A, $\overset{\frown}{EF}$ at B, $\overset{\frown}{FG}$ at C, and $\overset{\frown}{GH}$ at D. All of the arcs have a radius of 2 feet. What is the area, in square feet, of the shaded region?

252

A. $24 - 6\pi$

B. $24 - 8\pi$

C. $16 - \frac{9}{2}\pi$

D. $16 - 4\pi$

E. $16 - 8\pi$

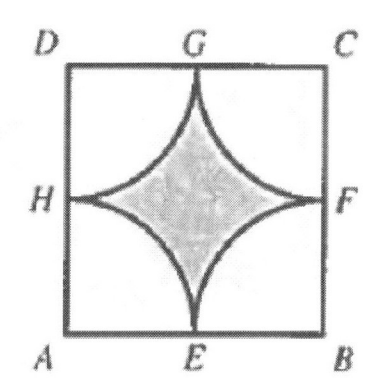

This one is not as hard as it looks. Notice that if you put the 4 white arc corners together they form a whole circle with radius of 2 feet.

That means the white area is just $\pi(2^2) = 4\pi$.

The length of the side of square ABCD is 4, which is twice the radius of the arcs. So, the area of the square is $4^2 = 16$.

Then the shaded region is $16 - 4\pi$. **D**.

37.

The rectangle shown in the figure below is partitioned into 3 triangles, 2 of which are shaded. What is the total area, in square inches, of the 2 shaded regions?

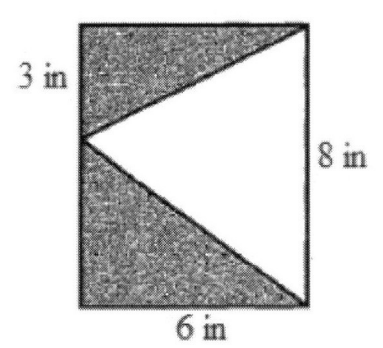

F. 20
G. 24
H. 32
J. 40
K. 80

The fastest way to handle this one is to subtract the area of the white triangle area from the area of the whole rectangle.

The rectangle area is just (6)(8) = 48, and the white triangle area is just (1/2)(8)(6) = 24.

Then, 48 − 24 = 24. **G**.

38.

A 2-inch-tall rectangular box with a square base is constructed to hold a circular pie that has a diameter of 9 inches. Both are shown below. What is the volume, in cubic inches, of the smallest such box that can hold this pie?

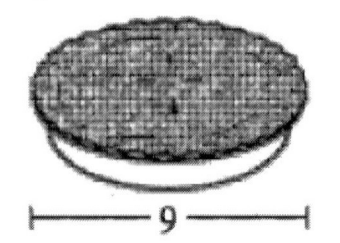

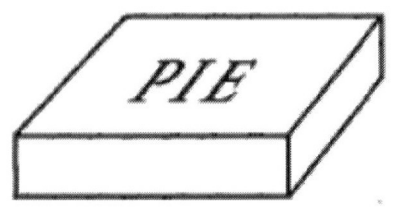

|—— 9 ——|

- **A.** 24
- **B.** 64
- **C.** 72
- **D.** 162
- **E.** 512

The smallest box would be one that touches the outer crust of the pie on all sides. That would require a box of equal length on all sides, which is a square.

The length of each side would be equal to the diameter of the pie. Then, the volume would be (9)(9)(2) = 162 cubic inches. **D**.

39.

Kaylina is constructing the kite shown below. The kite includes 2 perpendicular supports, one of length 32 inches and the other of length 18 inches. The ends of the supports are connected with string to form a 4-sided figure that is symmetric with respect to the longer support. A layer of paper will cover the interior of the 4-sided figure. Which of the following is closest to the area, in square inches, that Kaylina will cover with paper?

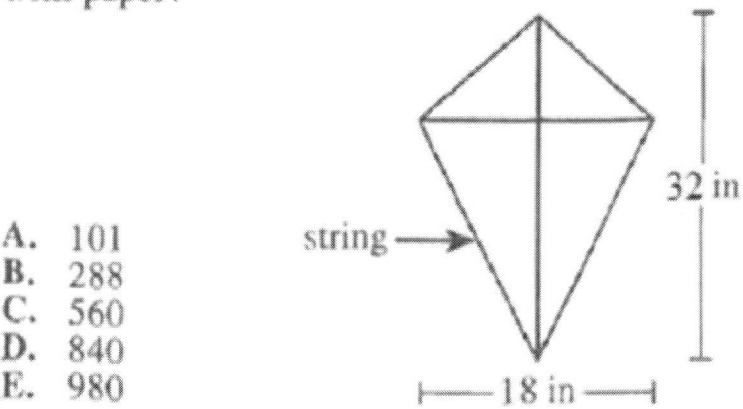

A. 101
B. 288
C. 560
D. 840
E. 980

There is a simple formula that will allow you to calculate the area of **any kite** when the perpendicular diagonals are known. The formula is simply **½ the product of the diagonals**.

So, in this case, the area = ½(18)(32) = 288. **B**.

40.

In the figure shown below, A, B, and D lie on a circle whose center is O, a diameter is $\overline{AB}$, $\overline{CD}$ is perpendicular to $\overline{AB}$ at C, the length of $\overline{AD}$ is 5 m, and the length of $\overline{BD}$ is 12 m. What is the length, in meters, of $\overline{CB}$?

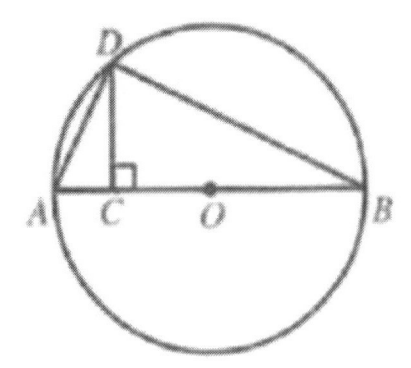

A. $\frac{60}{13}$

B. $\frac{65}{12}$

C. 13

D. $\frac{144}{13}$

E. 60

If you recognize that all the triangles shown are **similar right triangles**, then this one can be solved without too much trouble.

First notice that triangle ABD must be a right triangle because angle D is inscribed in a semi-circle. **Any** angle inscribed in a semi-circle must be 90° since it intercepts half the circle, which is 180°, and all inscribed angles are **one half** the arc they intercept.

Next, notice that triangle ABD is a 5-12-13 Pythagorean triplet, based on the given information.

Then, the diameter AB is 13, which is also **the hypotenuse** of triangle ABD.

Next, notice that $\overline{CB}$ is the long leg of triangle BCD.

Now, we can set up a proportion between the long leg and hypotenuse of triangle ABD and the long leg and hypotenuse of triangle BCD, since **corresponding sides of similar triangles are proportional**.

That means,

$$\frac{12}{13} = \frac{\overline{CB}}{12}$$

Cross multiplying and solving, $\overline{CB} = \frac{144}{13}$. D.

With that, we'll conclude this chapter on geometry word problems. Needless to say, there are many more examples that exist, but this chapter should have given you a decent flavor of what you might expect to see on the test.

Geometry covers a broad spectrum on both the SAT and ACT, and most of the problems won't be in the form of word problems. But every problem will test your understanding of one or more geometry concepts that you should have learned in your high school class.

Trigonometry

Like geometry, trigonometry on the SAT and ACT doesn't occur in the form of word problems as frequently as it does in straight mathematical equations and relationships. However, don't let that fool you into thinking there won't be a fair share of questions crafted as word problems.

The ACT tends to have more trigonometry word problems than the SAT, but that can change at any time. So, be prepared by studying the examples shown in this chapter.

1.

In a right triangle, one angle measures $x°$, where $\sin x° = \frac{3}{4}$. What is $\cos(90° - x°)$?

This one's a 2 second problem. Just remember this: Sine **always equals** cosine when their angles are **complementary**.

But what does complementary mean? It simply means that the two angles add up to 90 degrees. So, for example, sin 40° = cos 50° because 40 + 50 = 90.

They are complementary angles. In general, the complement of x is 90 − x , which is **exactly** what they are showing in this problem. So, immediately the answer is **3/4.** Done.

This would have been a grid-in problem on the SAT.

2.

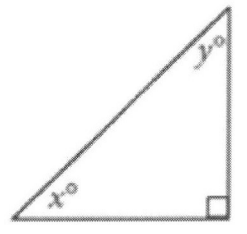

In the triangle above, the sine of $x°$ is 0.55. What is the cosine of $y°$?

Here again, we see a question about sine and cosine. Remember, the shortcut we used in the first problem to determine if the angles in question are **complementary, meaning they add up to 90 degrees.**

How can we tell in this problem? That brings us to another useful fact. **The acute angles of any right triangle are always complementary!**

Well, that makes our job so much easier. In this problem angles x and y are the acute angles of the right triangle. So, they are automatically complementary and, therefore, sin x = cos y.

Then, immediately, **0.55** is the answer. Be careful gridding in this one. You are not allowed to lead with a zero. Then, you would simply grid in **.55**.

3.

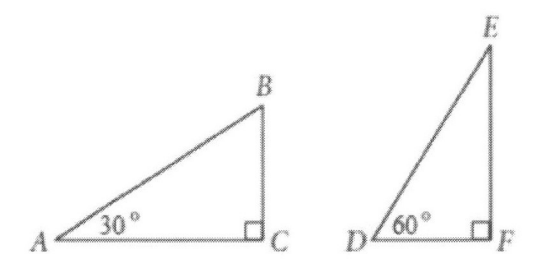

Triangles ABC and DEF are shown above. Which of the following is equal to the ratio $\dfrac{BC}{AB}$?

A) $\dfrac{DE}{DF}$

B) $\dfrac{DF}{DE}$

C) $\dfrac{DF}{EF}$

D) $\dfrac{EF}{DE}$

Once again we have a problem testing you on your understanding of the relationship between sine and cosine. Let's repeat it again.

The sine of an angle is **always** equal to the cosine of another angle if those angles are **complementary.** And recall that complementary means the two angles add up to 90 degrees.

Is that the case here? It sure is! 30 + 60 = 90! Therefore, sin 30 = cos 60. How does that help here?

Well, isn't the sine of an angle just the opposite side over the hypotenuse? That means sin 30 = **BC/AB**, and that's what the question is asking about. Now, immediately you know that must equal cos 60 which is the side adjacent to the 60 degree angle over the hypotenuse, or **DF/DE**, choice **B.** Done.

Are you seeing a pattern here? The SAT has been notorious about testing students on this relationship between sine and cosine. It would be wise to expect to see a problem of this type on your SAT exam, so take good note of it.

4.

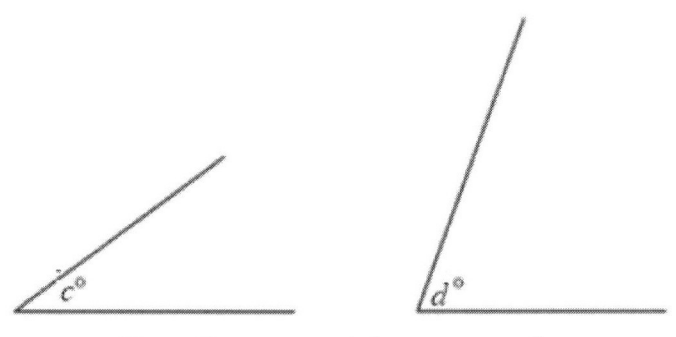

Note: Figures not drawn to scale.

The angles shown above are acute and $\sin(c°) = \cos(d°)$. If $c = 3w + 15$ and $d = 4w + 12$, what is the value of w?

A) 7
B) 8
C) 9
D) 10

This is a variation on the same theme. Do you see how?

Once again, the **only** time the sine of an angle equals the cosine of another angle is when the angles are **complementary.** That means, in this case, c + d = 90 degrees. Now, just substitute:

3w + 15 + 4w + 12 = 90

7w + 27 = 90

7w = 63

w = 9. Choice **C.**

5.

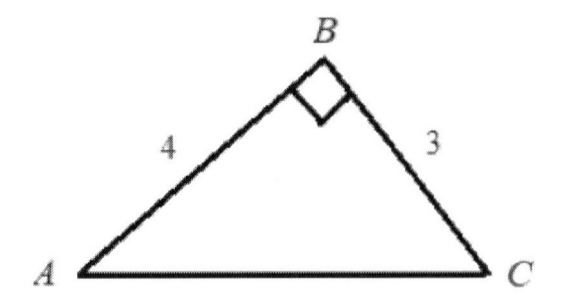

In triangle *ABC* above, point *D* (not shown) lies on $\overline{AC}$. What is the value of $\cos(\angle ABD) - \sin(\angle DBC)$?

Since point D has no specific location on AC, let's just randomly put it on that line segment and draw a line connecting it to B.

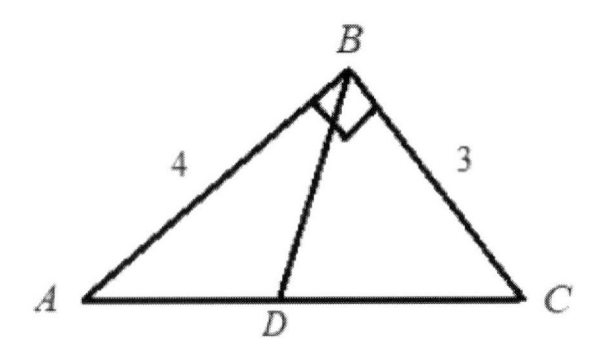

Now we should notice that it divides the **right angle B** into two angles. So then, we should know by now that any two angles which add up to 90 degrees are **complementary**. And we know that when two angles are complementary then the sine of one equals the cosine of the other, and vice versa.

That means **cos(<ABD) = sin(<DBC)**. Then subtracting them must result in **0**. Done!

Notice that the numbers 3 and 4 shown are irrelevant since we already knew it was a right triangle because of the box shown at angle B. Here again, the SAT is providing extra information which is not needed to answer the question.

Now that we've seen several examples of how the sine and cosine of complementary angles are equal, let's move on to other types of trigonometry related problems you might be tested on...

6.

In triangle ABC, the measure of $\angle B$ is $90°$, $BC = 12$, and $AC = 15$. Triangle DEF is similar to triangle ABC, where vertices D, E, and F correspond to vertices A, B, and C, respectively, and each side of triangle DEF is $\frac{1}{3}$ the length of the corresponding side of triangle ABC. What is the value of $\sin F$?

Pay attention to the word **similar**. All similar triangle have **the same angles.**

Here, **it makes no difference** that triangle DEF is 1/3 the length of the sides of triangle ABC because the ratio of the sides of both triangles are **the same**, no matter what the actual lengths are!

So **sin F = sin C** because **<F = <C.**

Now, let's draw out the triangles to have a clearer idea of what we're dealing with here:

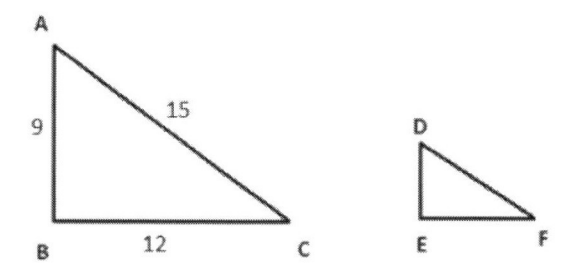

Where did the 12 come from? That's just Pythagorean's Theorem. Or, you might recognize those sides as a Pythagorean Triplet. Review these concepts if you don't know them already.

So, sin F = sin C = **9/15**, since <u>sin X = Opposite side/ Hypotenuse</u> in any right triangle, where X is one of the acute angles of the triangle.

Notice I did not reduce to the simplest form of 3/5 because it's not necessary! So long as it fits in the grid it's fine. The grid-in section does not require the answer to be in simplest form, so why take the chance of making a careless mistake by doing so?

You may be wondering whether a problem like this would be considered a geometry problem instead of a trigonometry problem. Perhaps, but sine, cosine and tangent are technically trigonometry terms, so they're included in this chapter.

6.

If rectangle $ABCD$ has an area of 324 and the tangent of $\angle BCA$ (not shown) is $\frac{4}{9}$, then which of the following is closest to the length of $\overline{BD}$ (not shown)?

A) 9.8

B) 27

C) 29.5

D) It cannot be determined from the given information.

The first thing to do is draw a diagonal in order to create <BCA as the problem states:

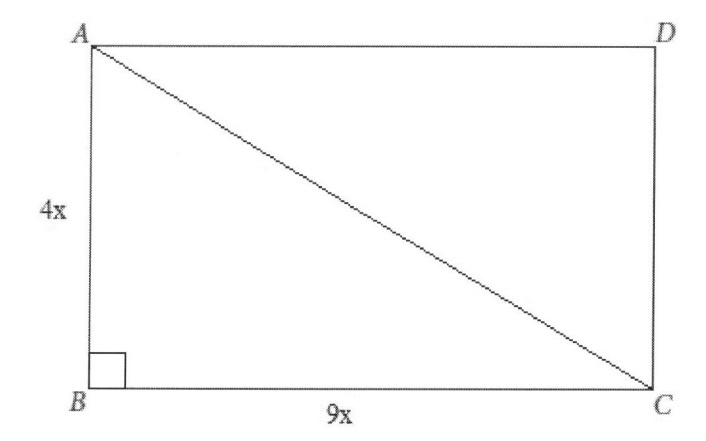

[Figure: Rectangle ABCD with A top-left, D top-right, B bottom-left (with right angle marked), C bottom-right. Diagonal drawn from A to C. Side AB labeled 4x, side BC labeled 9x.]

Since the tangent of <BCA is the opposite side / the adjacent side, we can set up the values of those sides as 4x and 9x since 4x/9x = 4/9 as the problem states.

Why 4x and 9x? Because they to be some multiple of 4 and 9 in order for the area to be 324.

Then, we can calculate x:

(4x)(9x) = 324

$36x^2$ = 324

x^2 = 9, so x = 3

That means the width of the rectangle is (4)(3) = 12, and the length is (9)(3) = 27.

The next thing to notice is that $\overline{AC} \cong \overline{BD}$ since the diagonals of any rectangle are congruent.

That means that if we calculate the length of $\overline{AC}$, using Pythagorean's formula, we will know the length of $\overline{BD}$ too.

So, $\overline{BD} = \sqrt{12^2 + 27^2}$ = 29.5. Choice **C**.

If that problem seems too complicated, don't worry. It's rare to see a difficult trig problem on the SAT. It was meant to introduce you to tangent, and how it can be used in a word problem.

7.

Ryan and Allison build a ramp to help their elderly cat, Simms, walk up to their bed. They need the ramp to make a 35° angle with their bedroom floor. How long must the ramp be to reach the top of their bed that is exactly three feet off the ground?

A) $\dfrac{\sin 35°}{3}$

B) $\dfrac{\sin 55°}{3}$

C) $\dfrac{3}{\sin 55°}$

D) $\dfrac{3}{\sin 35°}$

Here, like most geometry and trigonometry word problems, it helps to draw a picture:

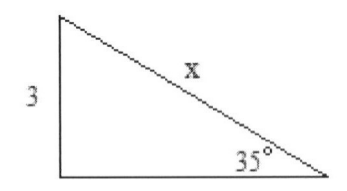

You can see that the situation describes a right triangle, with the length of the ramp, x, as the hypotenuse.

Then, it would be appropriate to use sine to calculate x since the side opposite the 35° is known. (Anyway, all the choices are in terms of sine, so that already tells you which trig function to use.)

So, sin 35° = 3/x. Then, x = 3/sin 35°. Choice **D**.

8.
Danielle is a civil engineer for Dastis Dynamic Construction, Inc. She must create blueprints for a wheelchair accessible ramp leading up to the entrance of a mall that she and her group are building. The ramp must be exactly 100 feet in length and make a 20° angle with the level ground. What is the horizontal distance, in meters, from the start of the ramp to the point level with the start of the ramp immediately below the entrance of the mall, rounded to the nearest meter? (Disregard units when inputting your answer.)

Again, if we draw out what's going on here it will help a lot:

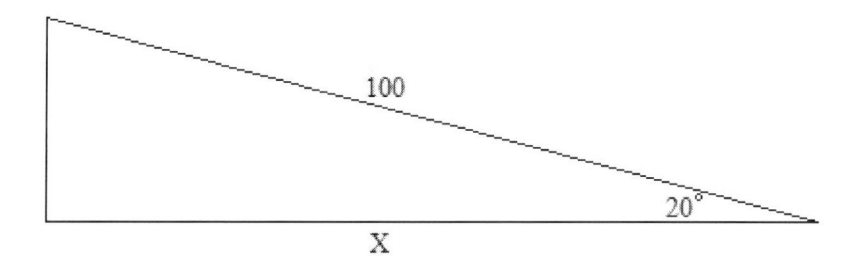

Since the distance in question is <u>adjacent</u> to the angle, and the hypotenuse is known, <u>cosine</u> would be the trig function to use.

Then, cos 20° = x/100

x = 100(cos 20°) = about **94**.

9.
Alyssa determines that a floating balloon is 1,200 meters away from her at an angle of 42° from the ground, as in the figure below. What is the height, h, of the balloon from the ground? (sin 42° = 0.669, cos 42° = 0.743, tan 42° = 0.900)

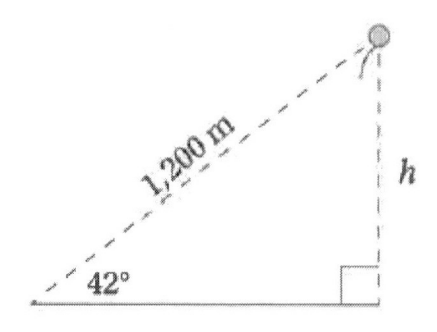

A) 802.8 meters

B) 891.6 meters

C) 1,080 meters

D) 1,793 meters

Here, again, we should recognize that when we're given an angle in a right triangle, and the side opposite and the hypotenuse are labeled, then we're dealing with sine.

So, sin 42° = h/1200

h = (1200)(sin 42°) = (1200)(0.669) = 802.8. **A**.

10.

A 20 foot ladder rests against a wall. The base of the ladder is 7 feet from the wall. What angle does the ladder make with the ground?

A) 55°

B) 69.5°

C) 73°

D) 81.3°

Let's draw it out so that we're clear about what the problem is asking:

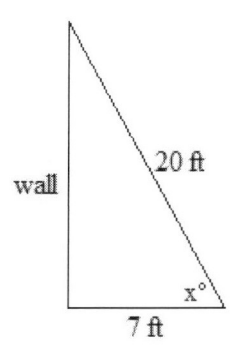

The only values given are the <u>side adjacent</u> to the angle and the ladder length, which is the <u>hypotenuse</u>.

That should immediately trigger in our mind "cosine".

Then, cos x = 7/20

x = cos^{-1}(7/20) = 69.5°. **B**.

If you're wondering what the cos^{-1} means, it's just the inverse of the cosine function which tells you what the angle is that the ratio of the sides represents. Your calculator has that function on the keypad. Just look for it.

That concludes the type of trigonometry word problems you might expect to see on the SAT. Obviously, it's not exhaustive, but meant to give you a general idea of the concepts you're expected to know. If you're a little rusty on these concepts, then the problems presented should give you a good idea of the areas you need to brush up on.

As I said, there are generally more trigonometry problems on the ACT. So, let's explore those now to see how they may or may not differ from the SAT.

11.

The triangle shown below has side lengths 25, 26, and 27 inches. Which of the following expressions gives the measure of the smallest angle of the triangle?

(Note: For every triangle with sides of length a, b, and c that are opposite $\angle A$, $\angle B$, and $\angle C$, respectively, $c^2 = a^2 + b^2 - 2ab \cos C$.)

The triangle shown below has side lengths 25, 26, and 27 inches. Which of the following expressions gives the measure of the smallest angle of the triangle?

(Note: For every triangle with sides of length a, b, and c that are opposite $\angle A$, $\angle B$, and $\angle C$, respectively, $c^2 = a^2 + b^2 - 2ab \cos C$.)

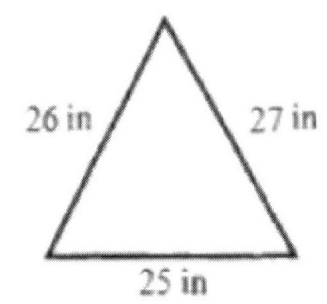

A. $\cos^{-1}\left(-\dfrac{27^2 - 26^2 - 25^2}{2(26)(27)}\right)$

B. $\cos^{-1}\left(-\dfrac{25^2 - 26^2 - 27^2}{2(26)(27)}\right)$

C. $\cos^{-1}\left(25^2 - 26^2 - 27^2 + 2(26)(27)\right)$

D. $\cos^{-1}\left(26^2 - 27^2 - 25^2 + 2(25)(27)\right)$

E. $\cos^{-1}\left(27^2 - 26^2 - 25^2 + 2(25)(26)\right)$

Well, here's something quite different from anything we've seen on SAT trig problems.

But, is it really harder? To answer that, let's examine it more closely.

From Algebra II, you should recognize the formula given in the parenthesis. It's called *The Law of Cosines*. It states that the missing side of any triangle (not just a right triangle) can be determined if we know one of the angles and the length of the two adjacent sides to the known angle. And, if we know the lengths of all the sides, then we can determine the degree of the angle opposite any side of the triangle.

The question here is asking for the measure of the smallest angle.

As we know from geometry, the smallest angle in a triangle is always opposite the smallest side. So, we're looking for the angle opposite the side with length of 25.

Then, applying the formula, $25^2 = 26^2 + 27^2 - 2(26)(27)\cos C$.

Solving for C:

$-2(26)(27)\cos C = 25^2 - 26^2 - 27^2$

$\cos C = \dfrac{25^2 - 26^2 - 27^2}{-2(26)(27)}$

$C = \cos^{-1}\left(-\dfrac{25^2 - 26^2 - 27^2}{2(26)(27)}\right)$

Choice **B**. The most difficult part of this problem was probably the algebra for many students.

12.

A 46-foot-long rectangular swimming pool with vertical sides is 3 feet deep at the shallow end and 8 feet deep at the deep end. The bottom of the pool slopes downward at a constant angle from horizontal along the length of the pool. Which of the following expressions gives this constant angle?

(Note: For $-\dfrac{\pi}{2} < x < \dfrac{\pi}{2}$, $y = \tan x$ if and only if $x = \tan^{-1} y$.)

F. $\tan^{-1}\left(\dfrac{5}{46}\right)$

G. $\tan^{-1}\left(\dfrac{11}{46}\right)$

H. $\tan^{-1}\left(\dfrac{5}{8}\right)$

J. $\tan^{-1}\left(\dfrac{46}{11}\right)$

K. $\tan^{-1}\left(\dfrac{46}{5}\right)$

Here's another one that's a little more challenging than you're likely to see on the SAT.

Again, it would help to draw it out to have a more clear idea of what to do:

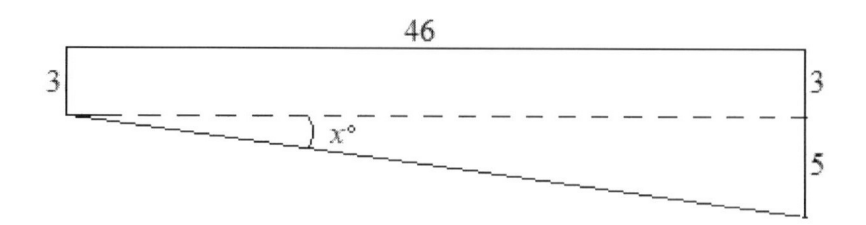

Now, it should be plain to see that, since we know the lengths of the two legs of the right triangle, we can use <u>tangent</u> to solve for x.

Then, tan x = 5/46

x = tan^{-1}(5/46). Choice **F**.

13.

As shown below, Pila walked her dog 300 feet due east from the entrance of a dog park to a trash can and then walked 800 feet in a straight line 35° north of east to a bench. Which of the following expressions is equal to the distance, in feet, between the entrance and the bench?

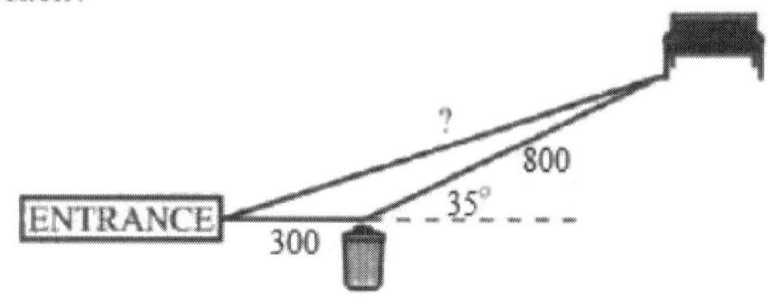

F. $\dfrac{1100}{\cos 35°}$

G. $\dfrac{300}{\cos 35°} + 800$

H. $\dfrac{300}{\sin 145°} + 800$

J. $\sqrt{800^2 + 300^2 - 2(800)(300)\cos 35°}$

K. $\sqrt{800^2 + 300^2 - 2(800)(300)\cos 145°}$

The triangle show is obviously not a right triangle. But we already saw that the Law of Cosines allows us to deal with such a situation. But this time the formula is not given, so it would be a good idea to memorize it before you take the test.

They don't provide the angle opposite the ? side immediately, but we determine what it is because it's supplementary to the 35° angle shown. So, the angle must be 145°.

Now we can use the law of cosines to solve for "?".

So, $?^2 = 800^2 + 300^2 - 2(800)(300)\cos 145°$.

Taking the square root of both sides we get:

$? = \sqrt{800^2 + 300^2 - 2(800)(300)\cos 145°}$. Choise **K**.

14.

A spherical droplet of ink strikes a vertical wall, as modeled in the figure below. The angle of impact is indicated by θ in the figure.

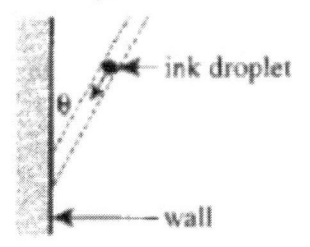

The stain the droplet leaves on the wall is oval-shaped. Scientists can measure the maximum length and maximum width of the stain to determine the angle of impact according to the formula $\sin \theta = \frac{\text{maximum width}}{\text{maximum length}}$. The figure below models such a stain. What was the impact angle of the droplet that left this stain?

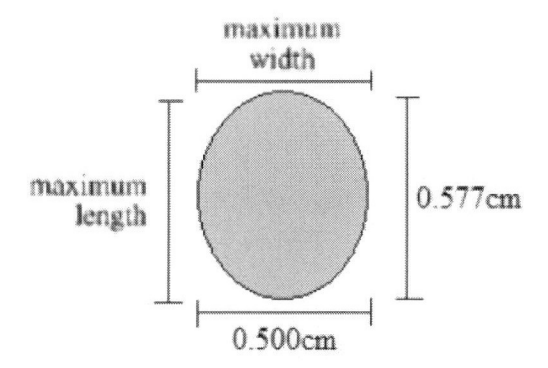

273

F) 35°

G) 45°

H) 60°

J) 90°

K) 120°

This one's not as hard as it looks, because all we have to do is plug the appropriate values into the given formula.

The maximum width is shown as 0.500 cm, and the maximum is 0.577 cm.

So, sinθ = 0.500/0.577

θ = sin⁻¹(0.5/0.577) = 60°. **H**.

15.

One angle measure and 2 side lengths, in inches, are given in the right scalene triangle below. In terms of a and b, what is $\cos\theta$?

F. $\dfrac{a}{b}$

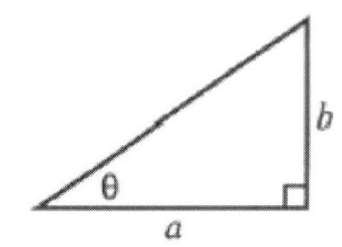

G. $\dfrac{b}{a}$

H. $\dfrac{a}{\sqrt{a^2+b^2}}$

J. $\dfrac{b}{\sqrt{a^2+b^2}}$

K. $\dfrac{\sqrt{a^2+b^2}}{b}$

Since the cosine of any angle in a right triangle is just the adjacent side over the hypotenuse, we must first find the hypotenuse using Pythagorean's formula.

So, if we call the hypotenuse c, the equation is $c^2 = a^2 + b^2$.

Then, $c = \sqrt{a^2 + b^2}$. Therefore, $\cos\theta = \dfrac{a}{\sqrt{a^2+b^2}}$. Choice **H**.

16.

Tia is standing 10 meters from a maple tree that is 15 meters from a willow tree, as shown in the figure below, in which the measure of an angle is given. Which of the following equations, when solved for x, gives the distance, x meters, between Tia and the willow tree?

(Note: For a triangle with sides of length a, b, and c that are opposite angles ∠A, ∠B, and ∠C, respectively, $c^2 = a^2 + b^2 - 2ab \cos \angle C$.)

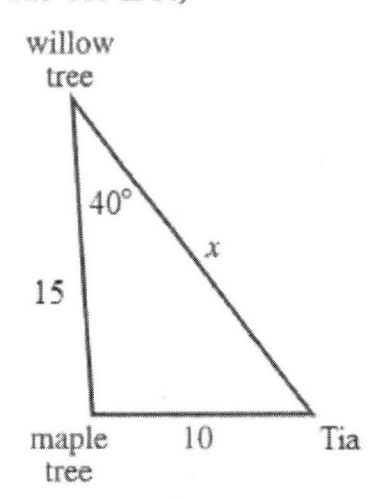

A. $10^2 = x^2 + 15^2 - 2x(15)(\cos 40°)$
B. $10^2 = x^2 + 15^2 - 2(10)(15)(\cos 40°)$
C. $15^2 = x^2 + 10^2 - 2x(15)(\cos 40°)$
D. $x^2 = 10^2 + 15^2 - 2x(15)(\cos 40°)$
E. $x^2 = 10^2 + 15^2 - 2(10)(15)(\cos 40°)$

One again, the formula for the Law of Cosines is given to you. All you have to do is identify the proper values and plug them into the equation.

The given angle is 40° and the length of the side opposite that angle is 10. That makes **A** the only possible choice. There is nothing to calculate.

As mentioned before, don't assume that these formulas will always be given to you. We have already seen a prior problem which needed to be solved using the Law of Cosines, and the formula was not given in the problem.

17.

In the figure shown below, a ladder 20 feet long forms an angle of 72° with the level ground as it leans against the vertical side of a building. The distance along the building, in feet, between the ground and the top of the ladder is equal to which of the following expressions?

F. $\frac{20}{2}$

G. $\frac{20\sqrt{3}}{2}$

H. $20 \sin 72°$

J. $20 \cos 72°$

K. $20 \tan 72°$

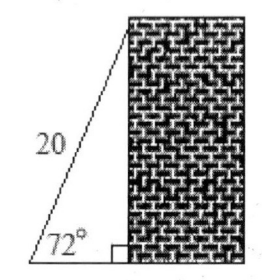

The ladder, ground, and building form a right triangle, as shown by the little box in the bottom-right part of the triangle. That means we can use the basic trig functions sine, cosine, or tangent to solve for missing sides and angles.

The distance along the building between the ground and the top of the ladder is the side opposite the 72° angle. Therefore, we must use sine to solve.

If we call the side opposite the 72° angle, x, then we have a simple equation:

$\sin 72° = \frac{x}{20}$. Solving for x we get 20 sin 72°. **H.**

18.

Emma, Amelia, and Aria are standing on a soccer field such that Amelia is 20 meters due west of Emma and Aria is 40 meters due north of Emma. Their positions are at the vertices of a triangle. Which of the following expressions gives the degree measure of the angle of the triangle at the vertex where Aria is standing?

F. $\cos^{-1}\left(\frac{40}{20}\right)$

G. $\sin^{-1}\left(\frac{40}{20}\right)$

H. $\sin^{-1}\left(\frac{20}{40}\right)$

J. $\tan^{-1}\left(\frac{40}{20}\right)$

K. $\tan^{-1}\left(\frac{20}{40}\right)$

Best to draw it out so that you don't make a careless mistake:

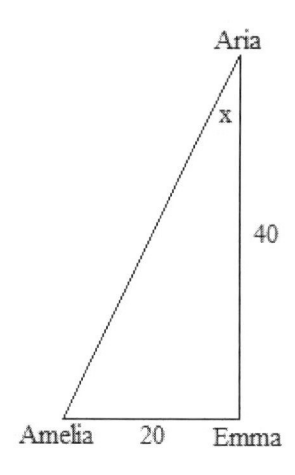

Now, it's easy to see that tan x = 20/40. So, x = tan⁻¹(20/40). Choice **K**.

19.

The clock shown below has a minute hand that is 4 inches long, and the center of the clock face is 10 inches above the bottom surface of the clock.

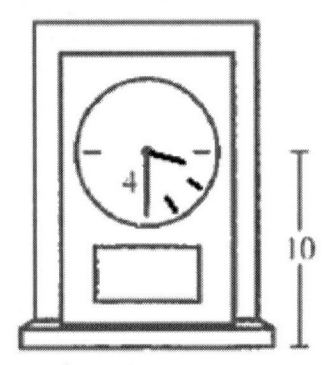

Let x be the time in minutes after the clock strikes 3:30. Let y be the height in inches that the end of the minute hand is above the bottom surface of the clock. One of the following graphs in the standard (x,y) coordinate plane shows the height, y, as a function of time, x. Which graph shows this relationship?

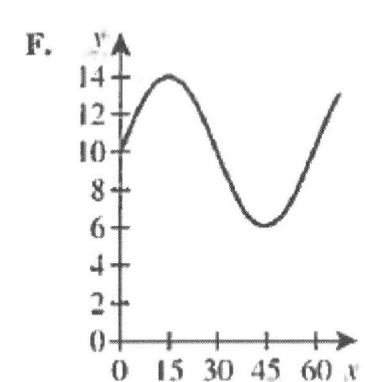

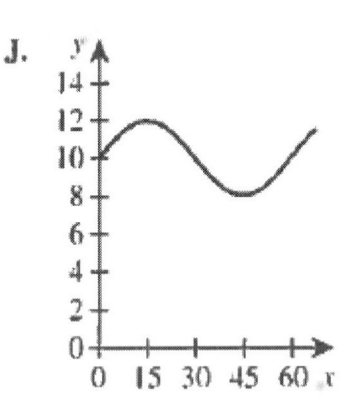

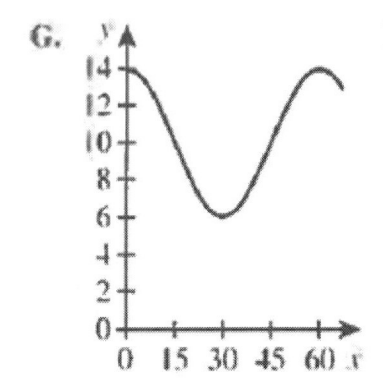

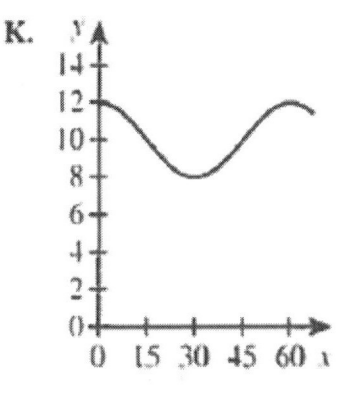

F.

J.

G.

K.

H.

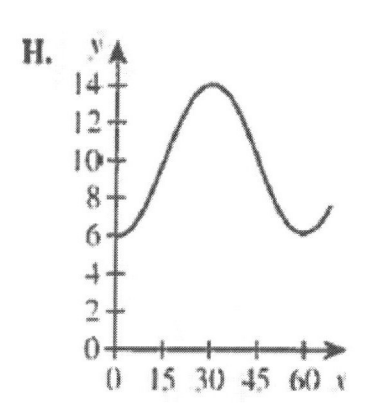

[Graph showing an upside-down cosine waveform with y-axis from 0 to 14 and x-axis marked 0, 15, 30, 45, 60, starting at y=6, reaching maximum of 14 around x=30, and returning to 6.]

At first, this may not seem like a trigonometry problem. But, if you'll notice the choices, they're all sinusoidal wave forms indicative of sine or cosine.

Fortunately, this problem is much easier than it looks. Notice that the minute hand **starts at the lowest point**, which is 4 inches below the center of the clock. That means it starts at 6 inches, since the center of the clock is 10 inches high.

A normal cosine waveform starts at the highest point. So, in this case, starting at the lowest point means that it's an upside down cosine function.

That immediately eliminates all the choices, except **H**.

But, to be sure H is correct, you can see that the minute hand will follow a circular and, therefore, cyclic path that is sinusoidal with the maximum height 4 inches above the center 30 minutes later at 4 o'clock.

20.

> Walter recently vacationed in Italy. While there, he visited the Colosseum, a famous attraction. Afterward, he took a 3.0-kilometer cab ride from the Colosseum to the Vatican. A tour guide named Amanda informed him that 25 million stones were used to build the main church at the Vatican, which is 136 meters tall.
>
> At a certain point, the angle of elevation formed by the level ground and the line from that point to the top of the Vatican church is 32°. Which of the following expressions is equal to the distance, in meters, between that point and the center of the base of the church?

F. 136 cos 32°

G. 136 sin 32°

H. 136 tan 32°

J. $\dfrac{136}{\sin 32°}$

K. $\dfrac{136}{\tan 32°}$

This question was taken from a multi-part problem. That's why there is information at the beginning of the problem that seems irrelevant.

Once again, drawing it out will help. Of course you don't have to draw it as well as shown here:

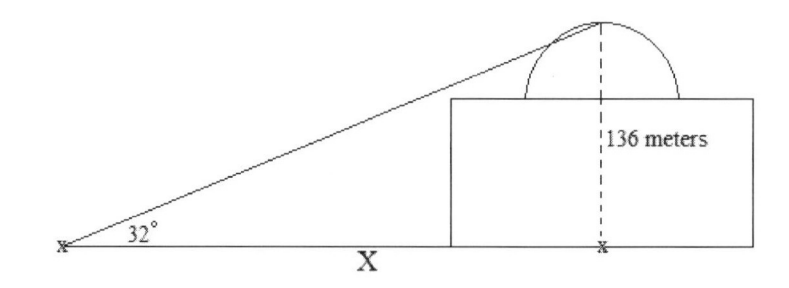

As you can see, the distance X between the two small x's is what the problem is asking for.

That can be found with the given information and the tangent function which gives us tan 32 = 136/X.

Then, X = 136/tan32. **K.**

21.

The hypotenuse of the right triangle △PQR shown below is 16 feet long. The sine of ∠P is $\dfrac{3}{5}$. About how many feet long is $\overline{QR}$?

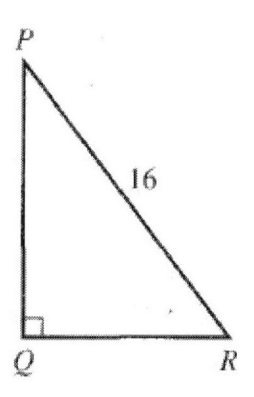

F. 8.0
G. 9.6
H. 12.4
J. 14.3
K. 15.4

This ACT problem is a little more complicated than a typical SAT trig word problem, but not too much more.

Any time they give you the sine of an angle in fraction form, you can draw a little right triangle and label the opposite side and the hypotenuse based on the numerator and denominator of the fraction since sine is always the opposite side over the hypotenuse.

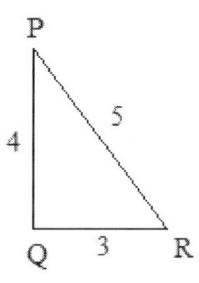

Even though it's labeled as triangle PQR, it is <u>not the same triangle</u> as described in the problem, but it is <u>similar</u>.

That means the sides are proportional and we can set up a proportion to solve for the side in question. If we call $\overline{QR}$ from the big triangle, x, then we have:

$$\frac{x}{16} = \frac{3}{5}$$

Cross multiplying we get:

5x = 48

x = 48/5 = 9.6. Choice **G**.

You could have also reasoned that, based on the given triangle, sin P must equal $\frac{\overline{QR}}{16}$. And, since they tell us sin P also equals 3/5, you could just equate them right away and get the same result.

22.

What is $\sin \frac{\pi}{12}$ given that $\frac{\pi}{12} = \frac{\pi}{3} - \frac{\pi}{4}$ and that $\sin(\alpha - \beta) = (\sin \alpha)(\cos \beta) - (\cos \alpha)(\sin \beta)$?

(Note: You may use the following table of values.)

θ	$\sin \theta$	$\cos \theta$
$\frac{\pi}{6}$	$\frac{1}{2}$	$\frac{\sqrt{3}}{2}$
$\frac{\pi}{4}$	$\frac{\sqrt{2}}{2}$	$\frac{\sqrt{2}}{2}$
$\frac{\pi}{3}$	$\frac{\sqrt{3}}{2}$	$\frac{1}{2}$

F. $\frac{1}{4}$

G. $\frac{1}{2}$

H. $\frac{\sqrt{3}-2}{4}$

J. $\frac{\sqrt{3}-\sqrt{2}}{2}$

K. $\frac{\sqrt{6}-\sqrt{2}}{4}$

As intimidating as this problem may seem, it's just a matter of substitution.

Once again, they are giving you the required formula, and they even give you values you need to plug in.

Since $\sin \frac{\pi}{12} = \sin(\frac{\pi}{3} - \frac{\pi}{4})$ we can immediately start plugging in values from the table based on the given formula:

$$(\sin\frac{\pi}{3})(\cos\frac{\pi}{4}) - (\cos\frac{\pi}{3})(\sin\frac{\pi}{4}) = (\frac{\sqrt{3}}{2})(\frac{\sqrt{2}}{2}) - (\frac{1}{2})(\frac{\sqrt{2}}{2}) = \frac{\sqrt{6}}{4} - \frac{\sqrt{2}}{4} = \frac{\sqrt{6}-\sqrt{2}}{4}. \text{ K.}$$

That problem could be considered more of an algebra problem than a trigonometry one. But it's indicative of how ACT trig word problems can differ from SAT ones.

23.

The lengths, in feet, of the sides of right triangle △ABC are as shown in the diagram below, with $x > 0$. What is the cotangent of ∠A, in terms of x ?

A. $\sqrt{4-x^2}$

B. $\frac{2}{x}$

C. $\frac{x}{2}$

D. $\frac{x}{\sqrt{4-x^2}}$

E. $\frac{\sqrt{4-x^2}}{x}$

Here's a term we haven't seen yet in this chapter, but you've probably seen it if you already took Algebra 2. It's <u>cotangent</u>. Cotangent is one of the <u>reciprocal trig functions</u>. All that means is that since the tangent of an angle inside a right triangle the opposite side over the adjacent side, the cotangent is the reciprocal, which is the <u>adjacent side over the opposite side</u>.

So then, based on the diagram, the cotangent of angle A (also written as cot A) is just the adjacent side $\sqrt{4-x^2}$ over the opposite side x. So, the answer is **E**.

Again, nothing earth shattering, but certainly more in depth than an SAT trig question.

24.

A right triangle that has its sides measured in the same unit of length is shown below. For any such triangle, $(\tan A)(\sin B)$ is equivalent to:

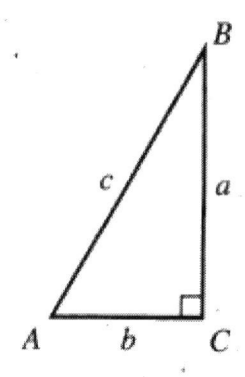

F. $\dfrac{a}{c}$

G. $\dfrac{ab}{c^2}$

H. $\dfrac{a^2}{bc}$

J. $\dfrac{b^2}{ac}$

K. $\dfrac{c}{a}$

This is just a variation on a theme. We can easily determine that tan A = a/b and sin B = a/c.

Then, we just need to multiply them (a/b)(a/c) = a²/bc. Choice **H**.

25.

For the function graphed below, the x-axis can be partitioned into intervals, each of length p radians, and the curve over any one interval is a repetition of the curve over each of the other intervals. What is the least possible value for p, the period of the function?

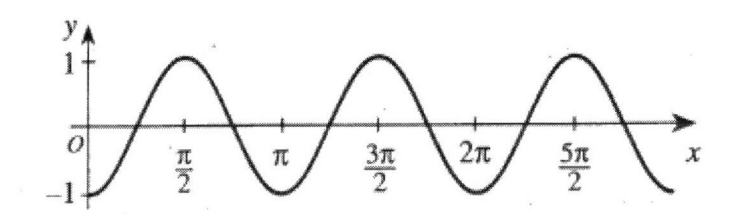

A. $\frac{\pi}{2}$

B. π

C. $\frac{3\pi}{2}$

D. 2π

E. 3π

The key phrase in this problem is the last sentence, "What is the least possible value for p, the period of the function?"

So, basically, they're just asking you to find the period. And that's easily found by looking at the graph and seeing how far along the x-axis you must go before the wave repeats.

The easiest way to do that is to go from one hump to the next. You should be able to clearly see that it spans an interval of π radians. **B**.

26.

The bottom of the basket of a hot-air balloon is parallel to the level ground. One taut tether line 144 feet long is attached to the center of the bottom of the basket and is anchored to the ground at an angle of 72°, as shown in the figure below. Which of the following expressions gives the distance, in feet, from the center of the bottom of the basket to the ground?

A. $\dfrac{144}{\cos 72°}$

B. $\dfrac{144}{\sin 72°}$

C. $144 \tan 72°$

D. $144 \cos 72°$

E. $144 \sin 72°$

tether line
144 ft

72°

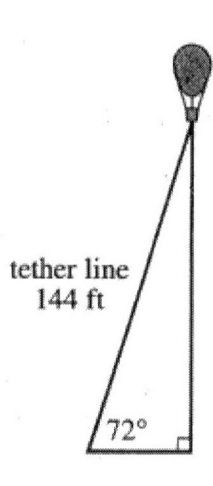

Here, the drawing is given to you, so you just have to interpret the wording correctly.

From the center of the bottom of the basket to the ground is the vertical distance.

Then we're interested in the side opposite the 72 degree angle. Since we're given the hypotenuse of the right triangle, we should use sine to solve the problem.

Calling the vertical leg x, the equation becomes sin 72° = x/144.

Therefore, x = 144 sin 72°. **E.**

27.

A trigonometric function with equation $y = a \sin(bx + c)$, where a, b, and c are real numbers, is graphed in the standard (x,y) coordinate plane below. The *period* of this function $f(x)$ is the smallest positive number p such that $f(x + p) = f(x)$ for every real number x. One of the following is the period of this function. Which one is it?

A. $\dfrac{\pi}{2}$

B. π

C. 2π

D. 4π

E. 2

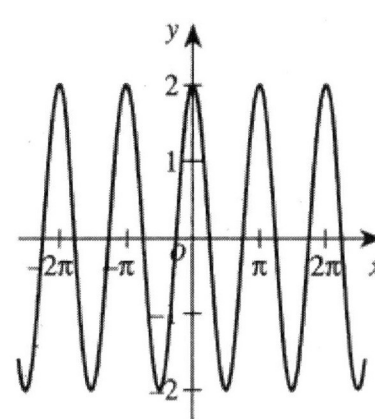

286

Once again, with all the fancy wording we only need to focus on the last sentence, "One of the following is the period of this function."

And again, the easiest way to determine the period is to simply go from one hump to the nearest adjacent hump and look at how far it spans the x-axis.

You should clearly see that it's π radians. **B**.

28.

The building below casts a shadow 24 yards long, and the angle of elevation from the tip of the shadow to the top of the building has a sine of $\frac{4}{5}$. What is the height of the building in yards?

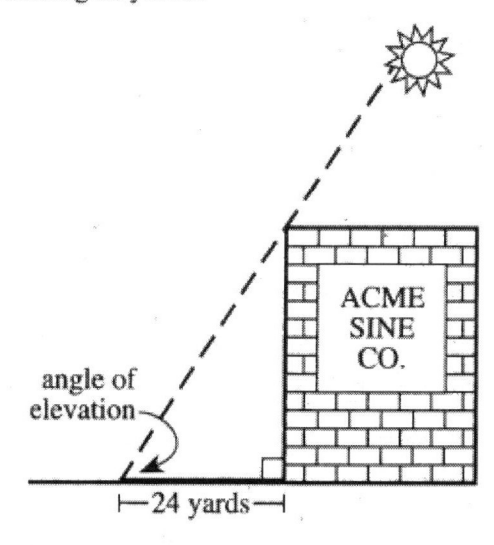

F. 14.4
G. 18.0
H. 19.2
J. 30.0
K. 32.0

In this problem we are given the value of the sine of the angle of elevation, but in the drawing we are only given the value of the side of the right triangle adjacent to the angle.

But, as we have seen before, whenever they give you the sine as a fraction, you can create a small right triangle that will reveal the other missing side. So, in this case:

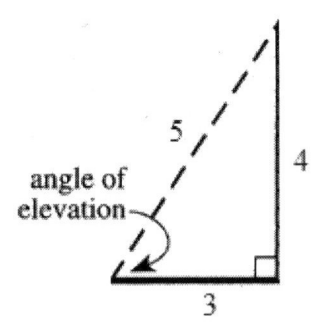

From that we can see that the tangent of the angle of elevation is 4/3.

Then, if we call the height of the building x, we can set up the following proportion:

$$\frac{x}{24} = \frac{4}{3}$$

Then, 3x = (4)(24)

x = 32. **K**.

29.

In the figure below, $\triangle ACB$ is a right triangle with legs of length a units and b units, where $0 < a < b$, and hypotenuse of length c units. The triangles $\triangle YCA$, $\triangle ZBA$, and $\triangle XCB$ are equilateral. The area of an equilateral triangle with sides x units long is $\frac{\sqrt{3}}{4}x^2$ square units.

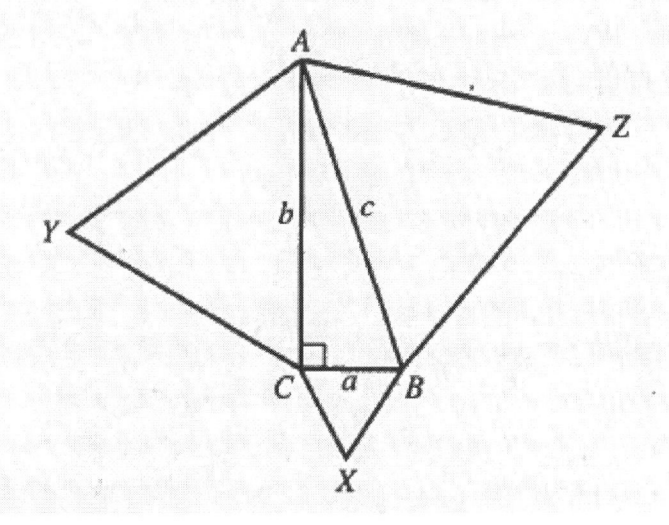

If $b = 2a$, what is $\tan(\angle ABC)$?

F. 2

G. $\frac{1}{2}$

H. $\frac{1}{\sqrt{5}}$

J. $\frac{2}{\sqrt{5}}$

K. $\sqrt{5}$

As you might suspect, this question comes from a multi-part problem. But the trig part here is pretty straightforward.

Since b = 2a, we can immediately substitute that for side $\overline{AC}$.

That means tan(<ABC) = 2a/a = 2. Done. **F**.

30.

In the standard (x,y) coordinate plane below, an angle is shown whose vertex is the origin. One side of this angle with measure θ passes through (4,–3), and the other side includes the positive x-axis. What is the cosine of θ ?

F. $-\frac{4}{3}$

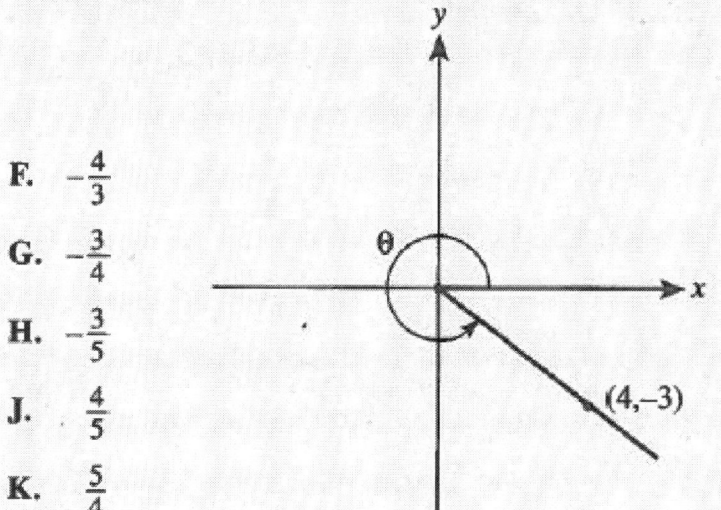

G. $-\frac{3}{4}$

H. $-\frac{3}{5}$

J. $\frac{4}{5}$

K. $\frac{5}{4}$

289

There are a couple of ways of looking at this problem. If you remember from your Algebra 2 class, the sign of the 3 trig functions follow the acronym ASTC, which can be easily remembered by employing a memory trick like, "All Students Take Chemistry", or some such phrase.

What it means is that All 3 functions are positive in the 1st quadrant, Sine is positive in the 2nd quadrant, Tangent is positive in the 3rd quadrant, and Cosine is positive in the 4th quadrant.

Clearly, the angle in this problem resides in the 4th quadrant, so that eliminates choices F, G, and H right away.

We can also eliminate K, since sine and cosine can never be greater than 1. So **J** must be the answer.

Another way to solve this is to draw a line straight up from the point (4,-3) to the x-axis. By doing that you create a 3-4-5 right triangle, where the cosine of the vertex at the origin is just 4/5. J again.

That concludes this chapter on trig word problems. There will surely be other trig problems on the tests that are not considered words problems, but will test you on the same concepts we reviewed here. Brush up on basic trigonometry if still feel unsure about this topic.

Statistics

Although we already had a chapters on probability and measures of central tendency which are sub-categories of statistics, there are other concepts in the broader topic that you may be tested on, such as samples of a population, characteristics of a normal distribution of data, and bias in sampling surveys, to name a few.

In this chapter we'll look at some examples that you might see on the SAT and ACT.

1. A study was done on the weights of newborn babies in a maternity ward. A random sample of babies were weighed and marked. The sample contained 30 babies, of which 30% weighed more than 7 pounds. Which of the following conclusions is best supported by the sample data?

    A) The majority of all the babies in the ward weigh less than 7 pounds.

    B) The average weight of all the babies in the ward is approximately 7 pounds.

    C) Approximately 30% of all the babies in the ward weigh more than 7 pounds.

    D) Approximately 30% of all the babies in the ward weight between 7 and 8 pounds.

This one is answered by understanding the concept of **samples**.

A sample is used to make predictions about a **population** (which is the entire group of anything where the sample came from).

So, when they tell you that in a sample (whatever the size) of babies at a maternity ward, 30% weighed more than 7 pounds, then you can predict that about 30% of **all** the babies in the ward weigh more than 7 pounds. **C.**

Samples are important tool in statistics, as long as they are not biased. We'll take a look at biased sampling in upcoming examples.

2.

A market researcher selected 300 people at random from a group of people who indicated that they liked a certain movie. The 300 people were then given a book to read upon which the movie was based and then asked whether they liked or disliked the book. Of those surveyed, 85% said they disliked the book. Which of the following inferences can appropriately be drawn from this survey result?

A) At least 85% of people who read books will dislike this movie.

B) At least 85% of people who watch movies will dislike this book.

C) Most people who dislike the movie will like the book upon which the move is based.

D) Most people who liked the movie will dislike the book upon which the movie is based.

Here's another example of statistical sampling.

Once again, a sample gives you data that allows you to make predictions about the population from which the sample came from.

So, in this case we have a sample of 300 people from **a population of people who liked a movie.** In that sample, 85% who read the book upon which the movie was based disliked the book.

That means you can predict that most people in the entire population of people who liked the movie will dislike the book upon which the movie is based. **D.**

292

3.

An advertisement for Royal Rat Rations states: "7 out of 8 veterinarians recommend Royal Rat Rations for your fancy rat." No other information about the data is provided by the company.

Based on this data, which of the following inferences is most valid?

A) Royal Rat Rations provides the best nutrition for fancy rats.

B) If you do not feed your rat Royal Rat Rations, your rat will be unhealthy.

C) Only one veterinarian does not recommend Royal Rat Rations for your fancy rat.

D) Of the veterinarians surveyed by Royal Rat Rations, the majority recommend Royal Rat Rations for your fancy rat.

A statistical inference is a logical conclusion you can draw from a given set of data and conditions.

In this case, we are told that 7 out of 8 veterinarians recommend a certain food for pet rats. We must take this information at face value since there is no counter or opposing data with which to compare. Then which inference is most valid?

Well, with problems like these, it's safest to look at the choices and eliminate the ones that are logically incorrect.

A) Does the recommendation of 7 out of 8 veterinarians means Royal Rat Rations provides the best nutrition? It might, but you really can't say for sure because there may be another rat food that 9 out of 10 veterinarians would recommend more. So, this is most likely not the correct answer.

B) Again, since there may be another good or better rat food available, you can't say your rat will be unhealthy if it doesn't eat this particular brand.

C) That would only be true if there were only a total of 8 veterinarians surveyed. But 7 out of 8 is only a proportion. If 80 veterinarians were surveyed then 70 would recommend Royal Rat Rations. That's still 7 out of 8.

D) That only leaves D as the right answer. But to be sure let's reason it out. 7 out of 8 is certainly a majority, no matter what the actual number of veterinarians surveyed was. So **D** would be the correct choice.

4.
A researcher conducted a survey to determine whether people in a certain large town prefer watching sports on television to attending the sporting event. The researcher asked 117 people who visited a local restaurant on a Saturday, and 7 people refused to respond. Which of the following factors makes it least likely that a reliable conclusion can be drawn about the sports-watching preferences of all people in the town?

A) Sample size
B) Population size
C) The number of people who refused to respond
D) Where the survey was given

And now we have a problem that tests your ability to find bias in a given survey.

Many students will scratch their heads thinking this seems like a perfectly fair survey. But is it really?

To determine if the people in a town prefer to watch sports on TV or attend the event in person, we to sample the right people. You may think that a random group of people at a local restaurant in town would be a fair group to survey, but think again.

Sporting events usually occur on the weekends, Saturday and Sunday. If the people surveyed are eating in a restaurant on Saturday, they are not attending the live sporting event that day. So, it is more likely that you will find the majority of the people there say that they prefer to watch the event on TV.

So, where the survey was given makes a difference. **D.**

These type of statistics problems frustrate a lot of students because in their opinion there may or may not be bias. However, students need to practice these type of problems to learn what the test creators consider is or is not bias.

5.
In order to determine if treatment X is successful in improving eyesight, a research study was conducted. From a large population of people with poor eyesight, 300 participants were selected at random. Half of the participants were randomly assigned to receive treatment X, and the other half did not receive treatment X. The resulting data showed that participants who received treatment X had significantly improved eyesight as compared to those who did not receive treatment X. Based on the design and results of the study, which of the following is an appropriate conclusion?

A) Treatment X is likely to improve the eyesight of people who have poor eyesight.

B) Treatment X improves eyesight better than all other available treatments.

C) Treatment X will improve the eyesight of anyone who takes it.

D) Treatment X will cause a substantial improvement in eyesight.

Like it or not, these type of problems turn up on the SAT from time to time. They can be very time consuming reading and trying to figure out the best answer. So, it would be a good idea to skip such a problem and return to it later after you have finished all of the easier problems.

Actually, the difficulty of this problem is very subjective. Some students will think it's easy, others not so much. Let's analyze it.

In the second sentence, it tells us that the research study was conducted on people with poor eyesight. From that fact, we can immediately eliminate choice C which claims Treatment X will improve the eyesight of anyone who takes it.

We can also eliminate choice B because it compares Treatment X to other available treatments, but the given information doesn't mention other treatments at all.

Now we're down to 2 choices. Even if you decide to guess on this one, you now have a 50-50 chance of getting it right instead of a 1 in 4 chance before.

So, now it's a choice between A and D. Choice A does seem like a reasonable conclusion to draw based on the information. But what about choice D? It seems reasonable too. Or does it?

Choice D uses the word "substantial" while the given information uses the word "significant" to describe the results of using Treatment X. While those 2 words may seem synonymous they may not be. How does "substantial" compare to "significant"? We don't really know.

So, the <u>best</u> choice would be A.

Often, with statistical word problems, you'll have to make a choice between two good answers, and choose the best one.

6.

A polling agency recently surveyed 1,000 adults who were selected at random from a large city and asked each of the adults, "Are you satisfied with the quality of air in the city?" Of those surveyed, 78 percent responded that they were satisfied with the quality of air in the city. Based on the results of the survey, which of the following statements must be true?

    I. Of all adults in the city, 78 percent are satisfied with the quality of air in the city.

    II. If another 1,000 adults selected at random from the city were surveyed, 78 percent of them would report they are satisfied with the quality of air in the city.

    III. If 1,000 adults selected at random from a different city were surveyed, 78 percent of them would report they are satisfied with the quality of air in the city.

A) None
B) II only
C) I and II only
D) I and III only

Most students assume that None is never the right answer to any math problem, but that's a wrong assumption as we'll see in this problem.

Let's analyze each of the given statements:

I. If you understand that a sample gives a reasonable prediction about the entire population but not an exact one, then you can throw this one out right away.

II. It is extremely rare that two different samples from a population would yield the exact same results. So, we can throw this one out too.

III. This one is obviously incorrect. It would be an amazing coincidence if adults from a different city had the exact same opinion of their air quality.

So, there you have it. None of the statements must be true. **A.**

7.
The members of a city council wanted to assess the opinions of all city residents about converting an open field into a dog park. The council surveyed a sample of 500 city residents who own dogs. The survey showed that the majority of those sampled were in favor of the dog park. Which of the following is true about the city council's survey?

A) It shows that the majority of city residents are in favor of the dog park.
B) The survey sample should have included more residents who are dog owners.
C) The survey sample should have consisted entirely of residents who do not own dogs.
D) The survey sample is biased because it is not representative of all city residents.

You should recognize the bias in this sample almost immediately. Do you see it?

The city council wanted to assess the opinions of all city residents about converting an open field into a dog park. But they only took a sample of residents who own dogs.

That just ignores the opinions of all the residents who don't own dogs. So this survey is obviously bias. Choice **D**.

8.

A survey was conducted among a randomly chosen sample of full-time salaried workers about satisfaction in their current jobs. The table below shows a summary of the survey results.

Reported Job Satisfaction by Education Level (in thousands)

Highest Level of Education	Satisfied	Not Satisfied	No Response	Total
High School Diploma	17,880	12,053	2,575	32,508
Bachelor's Degree	24,236	8,496	3,442	36,174
Master's Degree	17,605	5,324	1,861	24,790
Doctoral Degree	12,210	2,081	972	15,263
Total	71,931	27,954	8,850	108,735

Of the people whose highest level of education was a bachelor's degree who reported job satisfaction, 1,000 people were randomly selected to complete a follow-up survey in which they were asked about their salary satisfaction. There were 658 people in this follow-up sample who said that they were satisfied with their salaries, and the other 342 people were not satisfied. Using the data from both the initial survey and the follow-up survey, which of the following statements is most likely true?

A) Approximately 16 million people with bachelor's degrees would report salary satisfaction.

B) Approximately 24 million people with bachelor's degrees would report salary satisfaction.

C) Approximately 47 million people with bachelor's degrees would report salary satisfaction.

D) Approximately 72 million people with bachelor's degrees would report salary satisfaction.

Here again we're asked to make a reasonable prediction about the total number of people with bachelor's degrees across the nation who are satisfied with their salaries, from a sample of 1000 people with bachelor's degrees selected at random.

Since they were selected at random, we can assume this is a true sample, and can be used to make predictions about the population.

We are told that 658 out of the 1000 people surveyed were satisfied with their salaries. If we write that proportion as a decimal number, it is 0.658.

We can now apply that to the entire population who have bachelor's degrees . Looking at the table, that number is 36,174,000. (Remember, the numbers are in thousands as stated).

Then applying the sample proportion to the population we get (.658)(36,174,000) = 23,802,492. So, choice **B** is the closest answer.

9.

A researcher is trying to estimate the daily amount of time undergraduate computer science majors spend on nonrecreational computer activities. She surveys 120 students from among the computer science majors at a large state university and asks them, "How much time do you spend in nonrecreational computer activities each day?" The mean of these responses is 210 minutes per day, with a standard deviation of 16.5 minutes. If another researcher wishes to present the same question to a new set of subjects at the same university, which of the following subject groups would most likely yield a data set with a smaller margin of error for the estimated daily amount of time undergraduate computer science majors spend on nonrecreational computer activities?

A) 240 randomly selected computer science majors

B) 240 randomly selected liberal arts majors

C) 80 randomly selected computer science majors

D) 80 randomly selected liberal art majors

If your Algebra 2 course covered statistics, then you've probably seen the term margin of error before. If not, or even if you have and might have forgotten, let's review.

As the name implies, the margin of error is a range of values above and below the actual results from a survey. For example, a 60% "yes" response with a margin of error of 5% means that between 55% and 65% of the general population think that the answer is "yes." You can think of margin of error as a way of measuring how effective your survey is. The smaller the margin of error, the more confidence you may have in your results. The bigger the margin of error, the farther they can stray from the views of the total population.

So, back to the problem at hand, in general, the bigger the sampling the greater the chances of the results being a true reflection of the whole population, and therefore the smaller the margin of error.

Since the question asks for the group that would produce the smallest margin of error, we can see that it would have to be the higher numbers shown in choices A and B. To narrow down the choice further, you only need to notice that the researcher was surveying computer science majors.

That leaves **A** as the only logical choice.

10.

Year	North District	Central District	South District
2000	565	495	1023
2002	552	445	980
2004	503	376	924
2006	455	365	887
2008	406	278	842
2010	354	225	757
2012	343	201	624
2014	364	176	596

To better measure the effects of increases in poaching, the nation of Wakanda began a study in 2000 to track the number of elephants in each of the country's three administrative districts. Every two years, researchers performed a count of the number of elephants in each region; these counts were performed in January. The table above shows the results of the study.

Researchers determine that at a 95% confidence level, their margin of error for the population of elephants in 2010 was 17.4. If the actual population in 2010 is within the confidence interval, what is the lowest possible population of elephants in Wakanda in 2010 ?

A) 1,317
B) 1,318
C) 1,319
D) 1,320

This is an SAT problem, although it's unlikely you'll see one this complicated. But, if you can understand it, you'll be better off in case they ask something similar.

When statistics was covered in your Algebra 2 course, most probably the margin of error was always shown as a percentage. In this problem, however, it's shown as a quantity (notice no % sign next to it). There is nothing in the definition of margin of error that would preclude it from being such a number so long as it is relevant to the population from which it comes.

Here, the population is the number of elephants that the researchers counted in three different districts every two years.

They determined that the margin of error for the population of elephants in 2010 was 17.4 with a confidence level of 95%, which is another way of saying that they are highly confident that margin of error is correct. So, we will use it as fact.

Then, the lowest possible population of elephants in Wakanda in 2010 would be the total population in the 3 districts minus the margin of error.

We calculate the total by adding up the numbers in each district for that year: 354 + 225 + 757 = 1,336. Now we subtract 17.4 to get 1,318.6. Choice **C**.

Really, if you understand that the margin of error in this case is just a quantity, then this problem was relatively easy.

Now let's look at some statistics problems commonly found on the ACT that goes beyond mean, median, mode, and probabilities...

11.

The standard normal probability distribution function ($\mu = 0$ and $\sigma = 1$) is graphed in the standard (x,y) coordinate plane below. Which of the following percentages is closest to the percent of the data points that are within 3 standard deviations of the mean in any normal distribution?

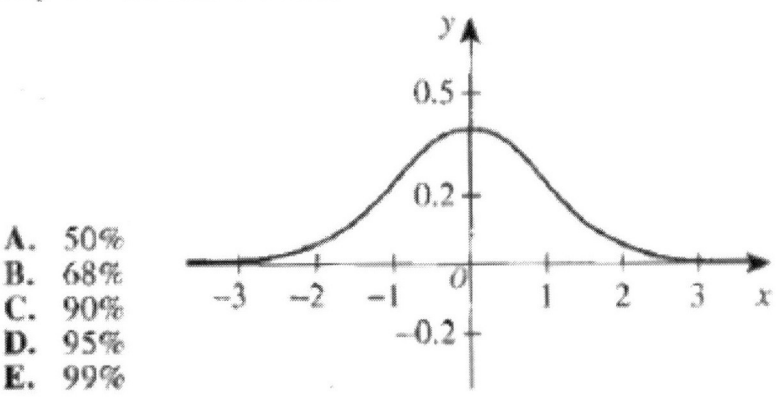

A. 50%
B. 68%
C. 90%
D. 95%
E. 99%

You can answer this one in a snap if you remember the 68-95-99 rule for normal distributions.

1 standard deviation from the mean encompasses 68% of all the data.

2 standard deviations from the mean encompasses 95% of all the data.

3 standard deviations from the mean encompasses 99% of all the data.

Therefore, the answer is **E**.

12.

The graph below depicts IQ scores of adults, and those scores are normally distributed with a mean of 100 and a standard deviation of 10. What percentage of the graph (to the nearest whole number) shows the total number of adults who have an IQ of 110 and less?

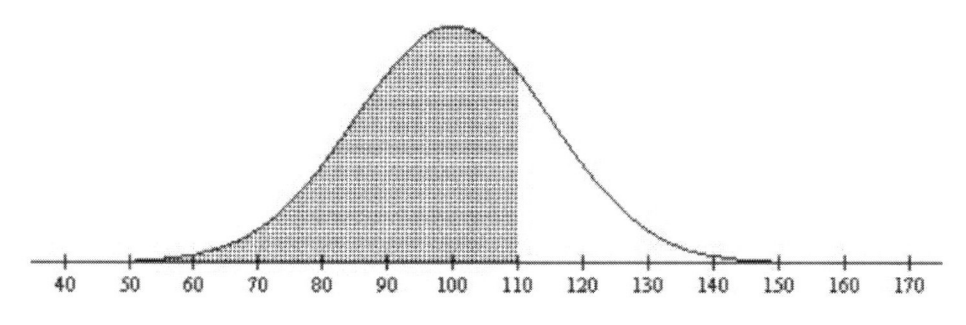

A) 68%

B) 75%

C) 80%

D) 84%

E) 88%

Remember the 68-95-99 rule. One standard deviation to the left and right of the mean represents about 68% of all the data.

In this case, an IQ score of 110 is one standard deviation above (to the right of) the mean, since the standard deviation is given as 10. But, one standard deviation above is half of the 68% spread, meaning it is 34% above the mean.

The mean always represent 50% of the data in any normal distribution. Therefore, one standard deviation above the mean represents 50 + 34 = 84% of all the data if we include all the scores below 110. Therefore, the answer is **D**.

13.

The scores on the Graduate Management Admission Council's GMAT examination are normally distributed with a mean of 530 and a standard deviation of 100. What is the probability of an individual scoring above 630 on the GMAT?

A) 12%

B) 16%

C) 24%

D) 32%

E) 50%

Again, let's apply the 68-85-99 rule. Once again, we see a value only <u>one standard deviation</u> above the mean, since the standard deviation here is 100, and 630 is 100 points above 530, which is the mean.

From the previous problem, we already know that all scores up to and including 630 represents 84% of all the data. But we want to know the probability (as a percentage) of all the scores <u>above</u> 630.

For that, we only need to subtract 84% from 100% to get 16%. Choice **B**.

And that makes sense, because you wouldn't expect very many people to score more than 100 points above the average.

14.

The annual precipitation amounts in a certain mountain range are normally distributed with a mean of 107 inches, and a standard deviation of 12 inches. What is the probability that the mean annual precipitation will exceed 131 inches?

A) 2.5%

B) 5%

C) 7.5%

D) 10%

E) 12.5%

This time the data in question is more than one standard deviation. How much more?

Well, to determine that we use a simple formula:

$$\frac{The\ given\ data\ point\ -\ the\ mean}{The\ standard\ deviation}$$

Plugging in the given values we get $\frac{131-107}{12} = \frac{24}{12} = 2$.

So 131 inches is 2 standard deviations above the mean.

The means we're dealing with the 95 percentile range of data, which means 2 standards deviations above and below mean.

Since we're only interested in the data point 2 standard deviations above the mean, we have to divide 95 in half, giving us 47.5.

Then, all the precipitation amounts up to and including 131 inches represents 50 + 47.5 = 97.5 percent of all the data.

So, probability of exceeding that amount is 100 – 97.5 = 2.5%. **A.**

15.

A 500-square-mile national park in Kenya has large and small protected animals. The number of *large* protected animals at the beginning of 2014 is given in the table below.

Large animal	Number
Elephant	600
Rhinoceros	100
Lion	200
Leopard	300
Zebra	400
Giraffe	800
Total	2,400

Due to an accidental fire, the office that contained the record of the number large protected animals tagged the previous year was destroyed and all the data lost. In order to obtain a reasonable estimate of the number contained in the record, park rangers took a random sample of 100 large protected animals and found that 18 of them had tags. Based on this information, about how many of the total population of these animals can they assume are tagged?

A) 330

B) 380

C) 430

D) 550

E) 700

This one is pretty straightforward if you understand that a statistical sample is designed to make a prediction about the total population from which the sample came.

So, in this case, the rangers found that 18 large protected animals had tags from a random sample of 100 large protected animals. That's a probability of 0.18 or 18%.

We can then project that onto the population of 2400 large protected animals. Therefore, (0.18)(2400) = 432. So, choice **C** is the most reasonable answer.

16.

In 2012, pollsters for the Gallup Organization asked a random sample of 1,014 adults, "On the average, about how much does your family spend on food each week?" The table below lists the percent of the sample that gave each response. For example, approximately 21% of adults in the sample responded that, on average, they spend no less than $200 but no more than $299 on food each week.

Average amount spent	Percent of sample
Less than $50	8%
$50 to $99	17%
$100 to $124	22%
$125 to $149	4%
$150 to $199	15%
$200 to $299	21%
$300 or more	10%
Did not give an amount	3%

If the number of adults nationwide was 138,568,821, about how many million would you expect to say that their family spends less than $125 per week on food?

F) 6.5

G) 11

H) 31

J) 35

K) 65

If you're careful not to make a careless mistake on this one, then it's just a matter of adding up the percentages of all that responded that their family spent some amount less than $125 on food every week.

From the table, we have 22 + 17 + 8 = 47%.

Even though those figures were based on a relatively small sample considering the size of the entire population, it can still be used to get a reasonable estimate of the total number of adults who would say their family spends less than $125 per week on food nationwide.

Therefore, (.47)(138,568,821) = about 65 million. **K.**

17.
After polling a class of 24 students by a show of hands, you find that 9 students play soccer and 21 students play basketball. If the class is indicative of all the students in the school, and the school has 987 students, about how many of them would you expect to play soccer also.

A) 300

B) 370

C) 450

D) 500

E) 530

Here again, there is nothing really tricky about this problem, which is typical of most statistics problems on the ACT.

The polling was done on a class of 24 students... <u>indicative of all the students in the school</u>. So, it can be considered a reliable sample.

The probability of random student in the class playing soccer is 9/24 = .375.

We can then apply that to the entire school. So, (.375)(987) = 370. **B**.

18.
In a poll, 25 people were randomly selected at a Little League baseball game and asked if they would be in favor of their town's tax money being used for the construction of a new high school. If the town has 50,000 residents, what is true about the validity of the poll taken?

I. It is biased because it is sampling people who are probably biased because they have children who will one day be going to high school.

II. It is unreliable because the sample is too small for such a large number of residents.

III. It is unbiased because it is sampling people randomly which ensures that poll taker is not influencing the outcome.

F) I only

G) II only

H) I and II only

J) II and III only

K) III only

Let's examine each choice:

F) While we should be able to determine that the poll would be biased for the reason stated in statement I, we can't say for sure it is the only true statement.

G) II is also true because 25 is extremely small compared to 50,000 and there are formulas which calculate the minimum size of a particular sample, although you are not required to know them. Here, common sense should tell you that such a small sample would be unreliable.

H) We can be fairly confident that this is the right answer, since III is wrong regardless of the fact that people at the game were selected randomly because the entire sample was biased to begin with for the reason given in statement I.

19.
A study recorded the birth weights of 1,630 babies born in the United States. The mean weight was 3,234 grams with a standard deviation of 871 grams. Assume that birth weight data is approximately bell-shaped. What is the approximate number of newborns who weighed between 2,363 grams and 4,105 grams?

A) 1108

B) 1275

C) 1398

D) 1450

E) 1520

Any time they tell you that data is distributed in the shape of a bell, immediately interpret that to mean it is normally distributed, since the graph of normal distribution looks like a bell.

Then all the rules of normal distribution apply, specifically, the 68-95-99 rule.

In this case, 2,363 grams is one standard deviation below (to the left of) the mean, since 871 grams is the stand deviation, and the difference between 3,234 and 2,363 is 871. And, 4,105 grams is one standard deviation above (to the right of) the mean, since the difference between 4,105 and 3,234 is also 871.

That means the 68 percent rule applies, and we can estimate that the total number of babies that fall within that weight range are approximately (.68)(1,630) = 1108. **A**.

You can see how many different ways they can test you on the same concepts.

20.

The true length of boards cut at a mill with a listed length of 10 feet is normally distributed with a mean of 123 inches and a standard deviation of 1 inch. What proportion of the boards will be less than or equal to 122 inches?

F) .25

G) .16

H) .33

J) .55

K) .45

You may think a fairly large proportion of the boards would be a little less than the mean of 123 inches. So, 122 inches is not far off. But you'd be wrong because the standard deviation is small. That mean most of the boards are right about at the mean. So, do not try to guess on a problem like this!

Just follow the 68-95-99 rule. One inch is one standard deviation in this problem.

And we already know that one standard deviation above and below the mean comprises 68% of all the data. So, one standard deviation below would be half of 68, which is 34%.

Then, 34% to the left of the mean is 50 – 34 = 16%. Choice **G**.

That means relatively few boards would measure 122 inches or less.

That concludes this review of statistics type word problems beyond mean, median, mode and probabilities. Although, not very many have appeared on past exams, they do tend to pop up from time to time and it would be best to be prepared in case your particular test has a higher number of them than usual. And, why miss out on an easy point if you get one or two of these questions?

Miscellaneous

In this final chapter, we will take a look at word problems that don't quite fit into any of the categories covered in the previous chapters, but have appeared on previous SAT and ACT exams in one form or another. They are still solved with solid mathematical concepts and logic, but they show up less frequently more randomly.

Let's examine some of these types of problems to top off this exploration of SAT and ACT word problems.

1.

Number of hours Tobi plans to read a book per day	5
Number of parts in the book	3
Number of chapters in the	75
Number of words Tobi reads per minute	200
Number of pages in the book	532
Number of words in the book	179,238

Tobi is planning to read a book. The table above shows shows information about the book, Tobi's reading speed, and the amount of time she plans to spend reading the book each day. If Tobi reads at the rates given in the table, which of the following is closest to the number of days it would take Tobi to read the whole book?

A) 3

B) 4

C) 5

D) 6

This type of word problem requires a deeper analysis than most others. However it is certainly doable if we reason it out properly with sound mathematical principles.

Notice that the question is asking for the number of days, which is a unit of time. So, if we go right to the choices and convert the days to hours and then minutes, we can use that information with the information on the table to find out how many words he will read and see if that corresponds with the number of words in the entire book.

A) 3 days = 5(3) = 15 hours of reading = 15(60) = 900 minutes of reading. If you're wondering where the 5 came from, it's given in the very first row of the table as the number of hours Tobi plans to read per day.

At 200 words per minute, Tobi reads (200)(900) = 180,000 words. Just about right. So, **A** is the answer.

Notice all the unnecessary information given in the table, such as the number of parts, chapters, and pages in the book! Often, tables on the SAT give more information than you need. You just have to decide which of the data is important and ignore the rest.

In this problem we were fortunate enough to only have to test the first choice, but even if were the last choice, the method of solving would still be the same and would only require a few more seconds to solve.

2.

A project manager estimates that a project will take x hours to complete, where $x > 80$. The goal is for the estimate to be within 5 hours of the time it will actually take to complete the project. If the manager meets the goal and it takes y hours to complete the project, which of the following inequalities represents the relationship between the estimated time and the actual completion time?

A) $x + y < 5$

B) $y > x + 5$

C) $y < x - 5$

D) $-5 < y - x < 5$

The best way to handle a problem like this is to substitute the variables for reasonable values.

312

For example, since x > 80, we could choose 90, which is a nice round number greater than 80. And if y is **within 5** hours of the x value, then y could be 94 for example.

Now that we have our values for x and y, we can just test them in the choices:

~~A)~~ 90 + 94 is **not** less than 5

~~B)~~ 94 is **not** greater than 90 + 5

~~C)~~ 94 is **not** less than 90 – 5

D) 94 – 90 **is** between -5 and 5

As you can see, although we are using sound mathematical principles, the method of solution requires using a bit of logic. Once you hit on the right approach, the math part is simple.

Needless to say, do <u>not</u> chew up a lot of time trying to figure out problems like these. I am presenting them here to show you that you can do them if use some common sense and logic. But if doesn't come to you, just skip them and move on. They're only worth one point each and there won't be many of them, so they're not worth wasting time that could be used to solve other problems.

3.
An artist will paint a mural on x walls in a housing project that has a certain number of apartment buildings. The artist's fee can be calculated by the expression $xDlh$, where x is the number of walls, D is a constant with units of dollars per square foot, l is the length of each wall in feet, and h is the height of each wall in feet. If the project manager asks the artist to use a more expensive brand of paint, which of the factors in the expression would change?

A) x

B) D

C) l

D) h

We can cut through the jumble and getting right to the heart of the question, which is "if using **a more expensive brand of paint**, what changes?"

The **only** fact you need to focus on here is which of the variables represents a **cost**. Clearly it's D because it has units of dollars per square foot. Choice **B**. Done.

4.
Arlene drives an average of 200 miles each week. Her car can travel an average of 40 miles per gallon of gasoline. Arlene would like to reduce her weekly expenditure on gasoline by $5. Assuming gasoline costs $3 per gallon, which equation can Arlene use to determine how many fewer average miles, m, she should drive each week?

A) $\frac{40}{3} m = 195$

B) $\frac{40}{3} m = 5$

C) $\frac{3}{40} m = 195$

D) $\frac{3}{40} m = 5$

Oh no. Problems like this make students hate SAT math. Just trying to figure out what they're asking can give you a headache!

But if we apply a little common sense, it's not as bad as it looks.

Basically they're asking how many miles of driving is equivalent to $5 of gas?

Well, we **already know** that each gallon of gas costs $3, and she can drive 40 miles on a gallon of gas. So for **$5** she can drive a little **less** than twice 40 miles. Let's say 70 miles. **You don't have to be exact!**

She wants to **save** $5 so she'll have to drive about 70 fewer miles. Now just **plug 70** into the choices and you'll see that choice **D** is the only one that comes close.

Of course you can also solve this algebraically, but you'll most likely forget how to do it on the actual test, so reasoning it out with a bit of logic will be more reliable.

5.

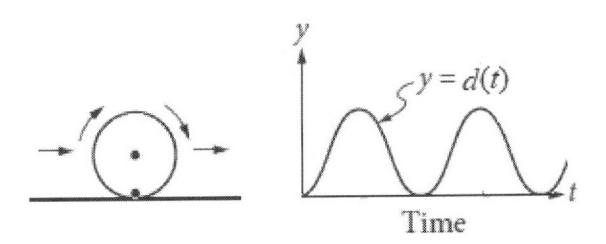

The figure on the left above shows a wheel with a mark on its rim. The wheel is rolling on the ground at a constant rate along a level straight path from a starting point to an ending point. The graph of $y = d(t)$ on the right could represent which of the following as a function of time from when the wheel began to roll?

A) The speed at which the wheel is rolling
B) The distance of the wheel from its starting point
C) The distance of the mark on the rim from the center of the wheel
D) The distance of the mark on the rim from the ground

The easy way to do this one is to just visualize what's happening to the position of the dot as the wheel rolls forward.

315

Can you see that it just goes up, reaches its peak at the top of the wheel, and then goes back down, and keeps repeating?

So, choice **D** describes that situation as shown on the graph.

6.

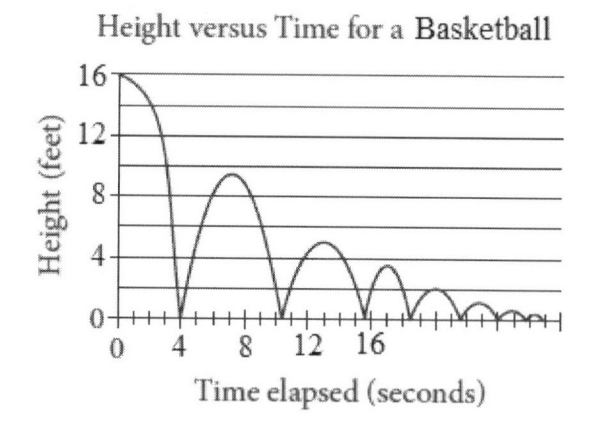

Height versus Time for a Basketball

As part of an experiment, a basketball was dropped from the roof of an 8 story building and allowed to bounce repeatedly off the ground until it came to a rest. The graph above represents the relationship between the time elapsed after the ball was dropped and the height of the ball above the ground. After it was dropped, how many times was the basketball at a height of 8 feet?

A) One

B) Two

C) Three

D) Four

Every horizontal line drawn from the y-axis represents a height. Now just focus on the line marked **8**. Circle the points where the graph crosses that line.

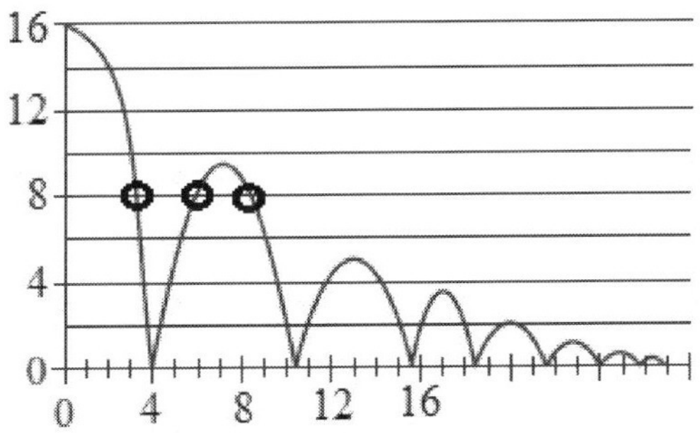

Choice **C**. Done.

7.

A gear ratio *j:k* is the ratio of the number of teeth of two connected gears. The ratio of the number of revolutions per minute (rpm) of two gear wheels is *k:j*. In the diagram below, gear A turned is by a motor which causes gears B and C to turn as well.

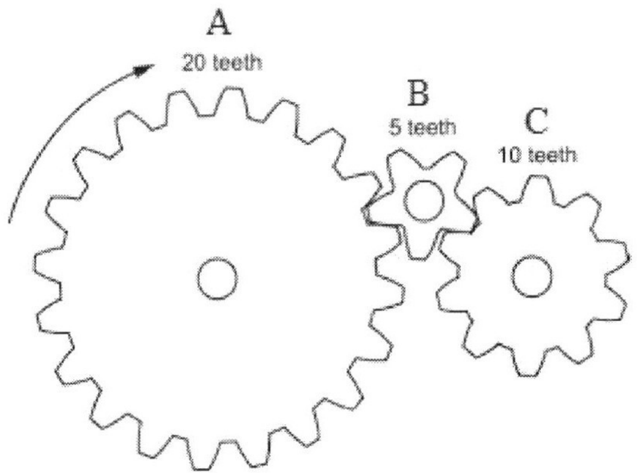

If gear A is rotated by the motor at a rate of 85 rpm, what is the number of revolutions per minute for gear C?

A) 100

B) 120

C) 170

D) 200

There is a beautiful shortcut to this problem which is overlooked by most students. As daunting as this problem may seem, it really boils down to a simple fact. The number of teeth on a gear and the speed that it turns another gear connected to it are **inversely** related, as indicated by the reversed ratios *j:k* and *k:j*. In other words, if one gear has twice as many teeth as another gear connected to it, then the other gear will turn twice as fast when they are connected together!

Now, here's the real shortcut to this problem. **Gear B doesn't matter!** That's right. That little gear right in between the two other gears doesn't make a bit of difference. It's just an interface between gear A and gear C. That is to say, its only purpose is to bridge the gap between the two gears and connect them. If gear A was connected directly to gear C, you would get the same result!

So, let's go back to that inverse relationship thing I mentioned. Since gear A has twice as many teeth as gear C, then gear C will turn twice as fast. So, if gear A is turning at a rate of 85 rpm, gear C must turn at twice that speed, or 170 rpm, which is choice **C**. Done!

Even grade A math students struggle with this type of problem. But now, for you, it's a cinch. You can see how this problem can chew up so much time if you think gear B needs to be accounted for. Sometimes they will make gear B very big to make it seem important. But don't be fooled. It still doesn't matter. Students often wind up giving up or just skipping a problem like this. And, if they are stubborn enough to waste minutes trying to answer it without really knowing how, they risk running out of time on the rest of the test, which is the worst thing that can happen.

8.

Seconds after submersion	Oxygen concentration (as a percentage of full saturation in the blood)
0	100
30	77
60	60
90	46
120	35

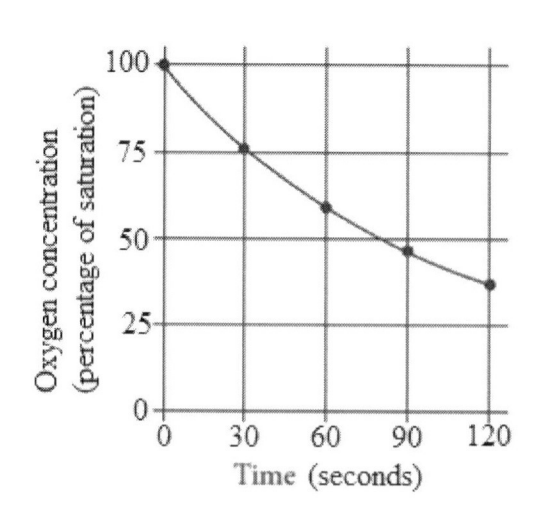

As part of their training, Navy pilots undergo breath exercises to enhance their ability to survive should they find themselves submerged underwater for an extended period of time. The table and graph above show the concentration of oxygen in the pilot's bloodstream, as a percentage of full saturation, at 30-second intervals immediately following submersion in a pool.

The oxygen concentration, as a percentage of saturation, in the pilot's bloodstream t seconds after submersion in the pool is modeled by the function S defined by $S(t) = 100b^{\frac{t}{30}}$. If S approximates the values in the table to within +/- 2%, what is the value of b, rounded to the nearest tenth?

Most students are completely befuddled by a problem like this, but it's not as complicated as it may seem.

To solve for b, we want b **to the first power!** That means b = b¹. Why is that important? Because the given function has the term b^t/30. So then, we need t = **30** in order that b^t/30 = b^30/30 = b¹ = b.

Now look at the table. At t = 30, the concentration of oxygen is 77. So, now we can just plug those values back into the function:

77 = 100b^30/30 = 100b

Therefore, b = 77/100 = .77 or **0.8** to the nearest tenth. Done. Grid in .8 or 8/10.

9.

The rotation rate of a mixing blade, in rotations per second, slows as a liquid is being added to the mixer. The blade rotates at 1,000 rotations per second when the mixer is empty. The rate at which the blade slows is four rotations per second less than three times the square of the height of the liquid. If h is the height of liquid in the mixer, which of the following represents $R(h)$, the rate of rotation?

A) $4 - 9h^2$
B) $1{,}000 - (4 - 3h)$
C) $1{,}000 - (9h - 4)$
D) $1{,}000 - (3h^2 - 4)$

This is obviously not a straightforward rate problem, but it **is** a straightforward translation of English into math.

Look at the 3rd sentence: "The rate at which the blade slows is four rotations per second less than three times the square of the height of the liquid."

Three times the square of the height of the liquid is just $3h^2$. And four less than that is just **$3h^2 - 4$**.

That amount represents "the rate at which the blade slows." Slows from what? Slows from the blade speed rotation of the empty blender, which is 1000.

Then, the rate with the slowdown is $1000 - (3h^2 - 4)$. **D.**

Problems like this one, if read carefully and translated methodically usually aren't too difficult.

10.
Reactant A is placed in a beaker, to which Reactant B will be added. Reactants A and B will not react unless B gets to a certain concentration. Once the reaction starts, both concentrations decrease until B has been consumed. Which of the following graphs, showing concentration in moles as a function of time in seconds, represents the reaction?

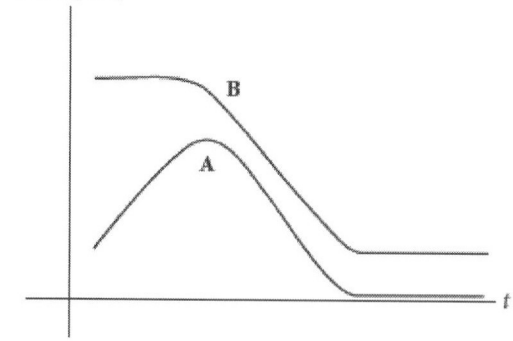

A)

B) Conc [mol]

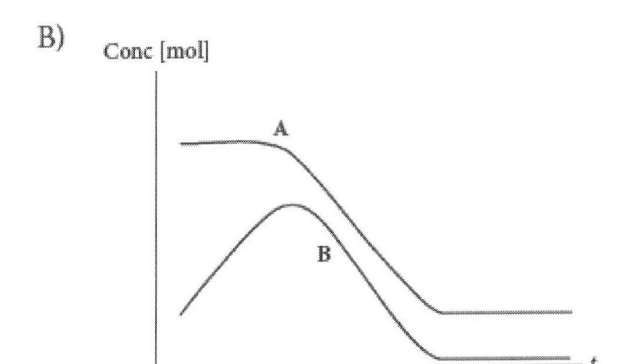

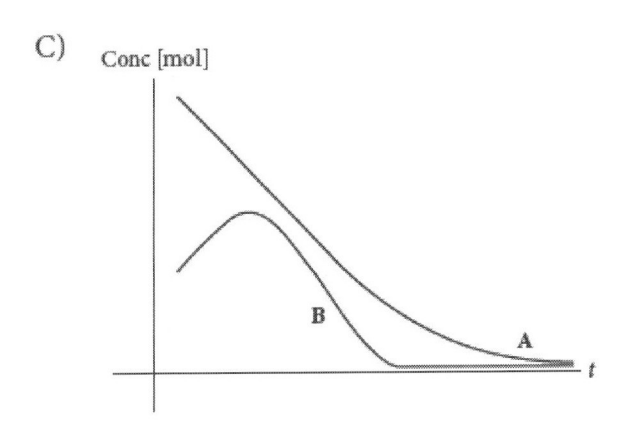

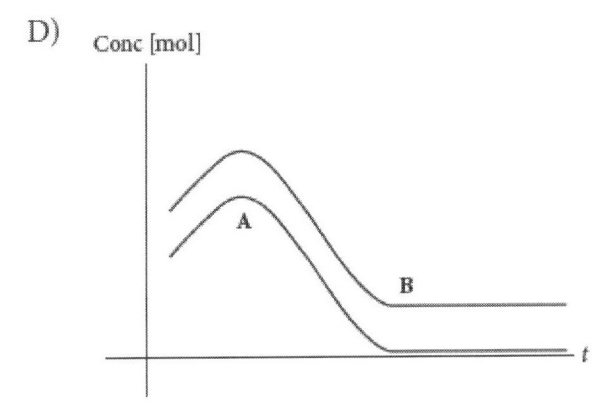

C) Conc [mol]

D) Conc [mol]

Again, this one just requires a proper interpretation of the English.

We're told that reactant A is placed in a beaker (at a certain concentration).

Nothing happens to A until reactant B gets to a certain concentration.

"Gets to" is another way of saying reaches or increases.

So, we're looking for a graph that shows reactant B's concentration climbing while A waits for B to reach a certain concentration.

The only graph that shows this scenario is **B**.

If you don't see that right away, then carefully examine the given graphs eliminating the ones don't correspond with given information.

11.

Luciano measured the amount of water that evaporated over a period of time from a container holding *w* ounces of water, where *w* is greater than 12. By the end of the first day, the cup had lost 2 ounces of water. By the end of the 7th day, the cup had lost an additional 8 ounces of water. By the end of the 11th day, the cup had lost half of the water that remained after the 7th day. Which of the following represents the remaining amount of water, in ounces, in Luciano's container at the end of the 11th day?

A) $\dfrac{w-2}{8}$

B) $\dfrac{w-2}{2} - 10$

C) $\dfrac{1}{2}w - 10$

D) $\dfrac{w-10}{2}$

A problem like this requires a methodical approach that breaks down each condition into mathematical parts.

We're told the container originally holds w ounces of water, but loses 2 ounces by the end of the first day. That is simply represented mathematically as:

$$w - 2$$

Then we're told that by the end of the 7th day, the cup lost an additional 8 ounces of water. So, the amount of water remaining is:

$$(w - 2) - 8 = w - 10$$

Then, they say that by the end of the 11th day, the cup lost half of the water that remained after the 7th day. Since we just determined that the amount of water after the 7th day is w – 10, half of that is:

$$\frac{w - 10}{2}$$

So, the remaining water must be that same amount. **D**.

12.

United States Investment in
Alternative Energy Sources

	Actual 2007 Investment	Projected 2017 Investment
Biofuels	0.31	0.34
Wind	0.40	0.32
Solar	0.27	0.30
Fuel Cells	0.02	0.04
Total	1.00	1.00

The table above shows the relative investment in alternative energy sources in the United States by type. One column shows the relative investment in 2007 of $75 million total invested in alternative energy. The other column shows the projected relative investment in 2017 given current trends. The total projected investment in alternative energy in 2017 is $254 million. Suppose that a new source of alternative energy, Cold Fusion, is perfected. It is projected that by 2017 that $57 million will be invested in Cold Fusion in the United States, without any corresponding reduction in investment for any other form of alternative energy. What portion of the total investment of alternative energy in the United States will be spent on biofuels?

A) 0.18

B) 0.22

C) 0.28

D) 0.34

Believe it or not, this problem only needs basic mathematical operations to solve. It's your job to find out how.

We should always approach a problem like this by going straight to the question at the end of the problem: "What portion of the total investment of alternative energy in the United States will be spent on biofuels?"

That directs us to the steps we need to take to solve the problem without getting lost in the weeds of information that we don't need.

According to the table, biofuels are 0.34 of the projected investment of $254 million in 2017 based on the information given in the problem.

Then, (0.34)(254) = **86.36** million dollars to be invested in biofuels in 2017.

Then we're told that a new source of alternative energy, Cold Fusion, is projected to be invested in 2017 in an amount of $57 million.

That means, the new total investment in alternative energy will be 254 + 57 = **311** million dollars.

Then, the portion of the total investment spent on biofuels will be 86.36/311 = **0.28**. Choice **C**.

As you can see, solving was just a matter of putting all the pieces of information together in the proper order and using basic math operations.

Notice all the information in the table that was totally irrelevant and would have led you astray if you thought you needed to take it into account.

13.

Melanie puts $1,100 in an investment account that she expects will make 5% interest for each three-month period. However, after a year she realizes she was wrong about the interest rate and she has $50 less than she expected. Assuming the interest rate the account earns is constant, which of the following equations expresses the total amount of money, x, she will have after t years using the actual rate?

A) $x = 1,100(1.04)^{4t}$

B) $x = 1,100(1.05)^{4t-50}$

C) $x = 1,100(1.04)^{t/3}$

D) $x = 1,100(1.035)^{4t}$

Here's another problem that will require some logic and common sense instead of just plugging numbers into formulas and spitting out a result.

There is one formula you need to know here- compounded interest when given the interest rate for a period time within a year:

$$A = P(1 + r)^{nt}$$

In that formula, A is the ending amount, P is the initial amount, r is the interest rate for the given time period, n is the number of times that interest rate is applied in a year, and t is the number of years.

In this problem, Melanie expects to make 5% interest for each three month period. So, r is 0.05. Then, plugging the values into the formula, she expects to make:

$1,100(1 + 0.05)^4$ = about $1,337.

Then, the problem states Melanie was wrong about the interest rate, and winds up with $50 less than she expected. That means she really only made 1,337 – 50 = **$1,287**.

All we have to do now is check which of the choices results in 1,287 when the actual interest rate is applied.

A) x = $1,100(1.04)^{(4)(1)}$ = **1,287**. Got it on the first try!

14.

Students in a physics class are studying how the angle at which a projectile is launched on level ground affects the projectile's hang time and horizontal range. Hang time can be calculated using the formula $t = \dfrac{2v \cdot \sin(\theta)}{g}$, where t is the hang time in seconds, v is the initial launch velocity, θ is the projectile angle with respect to level ground, and g is the acceleration due to gravity, defined as 9.8 m/s^2. Horizontal range can be calculated using the formula $R = \dfrac{v^2 \sin(2\theta)}{g}$, where R is the distance the projectile travels from the launch site, in feet. Which of the following gives the value of v, in terms of R, t, and θ?

A) $v = \dfrac{t \sin(\theta)}{2R \sin(\theta)}$

B) $v = \dfrac{2t \sin(\theta)}{R \sin(\theta)}$

C) $v = \dfrac{2R \sin(\theta)}{t \sin(2\theta)}$

D) $v = \dfrac{2R \sin(2\theta)}{t \sin(\theta)}$

This one seems atrociously cumbersome, but it's all just a matter of algebraic manipulation.

We can put g in terms of all the other variables in the second formula formula:

$$g = \frac{v^2 \sin(2\theta)}{R}$$

We can then plug that into the first formula:

$$t = \frac{2v \cdot \sin(\theta)}{\frac{v^2 \sin(2\theta)}{R}}$$

Reducing that gives us:

$$t = \frac{2R \sin(\theta)}{v \cdot \sin(2\theta)}$$

Then, putting v in terms of all the other variables we get:

326

$$v = \frac{2R\sin(\theta)}{t\sin(2\theta)}, \textbf{C.}$$

15.

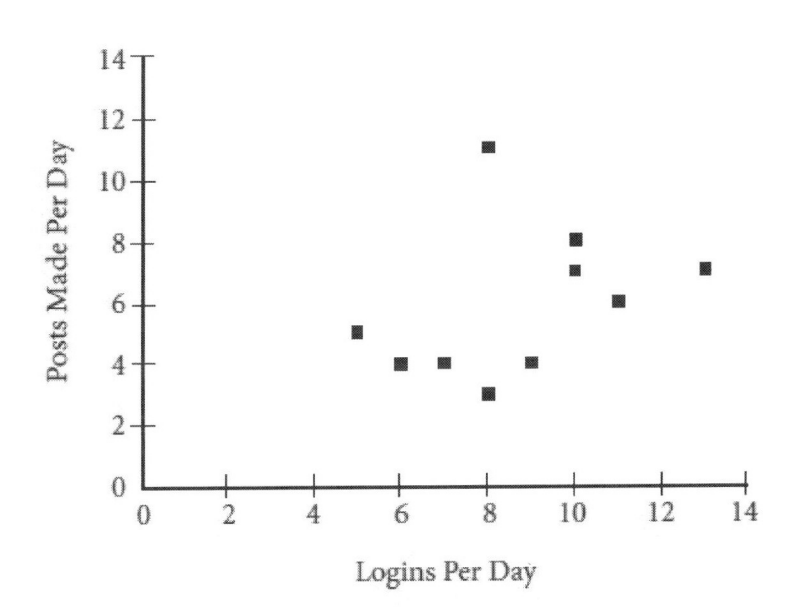

Given the scatterplot graph above, ten students at Welton Academy were polled at random about their usage of the school's new physics-centered social media app, E = MC Shared. The app was developed to encourage students to discuss physics curricula and concepts in ways that mirrored social media trends in 2013. Students were asked how many times they logged into the app each day as well as how many posts they actually made using the app. With the given data, what conclusions can be drawn about this group of students?

A) The majority of students polled logged in more times per day than they posted.

B) The majority of students polled posted more times per day than they logged in.

C) The majority of students polled logged in and posted an equal number of times.

D) No relationship can be drawn between logins per day and posts per day.

Again, skip the clutter and go straight to the question. Refer back to the given information if and when necessary.

The choices represent conclusions that can be drawn based on the data. So, let's look at each choice to see which one is true:

A) To determine if this true we have to properly interpret the graph. The horizontal axis represent the number of logins per day and the vertical axis represent the number of posts made per day.

So then, which data points show more logins than posts. Let's identify them on the graph:

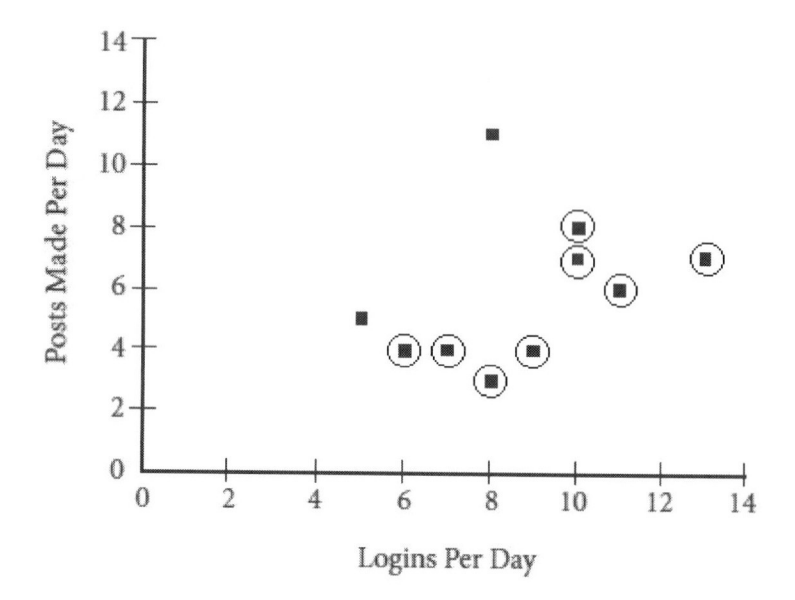

That really brings it into focus. It does indeed appear that the vast majority of students polled logged in more times per day than they posted.

So, **A** is correct.

This problem just required looking at the graph and identifying the points that match the conclusion.

Now, let's look at some ACT word problems that don't quite fit into any particular category...

16.

The number of decibels, d, produced by a siren can be modeled by the equation $d = 20\log\left(\frac{I}{K}\right)$, where I is the sound intensity of the siren and K is a constant. How many decibels are produced by a siren whose sound intensity is 100 times the value of K?

F. 4
G. 30
H. 40
J. 200
K. 2,000

You need not feel anxious when you see an unfamiliar equation or formula. Usually they are giving it to you to use with the information provided. In this case you only need to put the right value into the given equation.

Since they're asking for the value of d when the sound intensity is 100 times the value of K, we can immediately substitute 100K for I and plug that right into the given formula.

Then, the (I/K) part just becomes (100K / K) = 100.

Then it's just 20 log 100 which is (20)(2) = 40. Choice **H**.

17.

ABC Parking and Primo Parking both have an initial fee of a whole number of dollars to park a car in their parking lot. The fee increases a whole number of dollars at each whole number of hours the car is parked. The graphs below show the parking fee, in dollars, for both parking companies for parking up to 6 hours. When the fees of the 2 companies are compared, what is the cheaper fee for a car parked for 5 hours? (See graphs on following page)

ABC Parking

Primo Parking

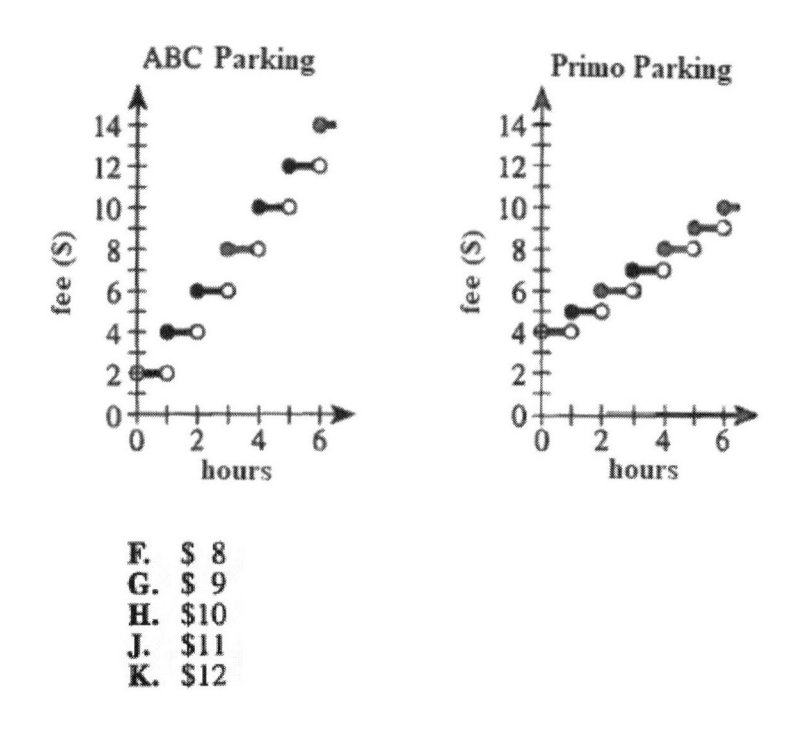

F. $ 8
G. $ 9
H. $10
J. $11
K. $12

This one takes much more time reading than actually solving. We only need to go to the 5 hour mark on each graph and go straight up **through** the open holes to the first solid black dot we encounter. See below:

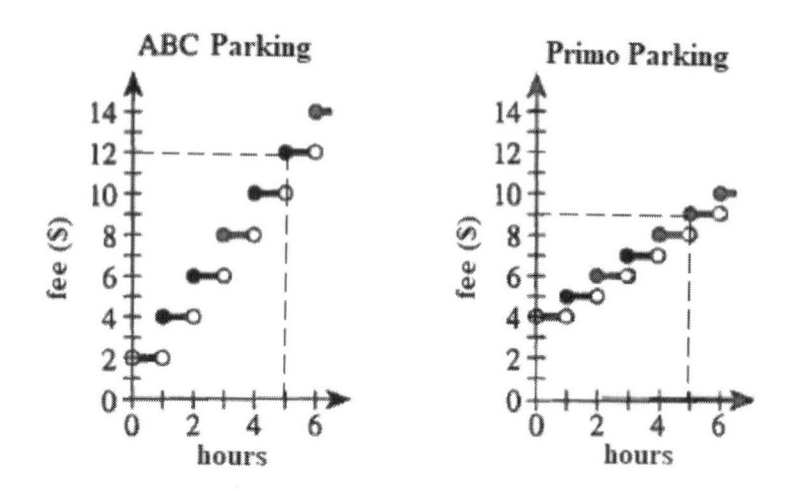

ABC Parking

Primo Parking

Clearly, Primo is cheaper at $9. Therefore, choice **G**.

18.

The sum of 2 positive numbers is 125. The lesser number is 15 more than the square root of the greater number. What is the value of the greater number minus the lesser number?

F. 20
G. 65
H. 75
J. 91
K. 121

This one's a real head scratcher for most students. Fortunately, there's a quick and easy way to answer this without resorting to setting up and trying to solve somewhat complicated equations.

Let's keep it simple. All the choices are **whole numbers** so we want the greater number to be a **perfect square** which always results in a whole number.

Since the sum of the numbers is 125 and the lesser number is quite a bit smaller than the greater number let's try 100 for the greater number. Its square root is simply 10. The lesser number **is 15 more**. So, the lesser number is 10 + 15 = 25. Hey, that works perfectly since the lesser and greater number add up to 125! Therefore, we have our numbers, 100 and 25.

Then the value of the greater number minus the lesser number is 100 − 25 = 75. Choice **H**. Done.

Let's say you made a mistake and chose 81 as the perfect square. Then you would quickly see that it wouldn't work since √81 = 9, and 9 + 15 = 24. But, 24 + 81 ≠ 125, so you would reject that choice immediately.

19.

At her friend's party, Michelle showed the guests a new game she invented. A player rolls three dice at the same time. They will be awarded 3 points for each die that lands on an even number. Let the random variable x represent the total number of points awarded on any given toss of the dice. What is the expected value of x ?

331

F. 1

G. $\dfrac{3}{2}$

H. $\dfrac{9}{2}$

J. 6

K. 9

Expected Value problems turn up from time to time on the ACT. If you know what it means, you can usually answer these type of problems very quickly. Expected value is simply the sum of the products of the numerical value of an event and the probability of the event. Written mathematically:

$$EV = \sum X * P,$$

where X is the value of the event and P is the probability.

Applying this to the given problem, the point value of a die landing on an even number is 3, and the probability of that occuring is **1/2** because half the numbers on a die are even.

Therefore, EV = (3)(1/2) + (3)(1/2) + 3(1/2) = 9/2. Choice **H**.

Use the following information to answer the next 3 problems:

In the figure below, a highway rest area (at D) and radar stations (at A and B) lie on a level east-west line; A is 20,000 feet due west of D. An airplane (at C) is shown directly above the rest area, flying due west at a constant speed of 400 feet per second and at a constant altitude of 24,000 feet. The airplane is located at a straight-line distance of 31,241 feet from the radar station at A and 25,000 feet from the radar station at B.

20.

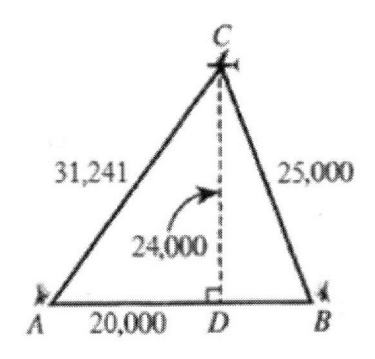

Let A, C, and D lie in the standard (x,y) coordinate plane such that A is at $(0,0)$ and D is at $(20,000, 0)$. Which of the following equations represents the line along which the airplane is flying?

A. $x = 20,000$
B. $x = 31,241$
C. $y = 24,000$
D. $y = 25,000$
E. $y = 31,241$

If we plotted this on a graph, we would see that C is at (20,000, 24,000).

Since the airplane is traveling on a **straight horizontal line**, that line is just y = 24,000.

Choice **C**.

21.

Which of the following values is closest to the number of seconds it will take for the airplane to fly from C to the point directly above the radar station at A ?

F. 17
G. 30
H. 40
J. 43
K. 50

Remember that distance = speed x time. Therefore, time = distance/speed.

We know the distance to go from C to a point directly above the radar station at A is 20,000 ft by looking directly on the diagram. And, the speed is given as 400 feet per second.

333

Then the time is 20,000/400 = 50 seconds. Choice **K**.

22.

When considering the changing triangle formed by A, B, and the moving airplane (C), which of the angles below increases in measure as the airplane flies due west beyond the point directly above A ?

  I. $\angle A$
  II. $\angle B$
  III. $\angle C$

A. I only
B. II only
C. I and II only
D. I and III only
E. II and III only

Here, just notice what happens to the angles as the airplane proceeds west:

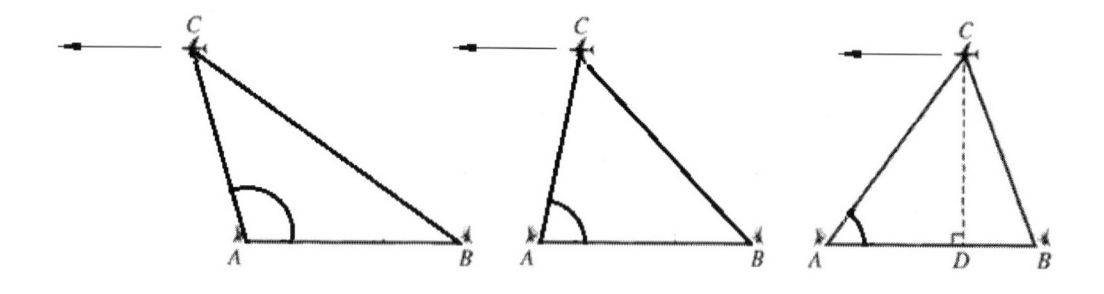

Only <A is growing. Choice **A**.

23.

Art and Abe started a landscaping job together. When Art stopped, he had completed $\frac{1}{4}$ of the job. When Abe stopped, he had completed $\frac{1}{3}$ of the job. Then Robin completed the rest of the job in 3 hours.

Assume that Art, Abe, and Robin all worked at the same rate. Which of the following values is closest to the number of hours it would have taken 1 of them to complete the entire job alone?

F. 0.32
G. 1.25
H. 2.74
J. 5.00
K. 7.20

Since Art and Abe already did 1/3 + 1/4 = 7/12 of the job, Robin finished the remaining 5/12 of the job in 3 hours.

If we let x = the time for the whole job, then (5/12)x = 3.

Solving for x, x = 3(12/5) = 7.2 hours. **K.**

24.
To graduate as an archeologist, a student must correctly order 4 artifacts by age, from youngest to oldest. The student knows which one is the oldest artifact, but randomly guesses at the order of the other 3 artifacts. What is the probability the student will get all 4 in the correct order?

F. $\dfrac{1}{16}$

G. $\dfrac{1}{6}$

H. $\dfrac{1}{5}$

J. $\dfrac{1}{3}$

K. $\dfrac{1}{2}$

An easy way to solve this is to set up a simple diagram:

_____ _____ _____ __X__

The X in the last space represents the position of the oldest artifact on the list. Then, let A = the youngest artifact, B = the second youngest, and C = the third youngest on the list.

So, the correct order on the diagram would be A B C X.

Since the student is randomly guessing, they could arrange the first three spaces as A B C or A C B or B A C or B C A or C A B or C B A. That's **six** possible orders, with only **one** correct order, A B C.

So, the probability is one out of six, or 1/6. Choice **G**.

Although this was technically a probability problem, it was so unique as to warrant a special place among the miscellaneous group.

25.

The nth term of an arithmetic progression is given by the formula $a_n = a_1 + (n-1)d$, where d is the common difference and a_1 is the first term. If the third term of an arithmetic progression is $\frac{5}{3}$ and the sixth term is $\frac{2}{3}$, what is the seventh term?

A. $-\frac{1}{3}$

B. 0

C. $\frac{1}{3}$

D. $\frac{2}{3}$

E. 1

Many students are drawn into thinking they need to use the given formula for an arithmetic progression. But, in this case, it's useless because they don't give us a_1, which is the first term.

Then we need to use an alternative method to determine d, the common difference. Really, all we need to do is subract the third term from the sixth term and divide the result by 3, because there are 3 terms between the third and sixth terms. So,

$\left(\frac{2}{3} - \frac{5}{3}\right) \div 3 = \frac{-3}{3} \div 3 = -\frac{1}{3}$. Then, the seventh term must be $\frac{2}{3} - \frac{1}{3} = \frac{1}{3}$. **C.**

26.
> Derek has 4 pairs of shoes, 3 pairs of pants, and 4 shirts, which can be worn in any combination. He needs to choose a clothes combination to wear to the school dance. How many different combinations consisting of 1 of his 4 pairs of shoes, 1 of his 3 pairs of pants, and 1 of his 4 shirts are possible for Derek to wear to the dance?
> A. 10
> B. 16
> C. 24
> D. 48
> E. 144

This problem is testing your understanding of the **Counting Principle**, which simply says that to find the total number of possible combinations you just multiply the number of choices in each different group.

Then, the total number of different combinations here are just (4)(3)(4) = 48. **D.** Quick and easy.

27.
> Lian has $6\frac{1}{4}$ yards of ribbon she will use to make bows. She will use $\frac{2}{5}$ yard of ribbon to make each bow.

After Lian has made all the bows possible with the ribbon, what length of ribbon, in yards, will NOT have been used to make bows?

A. 0

B. $\frac{1}{4}$

C. $\frac{21}{32}$

D. $\frac{2}{3}$

E. $\frac{7}{8}$

For this one, you can immediately divide 2/5 into 6 ¼ to find out how many ribbons can be made with the given amount of material.

Since you can use your calculator, convert everything to decimals. So, 2/5 is 0.4 and 6 ¼ is 6.25.

Then, 6.25/0.4 = 15.625 ribbons. So, the **remainder** is 0.625 ribbons which uses (0.625)(0.4 yards per ribbon) = 0.25 = 1/4. Choice **B**.

28.

Two dials are shown below. When the arrow on each dial is spun, it is equally likely to point at any of the numbered sectors on its dial after it has stopped spinning. After the arrows are next spun, the numbers in the sectors the arrows point at after they stop spinning will be added together. Which of the following values is NOT a possible sum of those 2 numbers?

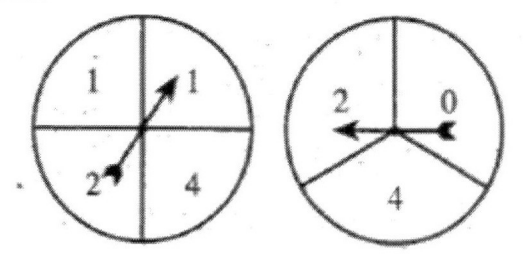

338

F. 1
G. 4
H. 6
J. 7
K. 8

This one only requires common sense and observation.

No number on the first dial when added to any number on the second dial will ever add up to 7. So, the answer is **J**.

29.

Kelsey invested $4,000 in a special savings account. The balance of this special savings account will double every 5 years. Assuming that Kelsey makes no other deposits and no withdrawals, what will be the balance of Kelsey's investment at the end of 30 years?

A. $ 80,000
B. $ 256,000
C. $ 400,000
D. $ 512,000
E. $1,024,000

Problems involving amounts that double periodically are fairly common. Be prepared.

The formula is simple: $A(2)^{t/p}$, where A is the initial amount, t is the given number of years, and p is the time period for the amount to double.

So, in this case, A = $4,000, t = 30 years, and p = 5.

Then, using your calculator, it's simply $4000(2)^{30/5} = 4000(2)^6 = 256,000$. **B**.

Memorize the formula and you'll answer a question like this in well under 20 seconds.

30.

A local golfing league established its handicap for golfers who have an average of 80 or more as 75% of the difference between 80 and the golfer's average score. If H represents the handicap of such a golfer and A represents his or her average score, which of the following equations gives H in terms of A ?

A. $H = 155 - A$

B. $H = A - 155$

C. $H = 80 - \dfrac{A}{0.75}$

D. $H = 80 - 0.75A$

E. $H = 0.75(A - 80)$

This problem really just requires you to translate the English into simple math.

The handicap H should be a positive number, so we want the difference between the golfer's average A and a score of 80, which is A – 80.

Then we need to take 75% of that, which is 0.75(A – 80). **E.**

That concludes this final chapter on SAT and ACT word problems. There are many, many more problems that have appeared on previous SAT and ACT exams, so you would do well to review this topic more by trying to do as many word problems from prior tests as you can. You can't overdo practicing this topic because word problems are sure to show up on your test. It's only a question of how many and which types.

Conclusion

This concludes our journey into the world of SAT and ACT word problems. The examples that were presented were not meant to be exhaustive. I could probably write three more books filled with more problems, but then it would become quite repetitive. No book could possibly contain all the word problems that might appear on future SAT and ACT exams. But, at least now, you should have a fairly comprehensive taste of what to expect.

Keep practicing the ones that you are still struggling with. Most solutions to these types of problems, as you have seen, use mainly basic math concepts. Some, more challenging ones, might require a little more creative thinking and deeper logic. But don't despair. The really hard ones are few and far between.

Avoiding word problems won't make them go away. So, you may as well tackle them head on, since they may be the only thing standing in the way of you and the college of your dreams.

Good luck!